BEYOND EUROCENTRISM AND ANARCHY

Culture and Religion in International Relations

Series Editors
Yosef Lapid and Friedrich Kratochwil

Published by Palgrave Macmillan

Beyond Eurocentrism and Anarchy

Memories of International Order and Institutions

Siba N. Grovogui

BEYOND EUROCENTRISM AND ANARCHY

First published in 2006 by
PALGRAVE MACMILLAN™
175 Fifth Avenue, New York, N.Y. 10010 and
Houndmills, Basingstoke, Hampshire, England RG21 6XS
Companies and representatives throughout the world.

PALGRAVE MACMILLAN is the global academic imprint of the Palgrave Macmillan division of St. Martin's Press, LLC and of Palgrave Macmillan Ltd. Macmillan® is a registered trademark in the United States, United Kingdom and other countries. Palgrave is a registered trademark in the European Union and other countries.

ISBN 978-1–4039–7254–5 (hardback)

Library of Congress Cataloging-in-Publication Data

Grovogui, Siba N. 1956–
    Beyond Eurocentrism and anarchy : memories of international order
and institutions / by Siba N. Grovogui.
        p. cm.—(Culture and religion in international relations)
    Includes bibliographical references and index.
    ISBN 1–4039–7254–0 (hc : alk paper)
    1. International relations—Cross-cultural studies. 2. Eurocentrism.
    3. East and West. I. Title. II. Series.

JZ1251.G76 2006
327.1'01—dc22   2005051309

A catalogue record for this book is available from the British Library.

Design by Newgen Imaging Systems (P) Ltd., Chennai, India.

First edition: April 2006

10 9 8 7 6 5 4 3 2 1

Transferred to Digital Printing in 2009.

*Aux feus Pétit Pié Sambri, Mamadi "Frank" et
Kolou-Kolou Grovogui
To Jann Grovogui—a measure of
skepticism is a good thing*

CONTENTS

Acknowledgments

*B*eyond Eurocentrism and Anarchy is the second of a trilogy aiming to reevaluate "international knowledge" in light of recent scholarship in the fields of hermeneutics, ethnography, and historiography regarding the "non-West," the "past," and the "present" of "international society." The first book of the trilogy, *Sovereigns, Quasi-Sovereigns, and Africans*,[1] explored the position of the non-West in international jurisprudence. The present book offers a view of the "present" in the form of a critique of Eurocentrism (the taking of Europe as sole reference for understanding international existence) and Occidentalism: the postulation of Europe as exclusive proprietor of legitimate science, universal morals and institutions and indispensable intellectual canons. In contrast, *Beyond* proposes empirical support for plausible inflections on modern ideas, norms, and institutions as bases for alternative political possibilities. It will be followed by an as-yet-to-be-named third book that bears on the "past" of international relations and society and their multiple agencies. Together, the three books should provide new insights into modern conceptualizations of power, interest, ethics, and subjectivity. Their objective is to offer plausible grounds for new norms and institutions through which to orient the study of international relations.

The present project began at the National Archives in Guinea with a review of primary source materials on nationalism, colonial policies, and the postcolonial imaginary. To supplement these data, I traveled twice in 1991–1992 to the National Archives of Senegal. Before Dakar, I received research support from the Center for Afro-American Studies of the University of Michigan, the Ford Foundation Project Research-Travel funds in 1990. It is only after Dakar that the RDA (also Democratic African Rally) and African intellectual movements in France emerged as the focus of my project. During this time, I also received institutional support from Eastern

Michigan University in 1995, in the form of a Spring-Summer Research Fellowship, and The Johns Hopkins University: a Faculty Summer Research Fund in 1998 and a Dean's Incentive Grant for Junior Faculty in 2001. This support afforded me four research trips to the Overseas Archives Center (CAOM) in Aix-en-Provence, in France; the French National Archives (CARAN), Paris, and the African Center for Research and Documentation (CRDA), Paris. It also led me to the Research and Training Center for Development (CEFOD) of Chad, in N'djamena.

I would like to thank the many professionals and staff members of these archives for their invaluable assistance. They are too numerous to list here. I would like to single out Vassiafa Touré who is primarily responsible for directing me to the writings of my principal subjects: Ouezzin Coulibaly, Gabriel d'Arboussier, and Boubou Hama among others. Vassiafa, his wife Claude, and children Christelle and Eric have since become members of my extended French family. Thanks.

This book would not have been possible without the inspiration of the late professors Murray Edelman and Lemuel Johnson. Along with Diane Rubenstein, Mary Layoun, and Michael J. Shapiro, Murray and Lem provided me with the intellectual curiosity and the language to think about the present project. I owe them the inspiration for the general direction of this book and I am forever indebted to all of them. I would also like to acknowledge the influences of Michel-Rolph Trouillot and Uzoma Esonwanne, particularly their comments to me on the postcolonial condition and postcoloniality. I am equally grateful to the participants of The Johns Hopkins University Institute for Global Studies in History, Power, and Culture, particularly Giovanni Arrighi, Sara Berry, Veena Das, Niloofar Haeri, David Harvey, Ali Khan, Felicity Northcott, Beverly Silver, and, again, Michel-Rolph Trouillot. I have learned greatly from them as well as other participating Hopkins' faculty, visiting scholars, and "distinguished lecturers." As always, my colleagues William E. Connolly and Margaret E. Keck served as mentors in this process. Ka mamma !

Further, I am indebted to a select group of graduate students, past and present: Simon Glezos, Daniel Levine, Andrew Ross, Cemalittin Hasimi, and Indira Ravindran. These young men and women helped me with various phases of editing and in the process challenged me in ways that I had not anticipated. They were preceded in their assistance by Bettina Ng'weno and Elizabeth (Beth) S. Hurd who aided in the initial organization of my archival notes. Bettina and Beth more than revealed to me the richness of my data. Their assistance was crucial to laying the foundation for the entire manuscript.

I sincerely wish to thank various members of the Leonard family for their kindness, open-mindedness, and understanding. I am grateful to Bill Leonard (Dad) for his patience and joviality and to Kay Leonard (Mom) for sending the muse my way. Mom, the muse really did arrive every time you wished it upon me. While I look forward to more happy moments with Ann, I owe more to Lynn Leonard than I can ever hope to repay. Lynn, thanks for organizing the bike trip to France and for showing your sister and me through example that kindness to others is neither weakness nor absence of courage and clear-mindedness. You are really special, Lynn!

I also wish to acknowledge some members of the Grovogui family. Although my entire family back home has lent me support and understanding, my life away from home would have been more arduous were it not for my brother Kékoura Grovogui. Mbemba, also Kégro, is at once my counsel, manager, and caretaker. I would be lost in the world without him and I am thankful to have him as a brother. And finally to the indefatigable Madeleine (Mado) Lamah, my sister-in-law: E Mamma E Hèghè!

The completion of this book has elements of happenstance, complicity, and joy. As stated earlier, it began in Guinea and drifted from there to Senegal, the United States, and then France. But it ended in Chad, thankfully. Chad is both a place and a metaphor. As a place, it is a country at the southern edge of the Sahara desert. It owns the oldest human skeleton and a vast reservoir of oil coveted by Western multinational corporations. But Chad is also a metaphor for a world of anguish, goodwill, and contingency. First, Chad exemplifies the often contentious meetings of black and Arab and/or Christian and Muslim Africans. It has born its share of civil wars fought over power, culture, and resources. No one knows yet what oil revenues will add to this situation. On the other hand, Chad has been at crossroads of another sort, bearing witness to the best of human sentiments: goodwill and solidarity. It is here that a black man from the French Antilles, Félix Eboué, articulated a new humanism that allowed the colonized to both rise in defense of a vanquished colonial power and join other communities around the world in defense of humanity. Chad also contributed to giving form to PanAfricanism by attracting outstanding members of the politically- active black diaspora. It was home to another Antillian, the much misunderstood and underrated Gabrielle Lisette, who dedicated his life to "giving voice" to the "black world."

Finally, Chad is the place where a young woman from La Crescent, Minnesota, ended up as an American peace corps volunteer. Now a Johns Hopkins assistant professor, Lori Leonard still spends the better part of her professional life in public health in Chad. She is the one who first took me to this part of Africa; and to her I dedicate this book as a tribute to love, ours.

INTRODUCTION

TRUTH AND METHOD: IDENTITY, SCIENCE AND POLITICAL HORIZONS

It is an ordinary requirement of the scientific enterprise that scholars occasionally revisit the epistemological and ontological grounds of their disciplinary approaches. This is the spirit of the present project. It seeks to revisit the methods and assumptions of the discipline of international relations (or IR). It is based upon the understanding that science, philosophy, and narratives often lag in their appreciation of the world. To paraphrase Michel-Rolph Trouillot, theoretical and historical accounts of global events (or "what is said to have happened") seldom correspond with what actually happened.[1] All accounts of international relations must omit crucial dimensions of the object of inquiry. These gaps between "accounts" and "reality" and their effects and consequences provide the space for inquiry. This is why "normal science" requires occasional revisiting of "what is said to have happened."

The most recent calls for revisiting disciplinary verities came in the 1990s, following the collapse of the Soviet Union. Their aim was to reexamine reigning orthodoxies on the international order, state, sovereignty, and nationalism as well as related identities, values, and interests. Then, as now, politicians and academics freely ventured that the world was entering an era of unbounded political possibilities. Charles W. Kegley, Jr., captured the mood when in 1993 he called on members of the International Studies Association to revisit their doctrines of "balance of power" and related theories of bipolarity, deterrence, and hegemonic stability.[2] He implored his co-practitioners to reject existing ideological pretensions in order to look beyond the regimes, institutions, and economies that underpinned IR. He anticipated that such reexaminations would bring about new intellectual horizons and, hopefully, contribute to a new ethos for international actions.[3] Kegley believed in an impending convergence of political philosophy, particularly Wilson's and Kant's, with the foreign policies of liberal states and vice versa.[4] Like many others, Kegley gave rationality and justification to the new order by placing his faith in the self-proclaimed Western[5] commitment to emancipatory and humanitarian goals.

From the 1990s onward, theorists examined previously unexplored dimensions of global politics for evidence of new political horizons.[6] The new impetus was exemplified by a collection of essays edited by Steve Smith, Ken Booth, and Marysia Zalewski laying out the stakes in prior disciplinary debates with sections on their "legacies," "silences," "openings," and "directions."[7] Gene M. Lyons and Michel Mastanduno initiated more focused discussions on the need to revisit the doctrines of state sovereignty.[8] Likewise, Mervyn Frost stressed the desirability of reassessing international norms with the aim of articulating new forms of international legitimacy.[9] Individual theorists, particularly rationalists, called for and invited a flurry of studies that highlighted the value and place of international norms and institutions in international society.[10] While moving methodologically beyond positivism, rationalists opened up the possibility of universal identities and obligations.[11] They joined feminists in these regards.[12] For their part, institutionalists pointed to previously omitted modalities of interaction as the basis for imagining new forms of politics.[13] They effectively captured the historical roles and agencies of transnational nongovernmental networks, multinational corporations, and international actors.

These findings had bearings on existing conceptions of sovereignty, citizenship, and territoriality but not the ones advanced by theorists. While they brought into focus useful values, institutions, and political processes and mechanisms, the new findings did little to elucidate the connections between modern identity, agency, and institutions. Nor did they pay sufficient attention to the political mechanisms and instruments of global politics. As a result, the new concepts of international society and morality remained nebulous. In the so-called West, theorists were content to point out the obvious: that the world had returned to sanity from the brink of nuclear self-annihilation; and the remaining superpower and its allies were liberal, democratic, and capitalist. Both these observations were accurate, but the conclusions to which they led were mistaken. Certainly, the doctrines, strategies, and military arsenals associated with the East–West antagonism made the cold war the most frightening moment of human history. Still, the East–West standoff was by no means exhaustive of the violence of modernity. Specifically, the architecture of the cold war did not mediate the relationships between the proverbial West and the Rest. Long before the Reagan doctrine, for instance, the Monroe and Jules Ferry doctrines had adopted historical forms of violence as political rationality toward African, Asian, and Latin American entities. These doctrines and others preceded the cold war and were likely to survive it.

From this latter standpoint, "Western" liberalism, democracy, and freedom had greater domestic than international application. With the end of the cold war, the world was not entering an era of unbounded political possibilities. Rather, it was awakening to a unipolar era in which a single hegemonic power had near absolute control in political, economic, and military matters. Thus, the post–cold war era bequeathed to the world a single superpower, one political and moral imaginary,[14] and an equally unflinching drive to incorporate all political entities within a single moral ambit. The emergent international order was more akin to a single-party regime, prescribed by the few for the majority, than a plural, democratic, and free international system. It left little room for ideological dissent, cultural pluralism, political initiatives, and economic experimentations.

It remains that theorists were unmoved by the strictures of the new international order. Indeed, canon makers and trendsetters deliberately skirted examination of the structures, processes, and rationales that guide the foreign policies of existing liberal states. For most, the collapse of the Soviet Union vindicated U.S. and European foreign policy rationales and doctrines. Thus, the general orientation of theorizing has not been to imagine new horizons in global politics; rather, it has been exaltation in optimism, fear, or fantasy. The first sentiment is typified by Francis Fukuyama's forecast of the end of history and the final victory of liberalism;[15] the second by Samuel Huntington's prophesy of a clash of civilizations;[16] and the third by Michael Doyle's thesis of a democratic peace.[17] In the final analysis, theorists merely exhorted Western powers (now synonymous with the international community) to act according to its values and inter-national morality. Related analyses were mystifying and tendencious at best and not simply because moral exhortation was not illustrative of political horizon. Nor was the new international morality fully scrutinized. Theorists seemed unwilling or unable to engage in the latter exercise: a revisiting of the nature of existing political structures, causes of their resilience, and global effects; and reexamination of the modalities and rationalities of relevant foreign policies. Even critical approaches failed to capture the implications of "international events" (for instance, the supremacy of one superpower and the institutionalization of global inequalities) for "international existence," especially the everyday existence of the vast majority of the constituents of the international community.

Related conceptions of nature, reason, and time were even more problematic. These originated from parochial recollections or memories of the experiences and trajectories of Europe and/or European-derived entities. Although they left out entire classes of events, experiences, and trajectories, most of them non-Western, these partial recollections and derivative observations served as bases for exclusive scientific verities. The attained verities on human nature, politics, and the available morality were also institutionalized as authoritative.[18] Regrettably, the institutional context of the academy lent itself to the proliferation of authoritative regimes of "truths" that were no less mistaken in their assumptions about non-Western understandings, lines of inquiry, and remedies to existential questions. These regimes of truths were favored by individuals and entities with power and influence over the determination of disciplinary identity, along with its essential ideas, concepts, and texts. This institutional context generated ambivalence toward outside truths and inquiries—including non-Western intentions and rationalities. Finally, it helped to obscure the relationships between identity and science, truth and methods, normativity and pragmatism.[19]

Traditions and Modes of Inquiry

The different IR perspectives can be grouped into two categories united by the twin belief in the infallibility of "Western canons" and the necessary and exclusive application of the "Western" gaze at international existence. The first category assembles social theorists of the self who envision "Europe" as proprietor of legitimate science, universal morals, and imperative institutions. The other category includes critical and reflexive theorists who position themselves against the historic self-representations in order to forward new theories. Neither group fundamentally questions the materiality or identity of the self. Self-consciously or not, they both appropriate the human genius for "Europe" or the "West." To be sure, social and critical theorists are cognizant of temporal and spatial intellectual pluralism and the hybridity and the fluidity of ideas and institutions.

But they assume Western origination of crucial ones. By implication, the methods and canons of analysis necessarily remain "Western" while the antiseptic gazes, the ones seeking cures for global pathologies, necessarily turn toward the non-West. Whether intended or not, this stance ensures that the body of disciplinary knowledge is constituted by impregnable Western representations of self and others. The result is that no disciplinary thought is possible without the filters of the Western gaze and its historical, anthropological, and aesthetic apparatuses.

The related social theory generalizes the pathos of historical Western rationalities into human nature or the human condition. Critically, they assume that the absence of structures of state or sovereignty amounts to anarchy. Leaving aside the colonial application of the assumption, it reflects a generalized state of cruel intercommunal wars that befell Europe upon the decline of the Catholic Church, leading to the Reformation and Counter-Reformation. Having taken the European experience for the human, theorists also assumed that "anarchy" necessarily generates one of two distinct moral reflexes and political responses: "realism" and "idealism." In actuality, both these postulations were founded alternatively upon mystifications of the nature of the international order and tendencious representations of power and interests within it. They also debased "non-Western" and "nonmodern" political rationalities.

Related deductions were mistaken about the nature of the international order as well as the intentions, interests, and values of existing political entities. They typically elevated political traditions that have contingent origins and trajectories into human nature and, conjointly, proposed the underlying rationalities as essential or universal political ethos. Indeed, many who would revisit disciplinary verities erred in taking their own ideological preferences and corresponding practices for an essential ontology. In short, presumed scientific claims and conclusions lacked the scientific qualities claimed by their proponents.

These views have persisted thanks to the weight of institutional culture, particularly of the academy, which privileges authoritative methodologies and regimes of truths, set in paradigms, norms, and rules that were not themselves up for consideration at that time.[20] These contexts of discovery and justification compel theorists and practitioners to forego open inquiries and contestations of the "scientific" validity of research and the affinity of representations or results with their objects. In exchange, the institutional culture encourages the mastery of parochial debates and their encoding in order to refine them as prerequisites of scientific investigation.

This culture of inquiry is compounded by the inadequacy of archives.[21] Specifically, IR accounts are founded upon incomplete archives and/or dubious recollections of international events; contestable classifications of international reality; and less than transparent understandings of international morality. To echo Marianne H. Marchand, disciplinary debates and their alternatives have not been sufficiently "cross-cultural" and cross-regional.[22] In fact, they have kept crucial regional perspectives, particularly non-Western and postcolonial ones, at arms-length. Again, I do not claim that knowledge may and must be empirically complete at all times. By necessity, international knowledge (including theory) seldom encompasses the totality of memories, understandings, and interpretations of international events and thought forms.

I wish to stress, however, that archives generate their own logics and that the lines of inquiry that emanate from the dialectic of *archives, memory, and recollection* necessarily reflect particular perspectives.[23] This is the case with disciplinary narratives of postwar events, which generally serve to refurbish the image of the West as regenerative, progressive, and redemptive in contrast to other variably regressive, repressive, and reactionary models of society.[24] The base narrative is straightforward: World War II destroyed Europe; exposed the weaknesses of the preceding international order; discredited existing Western institutions; and humbled previously great powers. The basic structure of the great divides of the war is also familiar. The war opposed the Allied powers—Western liberal democracies aided by the communist Soviet Union—to the Axis powers, assembling Nazi Germany, Fascist Italy, and militarist Japan. After the war, the story goes, the United States and the Soviet Union formed alliances with contrasting ethos, values, and interests. The United States offered to help reconstruct Europe under the Marshall Plan as well as constitutionally reform the former Axis powers into liberal democratic states. In contrast, the Soviet Union forced Eastern European countries into alliances dominated by Moscow for the sole purpose of world domination. Soviet aggression and repression in East Germany, Czechoslovakia, Poland, and Hungary proves this point. According to this story, the West responded to this aggression and related "provocations" by forming a security alliance, the North Atlantic Treaty Organization, and a supportive economic compact, the Organization for Economic Cooperation and Development. The Soviet Union responded in kind by forming its own alliances and compacts with countries that were subservient to it. The two blocs thus defined were bound to collide. They did, and their confrontation ushered in the cold war.

This general story has subplots that pertain to different regions of the world. These are also straightforward. They invariably begin with a recognition that the wartime events affected the structures, networks, and outcomes of politics beyond Europe and the West. It is also acknowledged that the war shaped the identities, interests, and desires of persons and communities everywhere in complex ways. Beyond these points, disciplinary verities and commonsense omitted significant dimensions of international existence during this time. Though the whole world participated in this war, the great majorities of the world population were given little will power, agency, interest, and imagination. Specifically, it is assumed that imperial fiats mandated the participation of colonial populations. The latter are said to have fulfilled their duties as per instructions. Afterward, the story goes, colonial entities sought independence upon which they wavered in allegiance between the modernizing "liberal West" and the "totalitarian communist East."

These partial recollections are not unusual. But archives become dubious when they are taken to provide comprehensive views of international reality and to encapsulate the totality of the intentions, motivations, and inherent qualities or defects of particular political entities, intellectual forms, and ideological formations. They are more so when they deliberately exclude competing perspectives. Take the date of May 8, 1945, that, to Western analysts, marks the end of World War II. In postcolonial perspectives, two other events occurred on that day that signaled another direction, this time away from the heroic global effort on behalf of democracy. These were the simultaneous reprisals by the formerly Free French Forces against anticolonial forces in Algeria (against the Party of the Algerian People, or PPA) and in Syria (against local officers of the peace), all formerly supportive of French resistance. The worst of the massacres happened in the Algerian town of Sétif. There, French troops massacred villagers who dared claim their humanity on a day that ended a war that Winston Churchill claimed was about the "Measure of Man." These events marked a different kind of transition as that noted in disciplinary narratives. Rather than merely symbolizing the culmination of human solidarity, May 8, 1945, also signified the resilience of a certain Western political rationality or determination to maintain its hegemony at all costs, including subverting the anticolonial agenda.[25] Multiple events confirmed this determination: the 1944 slaughter of African war veterans by French troops in Thiaroye, Senegal; French wars on decolonization in Vietnam and Algeria; American interventions from Vietnam to Guatemala, Cuba, Nicaragua, Angola, and elsewhere in the third world. None of these events were paradoxical, that is, reflecting momentary lapses by otherwise morally righteous liberal democratic states.

This brief synopsis is not intended to merely show the coexistence of competing memories and understandings of "international events." It is to show that Western misdeeds in the former empires—whether wars of aggression or otherwise—belong to the archives of international knowledge and not merely as happenstance. They are integral to a certain political rationality and a pathos of modernity whose outcomes are only intermittently acknowledged: the violence of modern institutions and their economies; the pathologies of colonial and neocolonial usurpation, expropriation, and oppression. To be sure, the causes of modern violence and usurpation are multiple, but the mechanisms of power developed by the West, including but not limited to conceptions of identity and interests and militarization and militarism, contributed largely to the related course of events.[26] Indeed, it is incumbent upon IR theorists to record them as such alongside other global pathologies in order to provide "empirically adequate knowledges"—ones that are appropriate to their contexts and legitimate in the eyes of the principal actors.[27]

Revisiting and Repositioning

Although this book is not intended as a complete rectification of disciplinary verities; it is a contribution to the ongoing revisiting of IR. In the interest of an alternative retrospective, this study brings to the fore non-Western appreciations of wartime events, ideas, and morality within the context of the thought forms of a particular set of actors. I focus on "Africa" and "Africans" for personal reasons but also because few Western theorists assume that Africans, their modes of thought, ideas, and actions have been integral to the dramas of modernity. They appear in Western narratives only as appendages of Western makers of history (Great powers); on terms defined by the latter (viz., the cold war or other great divides); armed with ideas springing from Western intellectuals (now great thinkers).[28] The unstated implication is that these "others" have not offered any valid discourses or practices outside of the strictures of the Western political languages and imaginary. Individuals such as Robert H. Jackson and Stephen D. Krasner openly cast doubt on the ability of post-colonial African entities even to absorb Western institutions to any satisfaction.[29]

The book is set in the period spanning the beginning of the war in 1939 and the formalization of the cold war in 1950, a time when politics was not only more plural, democratic, and cooperative, but also when multiple political horizons could be envisaged. This period remains unparalleled in modern history in its openness to pluralism and tolerance for experimentation. It may stand alone in modern history as the one when moral impetus and ideological initiatives flowed from all regions and when none fully controlled political outcomes. The period opens with the first shots of World War II and ends with the finalization of the structures and instruments of the cold war. It is rightly remembered as a murderous war for its untold atrocities. Yet, wartime events united multiple regions of the world in an uncoerced and unconstrained quest for new moral and political horizons. The reasons were structural, ideological, cultural, and political. First, the war unhinged empires in such a manner as to strip Great Britain and France of their capacity to maintain empire. Second, the idea of "Europe" as metaphor for progress and, as such, enactor of the collective good was momentarily indefensible. The resulting self-doubt was reflected in contemporaneous philosophical and political movements. Third, the United States and the Soviet Union had yet to exert truly global influence, except as models to those inspired by them. Finally, colonial entities everywhere joined (or confronted) their former masters with unparalleled confidence in discussions of world affairs.

The period therefore offers an opportunity to contrast the political imaginaries of a group of African politicians with those of French officials during and after the war. The contrast is facilitated by the fact that the protagonists were directly engaged in political contestations and intellectual deliberations over the design of the moral order. The book proceeds from a number of questions, complemented by some thoughts about their implications. For instance, in the summer of 1940, after defeat, occupation, and the advent of the Vichy state, which France might have asked Africans to fight for the Métropole? That summer, it must be recalled, Greater France—geographical France augmented by the empire and associated states—had disintegrated politically, metaphorically, and metaphysically. Outside the territory held by Vichy, the rest of France was under

German occupation. French West Africa was in the hands of a colonial administrator, Pierre Boisson, who aspired to keep that territory under French sovereignty in the interest of the French state, if not Vichy. French Antilles had been virtually cut off from the metropolis. De Gaulle had fled to safety in London in order to make his bid for leadership of an as-yet-to-be-formed dissident movement. The only part of Greater France that was constitutionally sovereign, autonomous, and legitimately republican was French Equatorial Africa. How and why did French-speaking Equatorial Africa—that is all it was then—decide to join the Free French Forces? Did its leaders merely intend to return to French sovereignty? Was the distinction established by anticolonialists between the French state and the republic simply whimsical? Why did the collapse of French authority not lead to anarchy or chaos? The answers to these questions not only defy disciplinary conventional wisdom, but they also point to distinct imaginaries and visions of the moral order.

Scholars of empire and international relations have assumed that the colonized entered the war to liberate. Accordingly, France produced a particular breed of colonial intellectuals committed to French ways who ensured the implementation of metropolitan fiats, injunctions, and/or mandates. Indeed, French colonialism produced culturally and intellectually hybrid entities known as the évolués. These were colonial intellectuals and elites sufficiently versed in French culture, ideas, and traditions to deserve a higher civil status than the rest of colonial populations.[30] However, this explanation fits more a cliché than a reality. Indeed, the defeat and occupation of France by Germany effectively blurred the symbolic line that distinguished the colonizer from the colonized. Now united in humiliation and political oppression, French nationals and colonial entities came to espouse open tolerance for political deliberation and mutual solicitation. They also converged in their ideological sentiments and political outlook. The related moral orientations and political interests rendered French and African agendas and their premises mutually intelligible, even if they remained at odds.

The result is that the colonizers and colonized felt jointly "responsible for the moral universes"[31] that they inhabited: whether fractured, war-damaged world, or colonized. This conviction led to a corresponding assertiveness of the évolués, including Félix Eboué, Gabriel d'Arboussier, and Ouezzin Coulibaly. These individuals were self-identified évolués, black men (*homme noir*), and PanAfricanists. The first two served in the colonial administration, only to disavow colonialism in favor of a postcolonial order. The three were self-proclaimed democrats, anti-imperialists, and eloquent defenders of "revolutionary" humanism and universalism. All three played a significant role in articulating a postcolonial imaginary with corresponding conceptions of identity, community, citizenship, and politics.

The relevant anti- and postcolonial appreciations and propositions significantly bore on the validity and legitimacy of the truths and commonsense that underpinned wartime and postwar pragmatisms. Related modes of thought, knowledge, and their justifications might considerably improve upon today's available moral universes and political horizons. Although the contexts of the relevant discoveries are not applicable today, the discipline has greatly erred by failing to fully incorporate these non-Western modes of appreciation and ethical propositions about international existence into its canons. It is my contention that the underlying experiences and reflections may provide valid grounds for rethinking disciplinary conclusions and views of modernity, modern foreign policy rationalities, particularly their approaches to sovereignty, interest, morality, and violence. Indeed, African discussions of the inadequacy of modernity and its ethical horizons provide useful grounds for thinking differently about international relations, modern political forms, their modalities, and implications.

Present At Creation: "Africa" in IR Narratives

The mood for political experimentation set throughout all regions during the war and afterward. Among Western powers, France went furthest in political experimentation. In Brazzaville, in 1944, France proposed to draft a constitutional union of the métropole and the colonies in anticipation of postwar colonial reform. The impending union was fitted with three legislative bodies where Africans could deliberate alongside their metropolitan counterparts. The proposed union appealed to colonizers and colonized alike to transcend their separate moral and cultural universes as well as the strictures of empire and statehood to establish a new political model for a new community of political entities, no longer estranged by colonialism, racial injustice, and economic and personal insecurity. French authorities intended the 1946 French Union, and later the Franco-African Union, merely as colonial reform, a shrewd move to redeploy colonial rule under new guises. But to limit the analysis to this simple point is to do gross injustice to the political reality it created. It is also to overlook the creative genius that preceded and followed postwar imperial institutions. Specifically, the framework of the proposed union exceeded the imagination of even the most optimistic of today's proponents of a post-Westphalian order.

The French Union opened up ideological and political spaces for ethical speculations and deliberations about the nature, place, and meaning of sovereignty, citizenship, and territory in modern life. The colonized necessarily expressed themselves in the French language due to the dislocation of so-called native languages. The result was twofold: French political ideas and concepts provided the conventional context for political discourses; and the terms of anticolonial discourses resonated necessarily with prevalent French idioms. But this convergence did not erase the differences between the political imaginaries and ethical inspirations of French officials and their anticolonial antagonists. There existed in regions under colonial rule compelling ideological sensibilities and political agendas that extended beyond the liberal-totalitarian dichotomy that prevailed in Europe and the West. Specifically, anticolonialist sensibilities and agendas corresponded to distinct imaginaries of order and morality.

To illustrate this point, I focus particularly on the evolving relationships between French authorities, French nationals, and the évolués. To summarize, in the French empire, following defeat, humiliation, and inertia in public life, the évolués, particularly black elites, emerged as the primary arbiters of metropolitan contestations and deliberations over postwar symbols and institutions: French identity, sovereignty, state, nation (*Patrie*), republic, and empire, on the one hand, and loyalty and patriotism, dissidence and treason, and liberty and democracy, on the other. Specifically in 1940, it was a black colonial administrator, Félix Eboué, who gave France its only autonomous and sovereign space, after its collapse before Nazi Germany. Eboué was aided by Chadian and French veterans of World War I in the colony.[32] Eboué also rescued the emergent French resistance from moral and ideological confusion by providing the political impetus toward the clarification of notions of state and republic, and thus patriotism and treason in the contexts of war and colonialism. As I show later, contrary to the authoritative common-sense, Eboué did not intend to save the French state, certainly not Vichy, nor resuscitate empire. His views of republicanism and freedom necessitated the dismantlement of empire and the restructuring of the state system to give way to new political entities.

Similarly, in 1946–1950, a group of African intellectuals from the Rassemblement Democratique Africain (Democratic African Assembly) (or RDA) tested the limits of post-Enlightenment French ideologies and the collective French will for a comprehensive and equitable reform of empire and the international system. Still under colonial domination, these intellectuals "surreptitiously" applied their knowledge of French idioms to their own everyday concerns to advance their views of modern identities—empire, France, Africa, and the international system.[33] As a necessary point of entry into "dialogue," the colonized necessarily abided by the metropolitan illusion that its primary mission was to integrate, absorb, and assimilate others into superior forms of culture and society. However, this posture was accompanied by a determination to articulate and fully deploy contrarian notions of persons, society, and law that undermined the colonial project.[34] To illustrate these points, I single out Gabriel d'Arboussier and Ouezzin Coulibaly, respectively secretary general and political director of the RDA during the period under consideration. D'Arboussier's political activism and intellectual reflections took place in the Assembly of the French Union, a legislative body instituted under the 1946 constitution of the French Union. There, d'Arboussier emerged as one of the most eloquent and forceful defenders of new forms and modalities of domestic and global democracy. Ouezzin Coulibaly too was elected to a post-1946 legislative body, the National Assembly, where he poignantly seized upon the spaces and ambiguities of postwar democratic politics and attempted a pluralization of international public life. His parliamentarian interventions and declared right to independent thought tested the limits of French tolerance of the moral coevalness of the colonized.

Eboué, d'Arboussier, and Coulibaly formulated and implemented alternative visions of the moral order, encompassing visions and imaginaries of community, state, and morality. Specifically, Eboué's conceptions of moral agency, subjectivity, solidarity, and the collective interest were received with relief in French and Western political circles during the war. But French and American officials rejected with equal vigor the underlying political reflexes and rationalities as bases for colonial reform. Likewise, French and American officials embraced d'Arboussier's and Coulibaly's visions and imaginaries of community, state, and morality only when they could be harnessed to reinforce the structures of colonialism in conjunction with European reconstruction and Western hegemony.

In contrast, Western officials could not rid their political discourses and actions of colonial understandings of the nature, function, and teleology of politics: self-interested, Occidentalist, and supremacist, both at home and abroad. In short, the postcolonial order envisaged by the évolués ran counter to French (and American) insistence on rights and privileges, on the belief that they were so entitled as "proprietors" and "adjudicators" of the ideas, standards, and institutions of order (signified by the state and the international system), society (domestic and global), and governance (international law and morality).[35]

In relating these events, my aim is to counter the conventional wisdom on the relationships between colonizers and colonized as well as to underscore that the évolués played a particularly crucial role during World War II in redefining the aims of the war, the future of French institutions, and postwar reform. In chapters 2 and 3, Eboué helps to bolster French resistance by providing it with the language with which to defy the state and retain legitimacy. He also lays down the foundation for the nucleus of anti-Vichy networks in the colonies. While revising preferred accounts of the war in relation to the colonized, chapter 2 also shows the errors of Eurocentric and state-centric perspectives regarding modern political identities, sovereignty, anarchy, and the international order. It shows that, in the absence of empire and state, the évolués could muster the cultural and ideological resources necessary to sustain and act on the temporal sentiments and ideals of solidarity, human dignity, and racial equality.

In chapters 3 and 4, I show that contemporary political ideas, practices, and languages have not flown unidirectionally from mythical Western centers to equally mythical non-Western peripheries. To this end I substantiate the following three points. The first is that the évolués elaborated distinct practices and languages of politics among coherent constituencies beyond the reach of the state. These were based on non-imperial and nonmetropolitan visions of community, solidarity, reciprocity, and mutual solicitation. Second, although they related their concepts to French republicanism, they opposed their referents and imaginaries to the metropolitan colonial imaginary. Third, the évolués transmitted these ideas to French dissidents who used them to great effect. Indeed, upon the defeat and occupation of France, Eboué and other évolués separated their sentiments toward the French state, which Africans associated with colonial oppression, from their humanitarian obligations to the French nation—which deserved support. This distinction was the basis upon which Eboué and others (including the dissidents themselves) privileged the defense of the republic over the immediate survival of the state. In this logic, loyalty to the nation—and thus support for all republican institutions—was a higher expression of citizenship than loyalty to the state. Patriotism was owed to the nation through the republic but not to a particular governing machinery. In short, Eboué's actions and comments conclusively proved that to rebel against the state in defense of republicanism was the highest form of patriotism—and certainly not treason.

Chapter 4 considers democracy and democratization within the context of the role and responsibility of liberal democratic states, on the one hand, and the nature and forms of democratic institutions, on the other. Its aim is to examine the official terms of democratization of domestic and international politics as well as the ideas of academics and other nonofficial practitioners on the reform of global politics. My account arises again from the context of the French empire and colonial reform with a focus on their overlapping spatial and temporal structures and processes of the international system. I pay particular attention to the connections between the dismantlement of empire, decolonization, and the advent of the global liberal order spearheaded by the United States. My primary goal is to illustrate the debates over the nature, form, and substance of domestic and global democracy in the emergent postcolonial world. It entails the particular discussions by Gabriel d'Arboussier, an anticolonialist deputy and African representative to the Assembly of the French Union, of the adequacy of French authority, interests, and institutions and values as exclusive grounds for a postcolonial order. D'Arboussier's discussions focus on the political rationalities and cultural prejudices embedded in the institutions proposed by France and leading liberal democratic states as bases for global governance.

Finally, chapter 5 addresses the questions of individual and communal liberties and privileges, with particular regard to the authorial and discursive rights of the formerly colonized. It explores the inherent tensions that arise when power, rationalism, and normativity confront freedom, the inevitable pluralism of discursive forms, and their corresponding methods. The chapter also explores the general discomfort that arose in the West with the *prise de parole* by the formerly colonized. Consistently, this chapter is based on two axes bearing on global governance and the practice of social sciences. The first is the sovereign insistence by postcolonial entities on their freedom of thought, thought forms, and modes of inquiry. The other is the equally notable insistence by Eurocentrists and Occidentalists on normativity in both science and discourses. The related clash is signified in the academy by the debates concerning the value and legitimacy of reverse ethnography, on the one hand, and the advisability of nonnormative speech acts such as sarcasm and irony in postcolonial criticisms, on the other. In their place, Eurocentrists and Occidentalists have counterposed ethnographic distancing and rationalism as valid alternatives to the forms and modes preferred by the formerly colonized. By way of illustration, I focus on the terms of discussion that opposed Daniel Ouezzin Coulibaly, an African deputy in the French National Assembly, to his metropolitan colleagues. French opposition to Coulibaly is a metaphor for the academy's reactions to postcolonial criticisms and modes of analysis.

Notes on the Organization of the Study

My concern in this study is to excavate a series of ideas and political experimentations in colonial French Africa that were important, but have been lost, marginalized, or depreciated in European and American political discourses. By drawing on these anticolonial perspectives, I hope, first, to challenge what might be called "the fundamentalism of international theory." This is a tendency to clamp general and fixed assumptions of the state, state interests, sovereignty, and so on, upon complex historical events involving a multiplicity of actors with conflicting desires and interests. In fact, theory is already a cultural product with inherent possibilities and limitations dependent upon its resources (including intellectual traditions and programmatic objectives); the institutional, cultural, and political context of its (re)production; and its intended uses (deployments) in policy debates.

To some the study might reflect Michel Foucault's ideas about the nexus between modes of power and theory.[36] My study is in fact a reflection on two distinct arsenals of theory. One combines the manner in which theorists identify their object (i.e., international relations), conduct research (ways of knowing), attach significations to events (representations), and narrate their findings (discourse). The other relates to the identities, values, and interests of communities of theorists and practitioners with particular reference to their institutional, cultural, political, and ethical environments. Specifically, I wish to show that international theory has been formalized to reflect peculiar histories, memories, rationales, values, and interests, all bound by time, space, and specific political languages and values. While I do not intend to impugn the legitimacy of theory or theory construction as an intellectual practice, it is my objective to take stock of the contingency of theory. My broader objective is to confront the reification that inevitably enter into dominant modes of theory over time—until events, discourses, and normative aspirations from elsewhere periodically press them to recoil back upon themselves again.

The organization of the study reflects my concerns with both reification and translation. Apart from this introduction and the first chapter, which are overviews of the problematic areas of disciplinary science and representation, the first section of each chapter opens with a critical assessment of disciplinary representations. The theorists involved in these discussions are too many to list in this introduction. The first section of chapter 2 discusses the impact of historicism in institutionalism. It challenges the construction of the "present" as the culmination of the Greco-European past alone, which is often reflected in the assumed temporal differential between the West and the Rest. This assumption allows institutionalists to insist on the unique pertinence of the intentions, insights, and will of the West over and above those of others. My primary interest in the first section of chapter 3 is to expand on the constructivist notion of the co-constitution of temporal horizons between and amongst contemporaneous Western and non-Western subjects and agents. Here I wish to debunk notions of intellectual and cultural authenticity, institutional incommensurability, and/or the inherence and exclusive legitimacy of the Western political imaginary. My arguments are organized around "European" narratives of republicanism, the origins and trajectories of ideas and institutions, and the resulting dynamics. While not contesting that the European state project has come to dominate international relations, I argue in the first section of chapter 4 that related IR theories of the international system and democracy have not been compellingly comparative to enrich our understandings of their temporal and spatial instantiations. I find fault with democratic peace theorists and cosmopolitans, in particular, for not entertaining translation from the standpoint of the internal laws of the new and unfamiliar. This assumption that non-Western institutions lack originality leads to superficial understanding of global dynamics, with grave consequences. Finally, in chapter 5, I consider the right, legitimacy, and necessity of non-Western gazes directed at the West. These gazes are not merely political exercises, replete with nonnormative speech acts as many critics have argued. They are indispensable to mutual understandings and to the construction of just worlds.

The discussions of the actions and thoughts of Eboué, d'Arboussier, and Coulibaly are reserved for the second section of each of the last four chapters. These are not, properly speaking, empirical sections because they are theoretically informed rejoinders to the "revisionist" projects contained successively in specific disciplinary approaches or perspectives, viz., institutionalism, republicanism, democratic peace and cosmopolitan theory, and normative theory. The aims of the rejoinders are the reformers' notions of politics, practices of science, and archival bases as well as their conceptions of power, interest, ethics, and subjectivity. All these notions and conceptions are countered effectively by the perspectives of anticolonial critics who not only proposed plausible alternatives to the historical postwar experiments, but also practiced the alternative models that they proposed. Specifically, I present the actions, political speeches, analyses, criticisms, and programs of Eboué, d'Arboussier, and Coulibaly as a coherent critique of modern institutions of order, conceptions of political interests, and instruments of peace and justice. These individuals hoped to propose new visions, imaginaries, and ethics as alternatives to those contained in modernity, whether in its Western liberal[37] or Soviet communist form.

The choice of these particular black figures is particularly pertinent. For long, Western scholars have made crucial assumptions about the hybridity of colonial elites. Based on notions of power, culture, and sociability, these assumptions have cast the West as initiator if not legislator of international morality and the non-West as adept pupils, students, and adaptors. The underlying diffusionist model of international socialization would apply to the évolués of the French colonial empire whose social imaginaries and political languages are said to gravitate around different strands of French political thought. This view has comparative strength but mostly liabilities. It is a view of institutional development that seldom represents ideal Western idioms of politics as contingent languages of power and communication that account for the political structures, interests and values that political languages must confront, capture, and mediate. It is in this context that I bring to the fore African actors, their intellectual resources, and their ideas of moral order. They provide a means to reformulate existing theories and to broaden international knowledge for a new ethics of engagement.

It would be erroneous to deduce that I wish to write about Africa or to make an exclusive plea that Africa and Africans be included on their own terms in the narratives of international relations. I am not interested in claiming humanity for Africans. Nor is my objective merely to revive the ethical premises upon which "Africans" founded their visions of the moral order. My primary concern rests in the actualization by anticolonial forces of a politics and ethics of "the now," one that assumed the co-constitution of temporal horizons between and amongst contemporaneous Western and non-Western subjects and agents.

The predicaments of the évolués and their political organizations can be edifying. One might contend that, politically, the single most important condition of international morality and legitimacy remains the willingness of international actors to apprehend the multiple idioms, visions, and imaginaries of society, government, and morality that either complement or contrast with their own. This means that political agents must be willing to engage in processes of indexation and translation across space and time of commensurate values, interests, and institutions regardless of the political languages, idioms, and forms of their expression. This endeavor must be complemented with the expectation of occasional incommensurability of object, function, and ends. These aforesaid criteria of political legitimacy apply equally to theory when it is projected as a medium of representation, exchange, and socialization. Indeed, if it is to be indispensable, IR needs to develop new methods of indexing international events, thought forms, and languages as a basis for their generalizations about the global moral order. Theorists must thus periodically evaluate the state of their discipline in regard to its teleology, epistemology, and ethics.

Concluding Remarks

By way of conclusion, this book underscores the relationships between political contexts, modes of appreciation, and ethical horizons. As Jens Bartelson has said, paraphrasing Michel Foucault, narratives of "where we came from, how we became friends, how we got where we are, and where we are heading" are historically and ontologically embedded in larger discourses: metatheories and metahistories of global existence.[38] The world, it must be remembered, seemed more in flux after World War II and the appeal of internationalism stronger than ever. The ravages of that fight and the subsequent collapse of imperial political institutions and economies created an unparalleled democratic space, characterized by deliberative contestations among a multitude of movements, organizations, and intellectuals from all regions of the world. Then, it was apparent to elites worldwide (including the French establishment) that multilateralism remained the most effective means to eradicating global pathologies. In this context, the call and pledge to multiple and concomitant modalities of sovereignty seemed a credible solution to modern pathologies. The proposed French Union (or Franco-African Union to Africans) too seemed to meet this view.

Why and how did the wartime project collapse? What sets of deliberation gave form to the institutions of Bretton Woods, the Marshall Plan, the North Atlantic Treaty Organization, and the European Union among others? What do these decisions say about their authors' visions of the world, its structures of identity, processes, and their teleologies? In the most agnostic of senses, it would seem that the decisions to initiate new hierarchies were not inconsequential to Western political and cultural dominance, military hegemony, and economic privileges. Nor were these particular decisions without consequences for the subordination and alienation of others today. This is to say that theorists must keep such questions in mind as they envisage the post–cold war era. Will this era bring about global democracy, peace, and justice or militarization of international society, militarism, economic disparities, and further subordination of others? In short, while philosophically speaking it is not a foregone conclusion that the post–cold war order will lead to one or another of these two poles, any judgement about its direction is founded upon explicit or implicit moral choices and ethical positions on crucial dimensions of international life and existence.

In conducting this analysis, I am not making a plea for sympathetic imagination or understanding of others. Through different illustrations, I wish to show even if one allowed for the sufficiency of theory as thought and method as mode of knowledge, both disciplinary knowledge and lines of inquiry about modernity and global politics would be inadequate. Indeed, disciplinary modes of inquiry thus far lack ontological and epistemological foundations commensurate with its ambitions. To be compelling and effective, IR theory must incorporate other modes of knowledge that are currently beyond its methodological and archival concerns. The discipline endorses the exclusivity and sufficiency of certain methods only at the expense of the pursuit and breadth of knowledge. Not only are the dominant modes of IR theory unavailable to significant constituencies of the moral order represented by them, but they also remain too allergic to close engagement with "strange places," "forgotten events," and "unfamiliar discourses," which might stretch and challenge them in multiple ways.

It is not simply that knowledge is necessarily grounded in specific linguistic and cultural resources that form the context of epistemological claims and intellectual credibility. The sources and distribution of institutional resources also hamper ontological claims. The latter no longer depend upon the *intrinsic* credibility of knowledge. Rather the credibility of knowledge hinges on its teleology as determined externally by larger institutional and political interests. These problems are compounded by the fact that disciplinary verities about the international order often rest on faulty methodologies, discoveries, and recollections. It is not incontrovertible to say that the totality of historical events far outpaces those evoked in disciplinary narratives and modes of signification. Still, the "international" exceeds its current disciplinary location within spaces between or among states.

Assuming that the purpose of IR is to generate knowledge for the adequate resolution of global problems, this book brings new lines of inquiry and forms of knowledge to bear on the moral universe of global politics; the struggles for political emancipation by the excluded; and the sources and causes of failures of related movements. This book is driven by two basic observations. The first is that IR does not serve its own purpose when its methods and narratives are parochial in their derivations, foundations, and perspectives. One crucial correction is that "international events"—or events of global significance—have occurred mostly within *overlapping structures* of spaces encompassing not only state boundaries but also empires, regions, and stateless "territories." My second observation is that the teleological subordination of disciplinary narratives and verities to specific foreign policy rationales docs not serve disciplinary interests. For a variety of reasons that are not all ontological, disciplinary objects—encompassing modernity and its material economies; the international system and sovereignty; the state and state-based international morality—are broader in scope, interest, and dimension than those of national foreign policies. Indeed, the declared objectives and self-representations of any state's objectives abroad seldom correspond to their embodiments and implementations as policy. Further, the effects of particular foreign policy actions may differ drastically from those intended by proclamations of policy rationales. None of these delegitimize the study of foreign policy, which remains a legitimate object of inquiry. I simply wish to stress that "realities" created by particular foreign policies are not exhaustive of "international reality."

A sense of irony traverses this book: that the brave new world of post–cold war theoretical innovations reaffirmed prior disciplinary practices and the political status quo. To be sure, theorists took stock of the collapse of the Soviet Union and the ensuing geopolitical transformations, including the elimination of bipolarity from the structure of hegemony. It did not follow, however, that they liberated themselves from cold war era institutional and political considerations. For instance, new theoretical insights led to constructivist and institutionalist revolutions, but the reformation and reformulation of disciplinary verities occurred within lines of inquiry that reflected old orthodoxies on international events and processes. These inquiries left out structures of power and a host of other important questions about the international order and governance. In addition, despite the new emphasis on the role of ideas and institutions, few really attempted cross-cultural or cross-national dialogue. Fewer still aspired to generate systematic rules for worldwide participation in defining disciplinary objects, subjects, and teleologies.[39] The rules of dialogue—mutual exchanges and adjudication of findings—had been forgotten in the process. As it happened, the politics of identity, recognition, and tolerance[40] primarily led individual groups and perspectives to negotiate their entry into disciplinary legitimacy and respectability.

My arguments would not be possible without an aspiration for global institutions and the pluralization of power within the moral order. However, my aspiration is not founded upon universalism in the rationalist sense of the term. It is founded, rather, upon the possibility and desirability of translation across cultural and geographical lines of differentiation. Eboué, d'Arboussier, and Coulibaly maintained ambiguous, ambivalent, and complex relations to post-Enlightenment ideologies of universalism. They acknowledged the unity of the human condition, but they insisted on temporality and multiplicity as human experiences. Their belief in the possibility of universal norms was contingent and conditional upon truth and values, themselves applied temporally and spatially. For these reasons, the Africans did not rely exclusively on Western canons and institutions as grounds for global standards and norms.

It is important to see that a critical politics of cultural translation is not reducible to relativism. A relativist seeks to leave each "place" alone as it is. A "translationist" seeks to place disparate and interdependent places and cultures into possible conversations. From this standpoint, for instance, the "human" cannot be said to conceptually exist in a single historical time frame charted by the Enlightenment and liberalism after it; nor is it ontologically singular as assumed by post-Enlightenment (secular) thought. These two points have been made by Dipesh Chakrabarty in the context of *Provincializing Europe* in reference to secular conceptions of the political and the social.[41] So, the human heritage finds its expression in multiple manners and forms of thought, reflecting human diversity. On this basis, I take the language of universalism to be plural and not uniform in its imaginary. Even in the case of the évolués, whose realization of the universal is formulated in the French language with French referents, the "universal" cannot be said to uniformly conform to related French imaginaries. To believe so would be to deny the plurality, hybridity, and richness of languages, on the one hand and their dependence on spatial and temporal necessities and conditions, on the other.

In sum, this book is a plea to disciplinary adepts to reconsider "what they think has happened" and how they think about it by first examining the errors of "how they happen to think" about international relations. It is intended to bring to disciplinary conversations a qualitatively fuller understanding of international relations through revisions of "international events" and disciplinary understandings of "international existence." While I do not intend to propose a theory or new methods for indexing international events, I hope to underscore the temporality and spatiality of international existence and thoughts by giving form to historical thought forms and political "languages" that originated in Africa and outside. Although not easily suited for existing theoretical perspectives, these thought forms and languages were intended to meaningfully "generalize" about the global moral order. This intention is embedded in their modalities, contexts, and sites of expression.

CHAPTER 1

ENCOUNTERS: THEORY, DIFFERENCE, AND REPRESENTATIONS

The goal of the present war is to restore the full measure of Man.

—*Winston Churchill, Centre des Archives d'Outre-Mer, 1944*

The essential sentiment that guides our native policy is the recognition by us French that there exist among [Africans] some general traits of humanity. But the foundation of the same policy has to be the relationship between this sentiment and the nature of things African, that bears on the internal differences of humanity: degrees of civilization and their observation of ancestral customs and traditional commandments.

—*Pierre Olivier Lapie, Centre des Archives d'Outre-Mer, April 1942*

The nature, purpose, and scientific ambition of IR come into focus whenever there appears a treatise that aspires to recast the terms of disciplinary debates. The publication of Alexander Wendt's *Social Theory of International Relations* triggered these effects.[1] While acknowledging the strengths of Wendt's arguments, I do not wish to engage them here. I am impressed that critics brought into focus several important points about the author's desire for a uniform meta-theoretical understanding of international relations;[2] his insistence on the necessity of a common methodological commitment to empiricism and positivist metaphysics;[3] and his undeclared teleology or drive to develop a social science centered principally on the state system.[4]

The consensus among critics has been twofold. First, Wendt's new science does not accommodate epistemological and ontological pluralism, although it is ironically labeled constructivism. Second, Wendt is only conditionally tolerant of "truths" and "methods" that emanate from outside the strictures of the American discipline of IR. To paraphrase Thomas Biersteker and David Campbell, the conditions of validity of practice are the positions and contentions of the "governing conventions of the field," particularly those relating disciplinary rules, methods, and teleology.[5] This claim builds a bias against nonconventional and external theoretical developments.

This chapter is inspired by these criticisms. It follows Friedrich Kratochwil's reflections on the enduring effects of linguistic, cultural, and intellectual artifices on professional practices and, ultimately, the grounds of disciplinary knowledge and authority.[6] Kratochwil insists, and I agree, that collective representations and commonsense are not easily overcome by will, whim, or consciousness alone. IR is a historically constituted object of methods and discoveries that define the axes of research and debates and, therefore, the grounds upon which contestants found truth and teleology. The authority of the discipline is founded upon the unquestioned acceptance of disciplinary narratives of origin as source of authority of its central ideas, concepts, and metaphors of science. The arguments are twofold. Disciplinary ideas, concepts, and metaphors are said to constitute a common heritage, a staple of intellectual and cultural life shared by the people of Europe. They are believed to have traveled in time from ancient Greece (with the likes of Homer, Herodotus, Thucydides, Aristotle, and Plato), to medieval Italy (where we meet Machiavelli), to the present. It is less important that they have not been consistently incorporated in political morality.

The will to theorize and to establish method has focused on an exploration of so-called Western traditions, trajectories, and political rationality along with related identities and institutions. Consequently, disciplinary memories and archives are shaped by historical representations of events, subjects, their teleologies and meanings that are derived solely from a certain understanding of Europe and its interpretations of international events. To reiterate an earlier point, the selection of events and their significations do not do justice to the ambition of the discipline to related global politics. Thus, disciplinary narratives often stand in stark contrast to the lived experiences of majorities in the world community.

In the following, I am not concerned merely with incomplete accounts of international relations. Rather I am interested in the instrumentality of partial mental pictures and resulting definitions and classifications of subjects, values and institutions, and entitlements. This focus also highlights the quality of disciplinary practice, narratives, and commonsense. I derive from them the conclusion that IR fails to capture the contours of international existence, particularly the moral visions, orders, and economies that have politics on a global scale. Disciplinary perspectives share responsibility in this failure, with varying degrees of intensity and complicity.

Eurocentrism, Occidentalism, and their Rationalities

This chapter begins with connections between identity, methodology, and truth. Disciplinary narratives are not only authoritative at the moment of their reception and iteration, but they also reflect Eurocentric and Occidentalist understandings of the roles, actions, and intentions of agents, actors, and subjects. Although the meanings and effects of Eurocentrism and Occidentalism have varied over-time, both concepts produce a fictionalized Europe for instrumental reasons. The most benign of the two phenomena, Eurocentrism reflects self-referentiality and self-understanding, both legitimate if not inherent attempts at self-reassurance.[7] It also presumes a higher status for Europe's modes of thoughts, its methods, and pragmatism.[8]

The idea of a self-contained and superior Europe did not become authoritative until after the seventeenth century when the Christian emporium of Europe was first projected metaphysically as a separate and self-contained civilizational sphere. This professed uniqueness of Europe was upheld by the Enlightenment and subsequent ideologies. Related discourses claimed that Europe alone possessed reason (rationality), science (positivism), and sensibility (pragmatism). These discourses did not merely disavow Europe's connections, debts, and relations with other regions. They cast other regions as sites of violent cultures. Then, European publicists and intellectuals progressively set Europe up as trustee for the rest of the "human species." This trusteeship was founded on the belief that providence (religion), morality (civil government and law), and knowhow (reason and science) bolstered Western claims.

With the advent of imperialism and empire, the ecclesiastical idea of trusteeship gave way to secular belief in the superiority of Europe and its preordination as savior and leader of the world. By the eighteenth century, there had emerged a near consensus that European traditions, rationality, and science were the necessary means to salvation and comfort for non-Europeans. The advent of the Industrial Revolution only reinforced this belief. Subsequent events led to the transmutation in the nineteenth century of Eurocentrism into something more formidable: Occidentalism. As I show later, in order to maintain that Europe was the exclusive proprietor of legitimate science, universal morals, and imperative institutions, Occidentalism conjointly depreciated the capacities, faculties, and achievements.

Occidentalism is presented by some in opposition to Orientalism as a set of ideas and images, if not stereotypes, of the West in the mind of others.[9] Some view it as a "historical fantasy of the modern" nurtured by the West and held by others in envy of the West.[10] The term is envisaged here in conjunction with representational practices that portray Europe as endowed with exceptional scientific and cultural faculties, technological capacities, and political institutions while conjointly making a case for non-Western compliance with Western will and desire.[11] Occidentalism thus requires the supremacy of the West (also Occident) as a necessary requirement of political rationality and international order and morality.

Although lacking ontological justification, related notions of time and space, "Man" and society, morality and law, remain central to political and social conceptions of geography and places—for instance, Africa, Near East, and Middle East—as well as authoritative views of "places," religions, and cultures. These are motivated by parochial visions of power (embodied by the state), social relations (reflecting society), and legitimate interests (now secured by law and constitutional entitlements). Yet, they have become the bases for discrete views of identity, values, norms, and institutions as fixed and determinate.

Related beliefs and ontology found their way into European discourses as historical justification for specific policies related to the conception and organization of the international order.[12] Thus, for instance, protagonists of post–World War II reconstruction drew explicitly on Occidentalism as a set of interrelated philosophical ideas and civilizational concepts in order to justify the need to reconstruct a unified West as a prerequisite of peace and order. The "West" reappeared then as the exclusive province of rational policies as well as a source and foundation of social theory and political experimentation.[13] In short, post–War European reconstruction was not merely a matter of pragmatism, it was founded upon the views of "Europe" and "the West" as the primary subjects of history and morality.

Although IR theorists are not exclusively and explicitly Occidentalist (the majority are not), disciplinary conceptions of political order, rationality, autonomy, and sovereignty frequently coincide with Eurocentric and/or Occidentalist conceptions of self and others and their ideas, thoughts, and discourses. Ideologically and politically distinct perspectives and approaches converge nonetheless on Eurocentric understandings of the terms and concepts of modern Western political discourses. This is to say that Eurocentric suppositions and conclusions are firmly embedded in disciplinary modes of thought, where it is now "established" that "Europe" is or must remain the foundation and principal agent of international order, morality, and knowledge.[14] As a result, my contestation of disciplinary practices and conceptions of politics, society, and institutions take their Eurocentric and Occidentalist constructions as point of departure. So too are my uses of geographical names and philosophical and cultural movements consistent with their Eurocentrist and occidentalist derivations.

The Eurocentrist bias is widely shared by both the so-called mainstream (represented by realists, idealists, institutionalists, and other rationalists) and disciplinary insurgents (including critical and postmodern theorists). Still, the degrees of Eurocentrism—and certainly of Occidentalism—vary across disciplinary divides and perspectives according to ideology, method, and affect. In the so-called disciplinary mainstream, Eurocentrism persists as a result of the unreflective definition of the collective good and the means to its realization according to Western self-references and self-interests alone. Particularly prevalent among liberal institutionalists and constructivists, this hubris is complemented by a conceit of omission from disciplinary discourses of non-European imaginaries of value, society, and institutions. Related perceptions of non-Western societies are seldom based on systematic knowledge derived from methodological and affective filters other than Eurocentrism and Occidentalism. The result is that non-Western societies—and "their" ideas, cultures, political experiments, and institutions—are subjected to sentiments ranging from curious admiration to misplaced misgivings and apprehensions.

Critical and reflective theories reject the Occidentalist instrumentalization of difference. For instance, feminists, critical theorists, poststructural, and postmodernist theorists have at times deliberately parodied disciplinary self-representations and scientific ambition on account of their erasure of human subjectivity and omissions of the wills, desires, and interests of significant moral subjects. Some dissenters have moved beyond highlighting the fictitiousness of self-representations to pointing out the sanitization of the archives, memories, and metaphors upon which the representations of self and/or the past are founded. In the event, dissenters recognize the hybridity and the fluidity of ideas and institutions across space and time, they have equally assumed Western initiation of the original or base ideas and institutions. Still, even in these instances, analysts have stubbornly clung to Eurocentrism, its archives and memories, as well as its metaphors, perceptions, and representations of self and others. A sign of benign Eurocentrism, the metaphysics of reflective and critical theories are replete with instances of attachments, affects, and prejudices. This is the case whether the analysts' interest lies in ontological or epistemological questions about the social world.

The following section examines the perniciousness and effects of Eurocentric and Occidentalist metaphors of time, space, and their subjects in IR. It explores the processes and teleologies of instrumentalization of difference along the lines prescribed by Richard Falk[15] and R. B. J. Walker.[16] I am particularly interested in their views on the naturalization of rationalism, modernity, and violence through metaphors of time embedded in disciplinary artifices of epistemology and ontology. According to Falk, for instance, disciplinary perspectives on sovereignty and rationalism epitomize "colonizing forms of knowledge associated with both evident and disguised structures of domination: statism, nuclearism, patriarchy, Western hegemony."[17]

Roxanne Doty concurs by arguing that the rationalism-modernity-violence convergence is more directly implicated in the colonial act.[18] With colonialism, partisans of conquest and empire began to dispense with anterior interpretations of transactions between Europe and other regions in order to instill in their place new justificatory representations of the new political realities and their policy rationalities. They no longer looked toward the other for evidence of the commonality of the human condition or the duplicability of human reflexes, intuitions, and wisdom. Rather, they sought to justify conquest and colonization by pointing to pathologies everywhere that demanded Europe's attention in order to prevent the corruption of the larger common order. These partisans also sought to marginalize elements of non-Western societies who did not support the imperial project: both Europe's claims to sovereign authority over others and the latter's marginalization within related moral orders. Because justifications of the colonial act found their

way in international thought, the imagination of any plausible
alternative to the present order and its political and ethical underpinnings must necessarily begin with an examination of the nature and
effects of the cultural, intellectual, and ethical arsenals of
Eurocentrism and Occidentalism.

"International Thought" and its Transmission

IR theorists and policy makers will likely react negatively to the idea
that their epistemology is shaped by, among other things, the modern
colonial ontology and the process by which its base moral universe and
relationships came into being. Indeed, the notion that scientific
imagination and high theory have served as justificatory ideologies for
less than honorable political practice is controversial. For instance,
philosophers, historians of ideas, and literary critics have protested
intimations that their questions, hypotheses, dependent variables, and
speculations often reflect political developments and not the other
way round.[19] The protestations have been louder when intellectuals
from the former colonies have proclaimed the need to turn their own
gaze on Europe, its intellectual practices, and institutions as means
to understanding modernity and colonialism. Thus, Tzvetan Todorov
defends the post-Enlightenment humanist/modernist project against
postcolonial detractors who would link it to such institutions as
racism, colonialism, and slavery.[20] He argues that such assertions "take
at face value" the claims of colonialists—a "propaganda; an attempt,
most often a clumsy one, to replaster the façade of a building
constructed for quite a different purpose. The reasons for the colonial
conquest were political and economic, rather than humanitarian."[21]

Todorov's comments suggest that it does not suffice simply to
point to temporal coincidence between the political ascent of
Europe to hegemony and the advent of the "international" to impugn
disciplinary discourses and their configurations. Any complicities
would have to be implicated and reflected in language, concepts, and
imaginaries. These are the bases for my contention that disciplinary
assumptions, theses, and propositions have converged on a colonial
ontology of difference. I am particularly interested in disciplinary
suppositions, first, that the West is the legitimate legislator and
adjudicator of values, norms, and institutions for the "international
community" and, second, that those (presumed) incapable of produc-
ing good government, good laws, and good morals should obey the
moral order bequeathed to them by the West, as a matter of deference.

The belief that the West has been "blessed" with good kings, laws, and reason, while others have not, has intensified and ebbed according to shifting conjectures of power and ideology, including understandings of "race," "religion," "custom," and "civilization." As Ivan Hannaford and others have shown, the "discovery" of the New World, the slave trade, and subsequent European imperialism enabled the symbolic projection of "Africa" as a counterpoint to Europe and civilization.[22] From the sixteenth century onward, Africa firmly became the land of heathens, "black," and the symbol of international dysfunction: a land without laws, without kings, without faiths. (The sixteenth-century French formula was "*terres sans loy, sans roy, sans foy.*") In contrast, the "West" became "white" and came to exemplify cultural adaptability, political competency, and ethical versatility. Related narratives are implicated in discourses and doctrines of subjects, rights, and justice.

So has the process of "racialization" of international thought shifted in time and according to regions. By the racialization of international knowledge, I do not mean to impute racist motives to international theorists. I simply mean to stress the use of analytical methods that uphold ethnographic allusions associated with a hermeneutics of race and culture. Often, such hermeneutics depend upon incomplete historiographic data that serve as central axes for understanding power (sovereignty) and subjectivity (self-determination) within the moral order. To the extent that they are evoked, disciplinary ontologies of difference—of civilized/uncivilized; modern/traditional; citizen/native; providential states/failed states; democratic/non-democratic—are seldom based upon a comprehensive comparative investigation of Europe and other regions in regard to "historical traditions," "political morality," and "cultural dispositions." More often than not, such distinctions appeal to racial (or ethnic) clichés and oversimplified notions of culture.[23]

The colonial ontology is therefore founded upon the prior belief of higher moral order in Europe, reflected by sovereignty, a constitutional order, and a consenting citizenry. Accordingly, there lies outside of the European order a less coherent space, a near anarchic one, of a lesser quality or civilizational form. This space must be nonetheless governed by rules, principles, and norms that depend ironically on civilizational goods: for example, the wisdom and necessity for respecting consensual engagements or promise (treaty rules); adherence to customary rules, precedents, and commonsense (precedent rules); compliance with the outcomes or decisions of adjudicating parties as means to stability (judiciary rules). Hence the need for (1) an orderly international system, or an identifiable structure as context for international relations; (2) an international community of states guided by the status and power of its members; and (3) an international society based on shared norms and values.

Related hermeneutics, historiography, and anthropology have served to mentally and politically organize the global moral universe throughout the modern era. Specifically, they provided the justificatory Western tropes for the hierarchies and structures of authority and legitimacy. Thus, in the eighteenth century, the principal justification for Western intervention elsewhere was that the concerned populations were led by kings but "without law, faith and/or reason." In the nineteenth century, the justificatory ideology for intervention was that, although local rulers possessed their own customs and traditions (and thus laws), they lacked sovereignty, derivable only from civilization now associated with reason. Thus endowed with imperfect laws and without reason, non-Western communities and their leaders lacked any legitimate claim to political autonomy and/or self-government. This formula was only slightly modified for the purpose of the cold war when the legitimacy of postcolonial governors and their modernizing nationalist ideologies were generally recognized by the superpowers, who nonetheless proclaimed some leaders and government to be unreasonably irrational and therefore ill-suited for power. Now in the post–cold war era, everyone is entitled to be "king," but only few have the proper faith—in liberalism, democracy, and secularism and its parallel rule of law on governance, property, human rights, and so on are the barometers of reason. Without it, no leader or government is legitimate in the eyes of the lone superpower and its Western allies.

The West and The Rest: Difference in International Thought

European or Western views of race, religion, civilization, and other modes of social existence are at once categorical, ambiguous, ambivalent, contradictory, tempered, and skeptical. They include justificatory as well as condemnatory ideologies of racism, oppression, and their forms.[24] This multiplicity of opinions allowed for multiple and distinct positions on the norms, values, and central morality of the relationship between and amongst the various constituencies of the moral order. Viewed in this light, the advent of the colonial epistemology and its "nomenclature" emerged progressively and paradoxically from the abandonment of open contestation and scientific pluralism on questions of race, culture, and the contributions of various communities to science and knowledge.[25] The prevalent institutional paradigm emerged as a result of the opportunistic choice to sidestep prevailing norms or scientific truths and wisdom in order to advance particular political and social agendas.[26] This move away from the rigor of scientific methods was itself the outcome of several occurrences in method and practice. For instance, when it came to the other, Anthony Pagden has noted that the European imagination was neither high-minded nor fully detached.[27] Pagden maintains that in such events scientists easily stepped outside of reigning scientific norms and wisdom when questions of race, culture, and civilization implicated the relationship between the West and the Rest.[28]

Pagden also argues that even high-minded scientists could not easily shed their attachment to things European.[29] Pagden's view is shared by Anne Laura Stoler, who shows that political rationality in the colonial context was often constructed out of affective knowledge and affective motivation.[30] This means that colonial *reason* was guided by *passion*, and not the other way round. Stoler further argues that the rationality of the colonial state was frequently used to produce a taxonomy of affect: an emotional economy that distinguished the West (likened to an adult guardian of children—godfearing believer, civilized moralizer, or rational modernizer) in order to oppose it to the non-West, whose inhabitants are then likened to children, heathens, barbarians, irrational beings.[31]

At any rate, once it conquered and colonized the rest of the world, Europe imposed an ontology of space and time, or territoriality and sovereignty, through a particular epistemology that displaced all others. European naval dominance and the establishment of merchant empires and colonial settlements in the New World and Africa gave rise to the idea of a self-contained and superior Europe with an original civilization. Although this was not generalized until the eighteenth century, it was anticipated succinctly by the Francis Bacon who asserted in the sixteenth century that Europe could gain little knowledge from others that it could not produce indigenously.[32] Similar narratives would be implicated in pre- and post-Enlightenment discourses and doctrines of subjects, rights, and justice as well. Thus, international theorists such as Pufendorf first used the term "international system of states" around 1675 to denote the province of a particular kind of morality, to be opposed to the norms applicable elsewhere in other systems.[33]

Post-Renaissance approaches to self and others survived the eighteenth-century Enlightenment debates on the nature of the moral order to affect nineteenth-century scientific racism. By this time, physical anthropology, literary criticism, biology, and history converged toward natural history to secure the epistemological standing of Europe and race in modern thought. This movement was formalized by anthropologists and ethnographers who capitalized on post-Enlightenment erasure of the views of the "racially distinct natives." (Similar scientific artifices continue to shape today's justificatory ideologies of Western unilateralism.)

Michel-Rolph Trouillot too maintains that the epistemology of race originated innocuously in the human and social sciences only to undergo several mutations according to circumstance and the relative power of the "West."[34] For his part, Walter Mignolo observes that, after the Renaissance, few European observers cared about "how an Indian or a Chinese could understand the far and the alien" much like theorists today pay little attention to "how encounters between Europeans and Chinese or between Europeans and the Amerindians in the sixteenth century" structured our present understanding of the moral order.[35]

From the seventeenth century onward, according to Ivan Hannaford, theorists inspired by Réné Descartes, Thomas Hobbes, John Locke, and others "[set] aside the metaphysical and theological scheme of things for a more logical description and classification that ordered humankind in terms of physiological and mental criteria based on observable 'facts' and tested evidence."[36] The methodological shift that they unleashed propelled Enlightenment ideas on the body, mind, and the national character, all related to race, and their later formalization in theory. The pervasiveness of racial and national attributes in political theory is manifest in the writings of the likes of Baron de Montesquieu, David Hume, Johann Blumenbach, Immanuel Kant, Gotthold Lessing, Johann Gottlieb Fitche, Johann von Herder, and Edmund Burke on government, society, and related institutions.[37] All of them helped to cleanse Europe and Western Christendom of its historical and intellectual and spiritual debts to other regions, cultures, and civilizations. They and their followers generally proclaimed the superiority of Christianity over other religions; of "Europe" over other regions; of Western rationality over non-Western belief systems; of property over use; of sovereignty over other forms of government associated with the inhabitants of territories conquered by the West.

These representations presented images of self and other that alternated between morally unified or internally disunited entities.

Whether the commentators belonged to the bourgeoning field of international law (e.g., Vitoria, Suárez, Freitas, Grotius, Pufendorf, Wolff, and Vattel); philosophy (Montesquieu, Locke, John Stuart Mill, Voltaire, Diderot, Rousseau, Marx); and politics (David Hume, Jules Ferry, William Gladstone, Frederick Lugard, William Jefferson); their views of the nature of the units of the moral order were seldom random. Political circumstance and material interest often determined whether the West or the Rest were projected as morally coherent, politically uniform, and legitimately constituted or, alternatively, lacking moral cohesion, political uniformity, and jural legitimacy. The trends that emerged then persist today with grave effects.

The overriding trend in these representations depend on whether individual theorists assumed moral unity and/or disunity, and according to the identity of the parties involved. Hence, the moral unity of Europe is assumed whenever and wherever the object of discourse is to project (1) a purposeful and conscious agent; (2) a modernizer with will and intentionality; and (3) an enterprising bearer of science and the essential values and institutions of the international order. Theorists still unconditionally and uncritically associate Europe or the West with civilization, giving them the proprietorship of political tolerance, democracy, and social and scientific progress. In all these regards, the Rest too is unified, but this time in contradistinction with the West. Regions beyond the West are metaphysically united in their traditions and cultures as deviations from Western standards. Africans, for instance, are said today to exhibit habits of mind, work, and social relations that render them prone to political and economic failures.[38]

Theoretical assertions of the internal disunity of the West and the Rest also produces an inversion of the order of moral properties. Once again, the contrast favors the West. Thus, the internal diversity and the temporality of political events in Europe has been accentuated with fervor when the object of discourse is the attribution of culpability or criticism for morally ambiguous actions. Hence, imperial Spain may be blamed for bringing death onto the New World, Germany for Nazism and the Holocaust, and Italy for Fascism; but few would assimilate enslavement, totalitarianism, Nazism, and Fascism with the West as essential features. In contrast, Occidentalist texts posit the moral incongruity and temporal discontinuity of non-Western entities in order to stigmatize the Rest. Such texts seize upon notable achievements—"success" or "progress"—as non-reproducible aberrations and evidence of acculturation and deviations from a supposed essence. Hence, when they are noted, "success" and "progress" are generally attributed to the exceptional qualities of their initiators, qualities often attributed to their bearers' embrace of the West or Western values.[39]

This racial epistemology survived even the best of intentions. Originating after the Renaissance, for instance, the emergent field of international law readily endorsed materialist explanations of European power that justified European violence and expropriation of the inhabitants of other regions. Thus, despite their comparative perspectives, Francisco Vitoria, Francisco Suárez, Seraphin de Freitas, Hugo Grotius, Samuel Pufendorf, Christian Wolff, Emerich de Vattel, and other pioneers of international law and ethics were swayed by political circumstances to overlook European expropriation of the infidels through discourses and discursive techniques that accentuated Christianity, civilization, and reason as the proper compasses to human affairs. Like philosophers and historians before them, international jurists relied heavily on religious and communal ideologies and understandings of society, government, and property to justify political and commercial institutions and norms. They did so with full intent to support the emergent colonial institutions and thus to envisage differentiated norms of rights, obligations, and duties corresponding to the racial and/or religious identities of the parties, to international or cross-communal exchanges, commercial contracts, and sovereign entreaties.

The encoded international law established different sets of norms to complement the European law of nations. By necessity the latter differed in substance and procedures from the emergent rules of engagements between Europeans and non-Europeans: old world infidels, Africans, and other New World heathens.[40] In a way, international publicists reaffirmed moral injunction by European powers to the non-European world. Thus, the principles of law and morality that applied to Europeans operating outside of Europe, as a unified moral entity, differed from those prescribed by the classical jurisprudence in inter-European affairs within that continent. The norms applied to intra-European relations (interactions among European communities within the boundaries of Western Christendom) formed a particular body of law known as Jus Gentilis. By design, this law differed from the rules and procedures applicable in inter-European relations (interactions among Christian merchants, settlers, and adventurers abroad). These two sets of laws bore scant resemblance to yet a third, which governed the dynamics between Westerners and non-Europeans.[41] The latter was the basis for unequal treaty obligations imposed by European powers or entities upon native populations, often in return of native hospitality and entreaties. The general sentiment of the era was best captured by Emerich de Vattel in the eighteenth century when he stated that the natives had no physical, legal, or emotional attachment to land or territory worthy of European respect.[42]

The means to this new cosmology was not only the instrumental-ization of knowledge, but also the omission of prior connections with other regions, which lay the foundation for more broadly construed notions of international morality. Thus construed, the new field of international law mirrored the gap between the myth of Europe and its actuality, on the one hand, and the deliberate omission of Europe's debt to other regions, on the other. Before the era of modern empires, for instance, European transactions in Africa and Asia depended principally upon local knowledge and practices of trade and diplomacy developed by indigenous classes, including the wangara in West Africa (a caste of black traders, brokers, teachers, and scribes)[43] and the dragomans in the Ottoman Empire (composed mostly of Armenian, Jewish, and Greek men of letters). Acting as interpreters and middlemen, these groups and many others participated significantly in the development of present-day diplomatic practices and cultures. European travelers and merchants depended upon these natives for mentorship regarding local standards as well as for their representation, functions now associated with consulates and embassies. It is to be noted that Ottoman rulers and traders as well as their Venetian, French, and British counterparts solicited the services of the dragomans. In great numbers, Europeans accepted the latter as teachers in the craft of interpretation and negotiation. The wangara played similar roles for Arab and Berber traders. In return, the wangara and the dragomans familiarized themselves with the practices and cul-tures of the foreigners whom they helped to introduce into their respec-tive societies. These moments of exchange witnessed great political, cultural, and economic transformations for all the participants.

Rather than reflect the aforesaid relationships and their processes, post-Renaissance accounts of world politics simply depreciated the non-West in order to provide intellectual sustenance to emergent capitalism and the colonial enterprise. Gone from the writings of international jurists were references to the roles played by Kurds, Ottomans, Moguls, and Venitians in the development of diplomatic institutions; the cosmopolitan ways of Chinese and Mande diaspora in East and Southeast Asia and West Africa; and Arab contributions to the development of global market relations, which included the letter of credit, the bussola or compass, paper money, and so on. In their place, jurists introduced instrumentalized notions and conceptions of government and society based on ambiguous and uncertain truths about Western achievements, its role in the advent of international society, the nature of political economy, and the causes of Western rise to hegemony. A central piece of the related story was the myth of the exclusive personal and collective industriousness of European societies, as encoded in Weber's thesis of the *Protestant work ethic* among others. Another is the idea that capitalism is or has been governed by fair rules of exchange based on mutually understood terms.

The West and the Rest: A Grammar of Authority

The racial epistemology survived in the social science because it was the only way to (1) elevate supposedly unique attributes of Europe as both reason and justification for its actions abroad; (2) depreciate the involvement of Europe in the violence associated with conquest, colonialism, and their aftermaths; (3) create a grammar and ethics of power and authority that legitimates the present international order and its affective economies. With the universalization of European reason and institutions, theorists could now talk about conquest and enslavement, colonialism and barbarism, and dispossession and expropriations strictly as outcomes of "natural" processes of expansion and war. So too did the naturalization of Europe's role in history come into being principally as a justificatory trope for a structure of authority according to which the Rest rightfully and legitimately deferred to the West on international morality. Finally, with the racialization of the other in theoretical speculations, theorists could set aside judgment on the outcomes of European actions abroad, particularly colonial processes. These included morally ambiguous activities, including fifteenth-century slave raiding in Africa (by Portugal) and subsequent transatlantic slave trade; the sixteenth-century conquest and plunder of the Americas (Portugal, Spain, England, France, and the Netherlands); seventeenth-century raids in Indonesia (Netherlands); twentieth-century plunder of Bengal, India (England); nineteenth-century opium trade in China (English); and nineteenth- to twentieth-century new imperialism and colonialism.

These processes did not just cause death and the defeat of the inhabitants of these regions. They fundamentally altered prior relations of production and exchanges across regions. They also initiated new modes of accumulating wealth on behalf of monarchs and states that were spearheaded by pirates, adventurers, and buccaneers. Related activities are the stuff of legends. For instance, the conquest of the New World and modern slavery initiated a new cartography of regions and identities and new lines of inquiry into the human sciences that led to the advent of anthropology. The new ethnography filled China, the Ottoman Empire, India, Africa, and the New World with contestable representations of cultures of autonomous and self-contained regions. These were now inhabited by Orientals, Arabs, Christians, Muslims, Hindus, Buddhists, and others. Western myths of progress, work, and ethic served to organize these relevant spaces hierarchically spanning from old world infidels (inhabiting China, India, and the Ottoman Empire) and heathens in Africa to other variously named categories elsewhere. Philosophers could then formulate rationales that bequeathed the West with the responsibility or obligation to fill the civilizational gaps separating the various communities.[44] Social theorists too could thus delegitimize any claims against the perpetrators of these activities.[45]

The realization of these aims depended upon affective attachments to a mystified order of beings, of Christians, Muslims, and others, moved by variable and detectable intentions of good or evil. Correspondingly, theorists developed an ontological, but frequently dubious discourses of contrasts of unbending righteous allies and fixed and wicked enemies. The latter category was either deserving of opposition and confrontation or undeserving of solicitation, consultation, and entreaty. Related discourses and narratives of security, war, and peace reflected the related historical (still regional) views on power, its functions, utility, and purposes: collective order and stability, protection and individual safety, preservation of collective and individual identities and of rights, and the preservation of individual liberty and personal property.

What has been mentioned in the previous paragraph suggest that, from the sixteenth century onward, the production of international thought did not reflect the complexity of the moral order.[46] European writings on international law and diplomatic history aspired to generate universal thoughts and norms, but they remained peculiar legal and political products, bound as it were, by parochial archives and memories reflecting the values and political loyalties of writers: Thomists (mostly Catholic), naturalists (initially Protestants and Catholics), positivists (modernists), and the like. Although they claimed to effect a symbolic universal order through corresponding legal or ethical regimes, post-Renaissance legal theorists invariably defended or justified parochial interests.[47]

International thought thus construed obscures the global contexts of international morality as well as the processes of hybridity and contestation that give form to modern institutions. Even if unimaginable today, European settlements survived the colonial environments thanks largely to their embrace of "local knowledge" and ideas as well as the empathy and sympathy of native populations.[48] In many instances, "local knowledges" found their way, unacknowledged, in Western thought and moral discourses. European philosophers and publicists too remained heavily indebted to contemporaneous non-European ideas. Indeed, Francis Bacon, John Locke, Voltaire, and Dénis Diderot and other post-Renaissance philosophers and scholars were also aspiring interpreters and translators of native "cultures," "customs," and habits. Consistently, international publicists like Grotius readily recognized that non-Christians had produced instruments of trade comparable to European ones.[49] Accordingly, Grotius and like-minded publicists advocated the extension of some forms of recognition and relative autonomy to "peaceful" non-European elites and rulers. Predictably, however, Grotius was unable to transcend the political conflicts and moral ambivalence toward non-Europeans afforded to him by his position as legal counsel for the Dutch East India Company. He vainly attempted to reconcile the notion of non-Western moral agency with the reality of an empire predicated on Christianity and European superiority. This dilemma presented him with theoretical and ethical difficulties and in the end he remained committed to both the moral unity of humanity and the greater Christian imperial claims within it. He granted moral agency to non-Christians but only so that they could engage in contracts and treaties with partners of their choosing.[50]

Throughout, scholars sought to reposition Europe and the West as dispensers of international morality and, therefore, their ultimate arbiters. They thus bolstered the authority of Western canons as the basis of international understanding and morality. With the modern ascendancy of archives as the basis of knowledge came illusions and misconceptions about both Europe and the Rest. The content of this knowledge has been neither neutral nor premised on the legitimacy of all human experiences.[51] To reprise an earlier argument, this knowledge was founded primarily upon modern inflections on historical accounts (originating from Homer, Herodotus, and Thucydides to travel narratives from imperial times) and philosophical understandings (from Plato and Aristotle onward). It emerges thus that the legitimacy of knowledge rested in its concordance with the deduced European experience and institutional development, from Augsburg (where that continent institutionalized domestic tolerance in 1555) to Westphalia (which sanctified princely authority in 1648), and Utrecht (which ushered in the balance of power and the terms of modern hegemony in 1713).[52]

Realism, Idealism, and their Derivations

To make sense of the gratuitous violence of Western expansion, imperialism, and colonialism, IR necessarily reaches deep into nineteenth-century natural history and its consecrated political ethics. This exercise puts a particular spin on the writings and ideas of the Greeks and Romans—particularly those of Homer, Herodotus, Aristotle, Plato, Thucydides, and Cicero among others.[53] These are complemented with those of post-Renaissance modern thinkers like Niccolo Machiavelli and Francesco Guicciardini (Italy); Thomas Hobbes (England) and Benedict de Spinoza (Netherlands); Jean Bodin, Baron de Montesquieu, and Jean-Jacques Rousseau (France); and Carl von Clausewitz, Friedrich Hegel, and Immanuel Kant (Prussia).[54] Thus mobilized, Greek topos and Roman metaphors and dictums of order, power, and sovereignty provide more palatable views into European actions abroad. The interpretations of Greek teachings and internalization of Roman practices by such diverse figures as Machiavelli, Hobbes, and Hegel helped to dress up dubious ethics—for instance, *raison d'etat* (or the national interest, in utilitarian Anglo-Saxon thought)—in the gloss of objectivity and nature, encapsulated by power and sovereignty against anarchy. It also helped that the more contemporary of these disciplinary precursors endorsed the projection of the imperial European will (or desire where applicable) and its morality as either universal rationalities or ethical imperatives. In either case, the conclusion was to establish the necessity of European control and leadership over the Rest and international affairs as legitimate universal goal.

Even in the nineteenth century, the production of an ethics of power alone was not enough to justify conquest and colonization.

Those who endorse the New Imperialism had to find fault with so-called natives. As president of the Royal Society of International Law, for instance, James Lorimer authoritatively defended the utility of the findings of ethnography on the attributes of the races to the inceptions of the "institutes of international law" and "jural relations of the separate communities."[55] Lorimer combined archival knowledge with crude ethnography to great effects, but his did not involve comparative analyses in cultures, ideas, and traditions worldwide. He was following in the footsteps of Niebuhr that "the true historical perspective of Greco-Roman life should be race, not politics': the temper and character of the races, as demonstrated in their close affections, common names, and kindred blood and color."[56]

Consistently, despite its diversity of opinions and perspectives, IR has converged upon recognizable epistemic nodes: (1) that the central problematic of international relations is anarchy; (2) that common-sense, rationality, values, and institutions are unevenly distributed across the moral order; (3) that, although all moral entities are entitled to equal rights, they do not equally possess the moral authority to legislate for the whole; and (4) that the privilege of legislating for the whole remains an exclusive privilege reserved to those with the proper moral disposition, intellectual capacity, and mental faculties. International theory also assumed prevailing notions of the unevenness of the political capacity (e.g., to form government and civil order) and cultural faculty (to reason) of the different constituents of the moral order. This differentiation of capacity and faculty has been the bases for distinctions between political society and civil society; rationalism and nonrational belief systems; and political pragmatism and moral corruption and fallibility.

Against this background, IR has sought to envisage pragmatic modes of existence. Here too, there is convergence around two primary reflexes corresponding to two modern ideologies: "realism" and "idealism." While clear about their purpose and teleology, these reflexes and ideologies have led to paradoxical, ambiguous, and overly simplistic conclusions about the nature of international politics and therefore policy. As a result, they have devolved into a number of subdisciplinary spinoffs during the latter part of the twentieth century to reflect shifting political pragmatism: for example neorealism, game theory, rational choice, neoliberalism, institutionalism, and the like.

According to conventions, political realism traces its origin to iconic figures and texts dating as far back as ancient Greece—particularly recollections by Thucydides, Herodotus, and others of war, its causes, and the foundation of lasting peace. Realists relate the political ideas and wisdom of these historic figures through the writing of intermediaries spanning the Middle Ages to the modern era: among them, Niccolo Machiavelli (medieval Italy), Thomas Hobbes (civil war England), Jean Bodin (monarchist France), and Count Charles von Clausewitz (embattled Prussia). These authors and others are credited with definitive pronouncements on the nondependability of human nature, the need for political order under a Leviathan, or a sovereign with statesman with total control of the means of violence and autonomy to determine the condition of use of violence. The sovereign, whether a prince or a man of the people, must cultivate particular kinds of virtue, and the contingency of fortune or opportunity. In the realist imaginary, Machiavelli is rivaled only by Thomas Hobbes in his insistence on order and the monopoly of the means of violence by the sovereign as its means.

Realism holds a number of generalizations which, according to Hans Morgenthau, for instance, represent "eternal verities" that are "able to guide the thought and action of our time as well as of any other."[57] These verities include the propensity of humans to want to dominate others through control of their minds and actions;[58] the inherence of violence to human nature and war to international politics; the endurance of competition and anarchy in both the state of nature and any international system of political sovereign or autonomous entities.[59] According to Morgenthau, "armed strength as a threat or a potentiality is the most important material factor making for the political power of a nation. If it becomes an actuality in war, it signifies the substitution of military for political power."[60] "Political ethics," in this context, "is indeed the ethics of doing evil" and moral courage is "To know with despair that the political act is inevitably evil, and to act nevertheless."[61] Again, these views are not uniformly shared by all realists. E. H. Carr, for instance, has argued that the oversimplifications of human nature and human condition is the result of "muddled thinking" that attributes everything to human wickedness while taking the latter to be a function of natural law.[62] Such a narrow account of human behavior, he argues, could not reasonably serve as basis for international morality and a world order.[63]

Political idealism too harkens back to the Greeks, Aristotle and Plato among them, before traveling a tortuous journey through time to the present. The major highlights of the road to Greece are the Renaissance rebirth of humanism, the Enlightenment gift of rationalism, and nineteenth-century constitutional liberalism. Whereas Aristotle must be a necessary reference for a republican order, idealists imagine Grotius and Kant as apostles of salvation of the political order from moral decay. Grotius and Kant provide the vision and the language with which to redeem collectives and individuals from anarchy and/or the abyss of war. The choice of Grotius and Kant is justified by their views on war (for Grotius) and peace (Kant). While Grotius reflected more closely on post-Reformation religious wars, the emergence of the sovereign state, and the consequences for Europe of expansion, Kant was more attune to the Enlightenment and the impacts of the French and American revolutions.

Idealism too has spun derivative perspectives, rational institutionalism and neoliberalism. Reflecting post-Enlightenment and postrevolutionary ideologies, these perspectives instrumentalize time in the service of policy. They envisage European civilization and cultures as progress and the latter as a necessary condition of human evolution. Progress thus envisaged is an improvement upon backward traditions and supposed unvarying ways of premodern Europeans and their latter-day non-European "native" prototypes.[64]

Idealism and its derivatives are not without detractors. Dubbing it utopianism, Carr faults its adepts for viewing progress as a universal commodity to be transferred to others through political trusteeship, self-determination, interdependence, collective security, democracy, and like institutions. This, he argues, is trying to create reality in the image of ideology.[65] Morgenthau too rejects the reliance of idealists (or rather rationalists) on "reason" and "logical deductions" alone for their conceptions of reason, the individual, and state.[66] Morgenthau agrees with Carr that idealists/utopians tend to be "oblivious to the corruption of power in the public sphere while still being conscious of its private manifestations."[67] They argue, in Morgenthau's words, that concepts like interdependence, collective security, democracy, self-determination, justice, pcacc, "are abstract generalities which may be applied to any particular situation but which are not peculiar to any particular one."[68]

The realist versus idealist classification itself has not be reassuring to all. Chris Brown, for instance, has argued that Martin Wight offers a "more elaborate classification" of international theory, which he divides into "Machiavellian," "Grotian," and "Kantian." According to Brown, Wight's classification does much to improve upon the inherent paradoxes and ambiguities of the prior classification.[69] To paraphrase David Campbell and Michael Dillon, the prevailing trend in international thought is to assume that the autonomous reasoning subject is capable of disclosing the rational character of politics (an epistemological claim) while centrally constituting politics in reality as violence (an ontological claim).[70] The connection between the two assumptions is itself constitutive of social practice. It allows theorists to apply reason (judgment for realists) to disclose that the nature of politics is anarchic and to envisage the corresponding political pragmatism: self-help or cooperation, both dependent upon the ultimate application of violence.[71] Related discourses posit the state and individual as a rational political subject that must by necessity divorce ethics and civil morality from politics[72] in order to naturalize violence as constitutive of politics and sovereignty.[73] Indeed, as Steve Smith has argued, international thought "promotes understanding via a 'reason' separated from ethical or moral concerns."[74]

The separation of reason from ethical concerns is more pronounced in regard to others. Carr's writings reflect the two dimensions of this disengagement. One holds that political progressivism—currently the norms, standards, and practices of liberalism–does not apply to other racial entities or nations, or peoples with immutable cultures and customs.[75] The other is that, as a result of the first, European powers should endeavor to envisage different regimes of morality that correspond to the racial and regional organization of the world. Hence, Carr cautions against the application in "civilized Europe" of a "Darwinian doctrine" that erroneously identifies "the good of the whole with the good of the fittest." Specifically, he stigmatizes as a form of "totalitarianism" the idea that violence may be used in all instances by the strong to coerce the weak.[76] Carr advises the alteration of Darwinism and the underlying totalitarianism in favor of a balance between power and a corresponding morality that upholds the "right of the strongest to assume world leadership" while preserving the interest of the weakest states. Correspondingly, Carr rejects the core assumption of realism on the ground that coercion must not be "turned by civilised peoples against one another."[77] In contrast, Carr is agnostic about "the brutalities" of the eighteenth and nineteenth centuries insofar as they "were confined to dealings between the civilised and the uncivilised." Subscribing to a selfsame logic,[78] Carr is unsure about the moral unity of the world as well as the possibility of fairness, justice, freedom, and human rights in the colonial context. He is not alone in this regard.[79]

As shown by Campbell, the dynamics and views of extraterritorial interventions today are foregrounded in an ontology of self and other, of identity and culture, religion and region that mirror colonial ones. Not only do metaphors of sovereignty culminate in the affirmation of the political order and settlements envisaged by the West, but the figure of the disorderly must logically be the other, signified by the absence of the institutions of the state in regions inhabited by natives.[80] It is there—in Africa, Asia, and the New World—that anarchy naturally reigns and that Western powers necessarily need to intervene.[81] There, according to Robert D. Kaplan, lies Sierra Leone in the outer reaches of civilization, "beyond salvage"; "within the *wall of disease*"; within "*nature unchecked*"; strewn with young toughs and private armies.[82] As in the Balkans, Kaplan claims, international morality on power and political agency, or sovereignty and autonomy, cannot be upheld here on the same terms as they are elsewhere.[83] Kaplan's recommendation is that the "civilized" must be prepared to relinquish familiar patterns of thought when dealing with these regions.[84] Rather, the former must decide whether there is anything they are willing to do for populations trapped in an unchecked state of nature.

The Next Stage: A Theory of the Subject

In revisiting disciplinary orthodoxies, critical theorists, Marxist or not, postmodernists, and feminists have sought to distance themselves ontologically and epistemologically from so-called mainstream truth claims. These perspectives took a fresh look at the relationships between modes of analysis, knowledge (or thought), and their objects. As they sought to detach themselves from their own circumstances to envisage broader contexts, these reflectivists also attempted to dispense with the instrumentalization of difference. Reflectivism, therefore, involves consideration of the relationship between theorists, thought, and its objects—for instance, community and ethics. I consider two kinds. One, self-consciously Euro-centered and, as such, is deliberately anchored in Occidentalist perspectives on the origins and properties of reason and political rationality. The other is more apprehensive of Occidentalism and is only implicitly Eurocentrist. The first may, for purposes of inclusion, allow for revision of knowledge and commonsense to account for diversity; but its forms of inclusion are grounded in assimilation or subordination to its notions of universality, rationalism, and the common good of other supposed lesser values, norms, and institutions.

This type of reflective theory is common among critical theorists and feminists for whom the teleology of criticism is improvement upon political practice, but not necessarily the recasting of the underlying modes of thought and knowledge. Andrew Linklater's views of the function of international theory and the mechanisms for extending rights illustrate the difficulties of critical theorists.[85] Linklater understands the need to rethink current conceptions of international community, morality, and relations by looking afresh at the "normative problem of the state," the "sociological problem of community," and the "praxeological question of reform." In these regards, Linklater has the advantage of being both theoretically reflective (critical) and politically inclusive. Consistently, he does not find any utility in the dichotomies of state versus nation, society of states versus community of humankind, citizen versus noncitizens, universality versus relativism, and commensurability versus incommensurability. He would therefore extend the privileges afforded to Western states and citizens to "noncitizens"—literally its own and metaphorically postcolonial entities: the state would offer protection to those previously excluded; state and political communities would create new spaces for the disenfranchised citizenry; the political order would allow for multiple expressions of views and sentiments to meet the requirements of cultural diversity.

Still, Linklater is unable to confront the actualized political division of human communities into differently positioned subjects, agents, and actors. There are two obstacles to such a move. The first is an insistence on the twin notions of "the uniformity of human nature' and "the timelessness of certain moral principles," beyond culturally-specific powers or needs.' Insisting that he does not mean to "devalue or denigrate' cultural norms that are cherished elsewhere," Linklater would draw diverse perspectives into a synoptic whole, with the aim of "striking a balance between the search for transcultural values and respect for cultural differences in modern international relations."[86]

The form of this generosity is as problematic as the absence of concrete proposals on mechanisms for eliminating existing privileges; for obligating the presently privileged to adequately respond to the underprivileged; for incorporating the moral imaginaries of variously situated subjects, agents, and actors into political and philosophical conceptions of power, agency, and political rationality. Linklater's generosity assumes full knowledge of postcolonial criticism of the problems of international politics. But he is mistaken about related criticisms of modernity, rationalism, and philosophical and political universalism. Such criticisms do not conceive prior misapplication or suspension of international morality (likened metonymically to a liberal constitutional regime) as a mere problem of exclusion. They involve considerations of the very terms of the constitutional order—the implicated political imaginaries, juridical and moral systems, and their base-notions of communities and obligations—as mechanisms of exclusion.

From this latter perspective, it is significant that Linklater sanctions the exclusion from disciplinary debates of those who would consider alternatives. He justified this exclusion as self-imposed exile: "challenging as they are, new theoretical departures will remain marginal unless they develop concrete empirical research programs which shed light on the central issues of world politics."[87] To be included, therefore, the critics must refrain from considering any issues that may reconsider existing representations of politics or the terms under which they are discussed!

There is another kind of reflective theory that involves contestations of the epistemological grounds of post-Enlightenment social knowledge, its structures of thought, and related constructions of political subjectivity.[88] Whereas rationalists once claimed to provide unity and sustenance to the moral order, more radical critics have recently aspired to fill the void left by the failure of Enlightenment-associated ideologies to bring about human emancipation, peace and order, and justice and equality.[89] Postmodernists are among the latter category. According to Richard K. Ashley and R. B. J. Walker, the postmodern agenda seeks to identify the "times" and "spaces" assigned by modernity to its various subjects of the moral order; the practices of power associated with modernity; the limits placed upon personal and political autonomy by political and economic structures and their implementations as traditions.[90] They show also that modern notions of time and space are implicated in post-Enlightenment humanist views of Man (or human faculties) and related notions of community (or society) and their needs (or desires).[91] Reason thus temporalized and localized ceases to be universal and becomes another historical construct purposefully enlisted to enact parochial orders.[92] In this light, Jim George and David Campbell have proposed an "agenda of dissent" that involves the opening up of "thinking spaces" in contemporary social theory, but its four major elements of critical analysis are "interdisciplinary."[93] They seek to explore "a space of thought to be exploited by a variety of dissident voices who would speak in reply to the dangers and opportunities" of modern political life.

Their views and goals are widely held among feminists, albeit on separate grounds. Consistently, V. Spike Peterson has contested the adequacy of IR construction of political identity, subjectivity, political rationality, all of them modernist in derivation.[94] She has argued also that disciplinary boundaries and their objects are imposed and not discovered and that they are better thought of as contingent practices and not transcendent "givens."[95] Speaking directly to post-positivism in the United States, Peterson proposes a revisiting of disciplinary "assumptions and tacit commitments" with the aim of evaluating the political effects of knowledge.[96] Peterson is in agreement with postcolonial critics in these regards, but for the absence of comparative approach to representation and social knowledge. Arjun Appadurai would complement Peterson's enterprise with a request for "acquaintance with the facts of modern life" more broadly in order to appreciate the "translocal processes" and "congeries of large-scale interactions" that have characterized the world for many centuries.[97]

The point of these reflections is not merely to show that traditional approaches to IR are mistaken. It is to show that the practices of interpretation, production, and normalization of IR theory are themselves implicated in larger social and political practices.[98] I therefore share postmodern and feminist commitment to seeking to understand the nature and manners in which discourses produce structures of domination and alienation. This commonality comes easily in part because postmodernist and critical feminist positions and views are much less Occidentalist in the traditional sense. They require metaphysical and affective distance from the self, or ethnographic distancing, as well as criticisms of the ideological grounds and political traditions of Eurocentrism and Occidentalism. Many like Ashley and Walker are deliberately *self-conscious* and inviting of others to offer their particular perspectives on the discipline and its regimes of truth. The postmodern and feminist introspection has received the scorn of disciplinary "gatekeepers" who view self-criticism as parody of sacred grounds, Eurocentrism and Occidentalism, always disguised as objective (scientifically), rational (ideologically), and universal (ethically).

Whither Postcolonial Vocality

I wish nonetheless to stress that even this thicker reflective theory is fashionably Euro-centered. Without hubris or malice, the relevant theories necessarily carry a residual Eurocentrism as a function of discursive traditions, contexts, and archives. Eurocentrism emanates thus from the absence of critical comparative approaches to self-study and self-representation. Barring comparativism, the best of analysts refer principally to what they know, or the familiar and familial. They develop perspectives logically by references to personal and collective experiences, memories of those experiences, archives, methods, and imaginaries. The result is that presumptive universal questions arise from contingencies of events (including regional, geopolitical, and cultural circumstances) and knowledge (ideology, method, and epistemology). As I show later, this basic reality is diminished by consciousness of the others, the desire to write about others or circumstances beyond their own, and the decision to rethink prior knowledge in order to accommodate imminence. The voices and agendas of self and others are already foreground in Western social theory, its views of (1) science, method, and questions of rationality, objectivity, and truth; (2) its constructions of agency and subject as opposed to structure and object; and (3) related linguistic and cultural terms of debates on identity, reality, and meaning.[99] Even in the event of imminent consciousness of others, reflectivist claims, pronouncements, and assumptions about the formerly colonized do not involve the latter's self-representations of their own wills, desires, and interests, on the one hand, and their political imaginaries, moral systems, and notions of identity, politics, community (or society), and law (also obligations), on the other.

This is not to be belittle the emancipatory move of criticism. As Walker has noted, the strength of individuals like Ashley is "to take the Anglo-American theory of international relations seriously as a ground for critical social and political exploration."[100] The underlying obsession runs the risk of getting stuck on Anglo-Saxon topos and accounts. By focusing singly on Anglo-Saxon or Western modernity and its terms, the critics have neglected other modernities, whether or not concurrent with the Western one. It is no secret, for instance, that after the Crusades Islam underwent a renaissance of sort and the Muslim political entities throughout the world spun empires and merchant networks extending from Asia to Africa to the doors of Europe. This "Renaissance" opened European eyes to ancient Greece and an era of admiration for the Muslim world. This admiration was illustrated by Roger Bacon's appeal to Europeans to "the study of oriental living languages . . . as a way of gaining knowledge from the Muslims in Spain and the Middle East."[101] Western modernity also countenances multiple identities and interests obeying a multiplicity of temporalities that texture its unfolding into separate spatial configurations. These spatial and political configurations included empires of conjoined regions from Africa to Australia through processes that were contested across space and time. They also produced uneven effects that gave varied inflections on colonial modernity itself. This is one of the reasons that international thought requires novel types of comparative history, hermeneutics, and ethnography to grasp the distinctiveness of modernity in colonial history as well as the complementarity in time and space of the various forms of modernity.

The other source of weakness in poststructural and postmodern criticisms is the rejection of notions of "deep structures, eternal truths, and perennial values" as they appear in rationalism (its liberal instantiation) and structuralism (including Marxism).[102] Again, critics have substantiated their positions with laudable demonstrations of the symbolic contexts of thought and identity formation. These have led also to speculations about political possibilities and their potential constituencies. There is much to be admired and taken from such speculations. As Ramashray Roy has indicated, suspicions of rationalism and structuralism are warranted especially when related discussions are designed to "absolve man of moral responsibility."[103] Still, Roy is concerned that scant attention has been paid to the manners in which cultural and material forces have interacted historically across competing modernities and their spaces of enactment. Roy's wariness is central to postcolonial criticism of both rationalism and its Western critics. In foregoing sustained analyses of the structures of power and social relations in the different spaces or sites created by Western modernity, critical theorists also dispense with historiographic, hermeneutic, and ethnographic questions that can only be addressed through a critical comparative approach.

The tendency to ignore the subjectivity of others is a residue of one of the darker sides of Western modernity—colonialism. Since its advent modern colonialism has shaped the encounters between the West and the Rest in multiple ways. For as long as it has lasted, colonialism has elicited criticisms and opposition from anticolonial forces as well as contrasting ethical projects. Like Western modernity, anticolonialism was the coming into being of a consciousness of self as well as a contestation of the structures of authority and legitimacy of the colonial order and its economies. It is born of a historical consciousness of oppression and denial of vocality to the colonized. The advent of anticolonialism marks an iconic moment of dissent. It also augurs a moral initiative in favor of repudiating the colonial act, Occidentalism, and their Eurocentrist imaginaries. This initiative was complemented with the desire of the colonized to *express their own wills, desires, and interests* as well as to autonomously interpret the moral universe through their own experiences. Anticolonialists also aspired to different forms of moral subjectivity and political agency, ones to be opposed to formulations of Western sovereignty and rationality that enabled violence against others. In short, anticolonialism culminated in decolonization, or the formal end of colonial rule. Although limited in its extent, decolonization held the promise of a new order in lieu of the one initiated by the Eurocentrist consensus and Occidentalist conceit. It therefore reopened international relations to new inquiries about the nature, function, and purpose of politics, values, and their institutions.

Postcolonialism, Time, and their Effects

Decolonization projected the formerly colonized into history on terms parallel to those of "Europe." After World War II, the colonized were no longer content to demand and wait patiently for moral consistency, juridical equality, or acts of generosity from Europe and/or the West. They were determined politically and intellectually to enact a new (postcolonial) order. The underlying idea of postcoloniality mobilized majorities of postcolonial intellectuals and politicians in the former European empires. To enact the postcolonial agenda, the formerly colonized laboriously challenged Western ideologies and their modes of thought and inquiry. To be sure, postcolonial analyses are not uniform as they diverge in their points of origination, disciplinary home, and ethical stands.[104] This diversity also reflects differences in colonial histories, linguistic and scientific traditions, and loci of enunciations of theorists and/or critiques.[105] During colonial rule, each mode of colonial administration allowed for distinct modes of native participation in imperial political economies of knowledge. Related trajectories affected the modes of inquiry and representation of colonial subjects as well as their accounts or memories of empire. These results are evident in postcolonial discourses and criticisms today. They account, for instance, for the fact that the South Asian subaltern variety of postcolonial perspectives originated in cultural studies. They also account for the origination of postcolonial criticism in the former French empire simultaneously in literature and political philosophy.

Like anticolonialism before it, the postcolonial struggle has its own temporalities and spaces of enactment. In the ontological instance, postcoloniality corresponds to a temporal fissure in modernity. It was through the ideological device of time that Europe and then the West elaborated a typology of a civilizational time according to which humanity and human development were cast into a single continuum of time lacking spatial dimensions. The metaphysic of time assumed a common human beginning in the dark ages (prehistory) but uneven spatial processes depending upon the capabilities and faculties of relevant human communities. In this light, each society was a thing, "moving in response to an inner clockwork."[106] This assumption allowed Europe politically to define history, society, and culture in such a manner as to confiscate political subjectivity for those assumed to lack the capacity to establish a viable order. Hence were born notions of trusteeship, protectorates, civilizing mission, and other "ethical" acts that relegated non-Europeans to "historical waiting room"[107] where they still linger in international theory.

Decolonization thus required confrontation of historicism, the primary instrument of Eurocentrism and Occidentalism, both of which absorb others as the inverse image of Europe.[108] Predictably in Africa, particularly among Francophone Africans, postcolonial criticisms have followed in the footsteps of anticolonial criticisms of Enlightenment-derived reason, post-Enlightenment rationalities, and their primary instrument: natural history. Their aim was to displace Europe from the center of history and consciousness in order to accommodate the experiences of others. This move necessarily required different ethical standards than those proposed by the extant Western ideologies of time and subjectivity.

In Africa, as elsewhere, anticolonial criticisms were shaped by modes of thought, languages, and practices that resided only occasionally in Western canons, idioms, and political traditions. Anticolonialism required ontological autonomy, even if only provisionally. As such, protagonists narrated historical events as a matter of sovereign act or authorial privilege. The emergent images of colonial acts and their justificatory texts are thus filtered through new ethical standards, some of which exceed the normative boundaries envisaged by the colonizers. The latter allowed anticolonialists and postcolonialists to legitimately affect their own subjective meanings to the rationalities of empire as well as the political sensibilities of colonial powers and their ideologues.

Postcolonialism too aspires to new hermeneutics, historiography, and ethnography. Accordingly, postcolonialism rejects post-Enlightenment notions of the proper and deviant as well as the accompanying views of non-European societies as inherently fixed, with immutable characteristics distributed temporally according to endogenous attributes. As I show later, this is not a wholesale disputation of Enlightenment belief in the possibility and desirability of universalism. It is simply to stress the contingency of any form of universalism. As I illustrate in what follows, postcolonial criticism also engages the universal while remaining skeptical of modern institutions that formalize narrow identities and parochial agendas, values, and interests.

Consistently, postcolonial discourses are ambivalent and skeptical toward modernity, universalism, and modern institutions. Their temporalities are distinct from those of postmodernism and post-structuralism, yet the former complement the latter in their teleology and aspirations. Thus, the latter cannot supplant the former. The postcolonial time is a decisive moment of revelation of the central but necessary myths of the colonial order. Key among them was the idea that, alone, "Europe" and "the West" stood for the universal and that their habits and institutions were self-evidently justified and in the collective interest. In IR, as elsewhere in the social sciences, "Europe" and "the West" still stand for many as short-hand for "goodness and universalism." This rendition of Europe and the West screens off their participation in international reality—not only universalism, pluralism, and the institutionalization of international norms, but also conquest, enslavement, colonialism, and other violent and coercive processes—in order to construct a self-image of benevolence, generosity, and humanitarianism. Yet, to reprise Dipesh Chakrabarty's formula, Europe and the West are revealed as "imaginary figures" albeit still "deeply embedded in *clichéd and shorthand forms* in some everyday habits of thought."[109]

Postcolonialism also has its conventionalized systems of ideas and idioms, or languages, and of politics which emerged from the collective ethos and style of anticolonialism. In Africa, they were inspired by 1920s anticolonial agendas developed in imperial métropoles in conjunction with comparable regional movements as well as postwar Afro-Asian initiatives such as the 1955 Bandung Conference. These agendas and fora formulated specific ethical requisites and political determinants that they understood as means to a unified foreign policy imaginary. In Africa, therefore, postcolonialism retained its focus on the identity and dignity of the formerly colonized as moral subjects, their integrity and autonomy as sovereign agents, and their will to freedom. These concerns also galvanized debates at the United Nations and associated institutions. There, the struggle for a postcolonial order has focused on political autonomy and authority within the international order; the right to speak for self and through the cultural resources on which individual participants draw their moral imaginaries; a quest for commensurable ideas, values, and objectives through which international morality can be formulated.

The agenda underlying postcolonial criticisms is postcoloniality, a time beyond colonialism. The underlying ethos emerged after decolonization partly in response to specific Western attempts at neocolonialism. This agenda has been mistaken as hostility to Western interests. This can only be true only if Western interests are undistinguished from neocolonialism. Postcoloniality is properly a bid to end all forms of colonialism by transforming the structures of the international order, its mechanisms of allocations of resources, and its value systems. These goals have brought to light the internal laws that thus far defined relations between the former colonial powers and the formerly colonized. To be sure, related undertakings by postcolonial states have varied in nature and intensity. Further, they have been executed with varying degrees of foresight, care, and appreciations of the mechanisms of the international political economy. However, policy flaws and failure of appreciations do not detract from the spirit of postcoloniality that survives to date in multiple forms.

This initial postcolonial agenda bore on such mundane matters as political power and control of natural resources. It includes the decisions by Gamal Abdel Nasser to nationalize the waterways of the Suez Canal (1956) and Iran's Prime Minister Mossadeq to nationalize the petroleum industry (1954). They were followed by similar decisions by Libya's leader Mohammar Khadafi (1969) and Chile's Salvador Allende (1970s). The immediacy of policy only masks the deeper structural and symbolic shifts in international morality that brought about these actions. Specifically, they were a direct rebuke of a mendacious claim, articulated authoritatively by John Locke and sustained through four centuries of international law, that denied *dominium* (lawful possession of property and political power) to non-Europeans on the ground that the latter had no affective attachments to their environments and no moral claim to their resources. Rebukes to colonial forms in international politics were never fully coordinated. Some were undertaken alone as did Nasser in the Suez Canal crisis. At times, postcolonial leaders reacted collectively as they did in 1995 in Bandung. They have also joined other leaders from all regions and political traditions as they did when they joined other leaders of so-called non-aligned countries in 1961 in creating the Non-Aligned Movement. In any case, these actions nonetheless were direct responses to emergent neo-colonial forms around such issues as material justice, the use of force, and the authority to legislate globally.[110]

Difference, Disclosures, and the Moral Order

In the next four chapters, I illustrate a particular form of postcolonial criticism and its visions of postcoloniality. I explore the efforts of a community of intellectuals from the French colonial empire who engaged France, on the one hand, and the United States and Great Britain, on the other, from 1939 to 1950 on the central themes of the war and the form and purpose of the emergent international order. My point is not simply that French defeat and the disintegration of the imperial order allowed these so-called évolués to play a central role in the liberation of that country. I wish to demonstrate that they helped to redefine French politics, French thought, and by this token the terms of international politics. Because of their location on the political left, theorists have long maintained that these colonial subjects derived their visions, imaginaries, and referents from French universalist ideologies. This is only partly true. The colonized may have frequently referred to French universalist idioms and concepts, but they did so only because such idioms constituted a vehicular language capable of countenancing the visions, political imaginaries, and ethical referents of the postcolonial order envisaged by the colonized. Theirs was universalist too but not in the ways that the term had been understood in Enlightenment and post-Enlightenment French and Western traditions.

The project focuses on the relationships between French authorities, French nationals, and the évolués, who played a particularly crucial role in redefining French institutions and bolstering the French resistance and, in the process, established distinct practices and languages of politics among coherent constituencies beyond the reach of the state. Following the defeat and occupation of France by Germany, they were most instrumental in establishing wartime networks in defense of France and against Nazism and Fascism, emanating either first or, if not, conjointly from colonial subjects and French nationals, both liberated from the authority of the French state.

Prodded first by Félix Eboué and, then, Gabriel d'Arboussier and Ouezzin Coulibaly, the évolués developed doctrines and visions of state sovereignty and global interactions, of moral agency and subjectivity, and of the collective good that differed greatly from Western ones. These doctrines and visions were constitutive of a distinct "language" of international relations, founded upon a discernible political imaginary: a vision of the moral order and political community. Theirs allowed them to develop distinct imaginaries of peace, freedom, security, justice, and interdependence that permeated wartime and the postwar era. I am also interested in their use of symbols, figures of speech, and metaphors pertinent to power and interest, on the one hand, and to international morality and law, on the other. I propose their conceptualization of power, interest, ethics, and subjectivity forwarded as an exemplary constellation of political idioms through which one might productively orient both the study and practice of international relations. This is not just an academic interest.

The interventions of the évolués warrant engagement as alternative sources of international morality. Their imaginaries of identity, society, and social relations contrast positively with those of ruling coalitions of France, Britain, and the United States. The contrast with the French left is particularly interesting because, as the core of ruling coalitions under the Fourth Republic was left-leaning, coalitions were the primary initiators and benefactors of transimperial alliances with the colonized. Beginning with Félix Eboué's ideas and actions during tenure as governor of the French Equatorial African empire, I focus later on those of key elements of the Rassemblement Democratique Africain or RDA. I am particularly interested in their political declarations or speech acts and the possible connections they may have with reigning intellectual conventions and their canonical inspirations. As a matter of economy of space and arguments, my references to the American and British are minimal. I am assuming a common repertoire of knowledge in their regard. References to France and French politics are substantive only in regard to subjects and events less present in disciplinary narratives. Otherwise, the bulk of the book concerns my selected black (mostly African) intellectuals and politicians, who developed a plausible vision of the moral order to be opposed to the ascendent Western one as basis for international relations.

The moral vision enacted by the évolués corresponded to a different political ethos, one aiming to effect a politics and ethics of "the now." Even as France lay defeated and, later, the United States emerged dominant and uncompromising, these black intellectuals understood the co-constitution of political (and temporal) horizons between and amongst contemporaneous actors, agents, and subjects. Specifically, the RDA pursued its goal through its involvements in postwar reconstruction, when it sought to implement different conceptions of politics, justice, and economies based on distinct notions of solidarity, interdependence, and security.

The larger empirical point is that Europe and the West were not alone in the postwar era in reflecting upon the consequences of the war—specifically the chaos, horrors, and disintegration of social order engendered by the war. In Europe, I show, questions about the past and the future were framed in light of either a blend of post-Enlightenment universalist views or a pragmatism constructed from Anglo-Saxon intellectual and political traditions. These ideological blends and their intellectual sources provided the context for peculiar understandings and formulations of law, freedom, justice, solidarity, community, and peace. These are reflected in the 1941 Atlantic Charter, proclaimed by Franklin D. Roosevelt and Winston Churchill, and the 1942 Declaration by the United Nations, the antecedent to the UN Charter.[111] Here, as elsewhere, postwar questions arose from specific political and cultural contexts to reflect distinct teleologies and ethical domains of applications.

The war brought into relief new subjects and new conceptions of subjectivity that only partially depended upon Western idioms. These subjects comprised anticolonialists who joined Western skeptics in asking whether Western values (culture), science (reason and technology), and institutions (social organization) were adequate or uniquely suited to meet the requirements of the imminent world.[112] They too confronted the near-uniform existential questions about modern times within their own particular contexts. Like colonial elites everywhere, the political class in Africa approached related issues from their subject position as colonized. They spoke from various positions in the colonies and the Métropole with diverse intellectual, cultural, and political sensibilities. In Francophone Africa, elites with formal French education, known as évolués (explained earlier) benefitted from an ambiguous identity that placed them at the intersections of imperial and anticolonial politics. As I show later, some were elected to representative legislative bodies in

France, positions that they cumulated with elected and administrative posts in Africa. Their interests were thus spatially distributed across the structures of empire and the international system. As such, they thought of themselves as equally implicated in the terms of postwar resolutions as their metropolitan French counterparts. Further, the African or black elites under study in the body of this book were of ideological and political sensibilities that situated them on the political left, in metropolitan terms.

These Africans nonetheless maintained their own singularity and individuality from the French left, with corresponding positions on world politics. These positions were founded upon specific ethno-graphic, cultural, and political referents that accounted for their own modern experiences. To them, the "sclerosis" of the international system included the advent of Nazism, Fascism, and other forms of totalitarianism. But it also included larger crises of empire, state, and governance that had at their core institutions and structures of values and interest that belied Western humanist and universalist proclamations regarding freedom, political autonomy, sovereignty, and self-determination. These factors gave form and substance to African deliberations such that they asked different questions and offered distinct interpretations of international events than the French left. Related differences in political lexicon and discourses and political languages and their grammar of engagements (or ethics) are the object of the chapters in this book. They provide the empirical basis for further comments on the global moral order, ethics, communication, and other languages of international relations that are obscured by prevailing disciplinary narratives and international theory.

The other more ontological point is that the postwar era is decidedly postcolonial: the advent of a generalized consciousness of the common fate of humanity; the rejection as unfounded and dangerous of cultural and racial ideologies that ranked humanity and political subjects hierarchically according to arbitrary but self-interested criteria of human and political subjectivity; and the realization that official Western proclamations about national political rationalities had little basis in a reality characterized partly by imperial ambitions and colonial logics. The teleology of this post-colonial consciousness conflicts today with the moral vision and political ethos imposed today by hegemonic powers. As stated earlier, postcoloniality assumes the possibility for all moral entities to form beliefs, to pass judgment, and to will the application of their values to their own contexts. It also postulates that modes of inquiry must be appropriate to their objects. Relatedly, this book (1) accounts for the emergence of the formerly colonized and their structures of thought as ontological categories in international relations; (2) maintains an ambivalence and skepticism toward modernity, universalism, and modern institutions, although it does not totally reject them; and, to these ends, (3) remains firmly grounded in a multitude of times. The book reflects ruptures in modern temporalities that belie modernist narratives in the social sciences. The assertion by the formerly colonized of their political identity, and thus subjectivity, marks the first feature of postcoloniality: the advent of new political subjects on the world stage. Unlike Western foreign policies that have actively combated this time-interruptive event of postcolonial consciousness in the postcolonial world, disciplinary narratives have yet to properly realize its implications for history: still misnamed international relations.

It remains an open bet whether disciplinary practitioners would warrant equal ontological status to narratives of "international developments" that take postcolonial "histories," memories, and like references as their points of departure. It remains, however, that postcolonial consciousness and criticisms of Western modernity, rationalism, the colonial act and their structures will persist. These criticisms hold compelling revelations about international relations today that are unrepresented in disciplinary narratives. These include *inter alia* (1) the inherent dangers represented by modern foreign policy rationalities and the corrupting effects of Western foreign policies in global politics; (2) the corrosive effects of technologies of violence, militarism, and the militarization of public life—symbolized by the militarization of prewar Europe, the militarist ambition of Nazi Germany, the holocaust, and later the cold war-related nuclear arms race and subsequent proliferation of weapons of mass destruction; and (3) the related trend toward the militarization of space.

Conclusion

This book seeks to revise IR discourses and to align its narratives with the experiences, memories, and archives of anti- and postcolonial intellectuals. It fully recognizes disciplinary diversity. As with any intellectual enterprise, IR contains divisions and divergences based on methodology, ideology, and politics. So it is that *our* discipline has generated "dissenters" and "insurgents" who have taken aim at disciplinary epistemology, ontology, and teleology. They include neo-Kantian rationalists and an assortment of postmodern and poststructural theorists. Collectively, they are inspired by the existential conditions of human diversity and multiplicity. Correspondingly, they have formulated theories that serve as a guide to corresponding ethics of engagement.

It will be evident in the following chapters that the critics themselves have not sufficiently dealt with the asymmetry of power that characterizes international politics. Nor have they coherently reflected upon the relationships between power, method, and truth. More often than not, theorists have failed to sufficiently detach themselves from their own cultural and theoretical context to cross over to "the other side," that is, to recognize the merits of otherwise constituted identities, values, and interests for the purpose of correcting or amending disciplinary narratives. Traditional or institutionalized modes and forms of inquiry have been particularly scornful and contemptuous of alternatives. Disciplinary contempt has been greatest toward approaches and perspectives that are explicitly constructed in opposition to Western values, interests, and institutions or those whose structures of recollection, affect, and practices do not conform to the institutional, epistemological, and aesthetic requirements of disciplinary forms and narratives. Thus, for instance, IR has relegated the theories of dependency, neocolonialism, imperialism to its canonical margins even as historical processes confirm the worst case scenarios of the concerned theories: that Western political, cultural, military, and economic institutions and organizations would supplant all others and thus bring about an authoritarian and less just international order.

Likewise, IR has been unable or unwilling to countenance analyses identified in the social sciences today as postcolonial in approach and/or perspective. The reason is not that the objects of postcolonial analyses lie outside disciplinary preoccupations. As discussed in chapter I, disciplinary scorn and contempt for such perspectives are partly motivated by deference to political and cultural forces, particularly to the state (in recognition of its sovereign authority and interests), foundations, and the like. Deference to these institutions is enforced both within and without the academy.[113] Yet, disciplinary scorn and contempt for postcolonial inquiries and perspectives are also motivated by ideological, cultural, and regional orientations that shape approaches to and perspectives on methods and practice.[114]

The exclusionary actions are still astonishing for a discipline that remains universalist and totalizing in its ambition. They are particularly unfortunate when they are founded upon contestable charges, for instance, that (1) the methods of postcolonial analyses are nonnormative, eclectic, and nonsensical; (2) postcolonial critics are disinterested in good faith and free exchange of ideas; and (3) Western intellectuals exclusively possess the cultural "dispositifs" for cross-cultural interlocutions and translations that promote a convergence of values across cultures and regions.[115] While I do not offer postcolonial criticisms as constitutive of an alternative theory, I wish to insist that it is a mistake to not weave postcolonial experiences and postcoloniality into disciplinary commonsense.

Again, the next four chapters show that the colonized developed plausible doctrines and visions of state sovereignty and global interactions, of moral agency and subjectivity, and of the collective good that differed greatly from Western ones. These doctrines and visions were constitutive of a distinct "language" of international relations, founded upon a discernible political imaginary: a vision of the moral order and political community. This language is in evidence in their symbols, figures of speech, and metaphors which are all pertinent to their conceptions of power and interest, on the one hand, and international morality and law, on the other. Their conceptions of power, interest, ethics, and subjectivity, contained in specific constellation of political idioms, allowed them to attach distinctly functional meanings to postwar idioms of peace, freedom, security, justice, and interdependence.

In a nutshell, it is not my desire to invalidate international theory or negate its possibility. Such a reading would be hasty and/or ungenerous. To repeat a point made in the introduction, I am not interested in remedying aporias in international knowledge so as to vindicate any particular intellectual, ideological, and/or methodical traditions that currently contend to disciplinary or epistemological hegemony. I merely wish to reconcile IR with international existence or reality to the extent possible by exploring the ways in which theorists might diversify their resources, ways of knowing, representations, and discourses. The purpose is to sharpen the disciplinary gaze in relation to international reality; to improve upon analytical instruments during the conduct of research; to attach equal significations to like events; and to narrate their findings in manners that are meaningful to all implicated political subjects.

CHAPTER 2

LECLERC'S MOSAIC: HISTORICISM, INSTITUTIONALISM, AND MEMORY

From Fort Lamy, Douala, Brazzaville, Bangui, from the bushes to the combatants of the hinterlands, there formed a community of faith who brought us action and success. These are the children of the same people guided by the same instinct in Africa and in the maquis who pulled France from the worse nightmares to restore it to enlightenment and grandeur.

— Réné Pléven, *Centre des Archives d'Outre-Mer, August 1944*

France could not forget the debt that she owes to men of all races and of all religions that came to fight on its soil on the side of its sons for our liberation.

— Vincent Auriol, *Centre des Archives d'Outre-Mer, April 1947*

In 1995, the American Public Broadcasting System (PBS) produced a month-long televison series commemorating the fiftieth anniversary of the end of World War II. The PBS series was one of many events that sought to recapture the high moments of the "great war." According to PBS, these were *inter alia* the collapse of France; German invasion of Belgium; the march of Werhmacht toward the Low Countries; the Russian Front; the Stalin–Hitler Pact; the blitzkrieg or bombing of London; the Normandy landing; the Pacific Front; the fall of Germany; the liberation of death camp survivors; the division of Europe; and above all the selfless entry of the United States into war to defend democracy. Except for sequences on the loyalty of colonial troops to the Allied cause, the series characteristically omitted the role played by colonial populations. Africa was shown merely a theater for motorized battles opposing the ultimate victors to their Nazi and Fascist antagonists. Where it was mentioned, African participation was attributed to loyalty to the métropoles and/or compliance with metropolitan fiats. By a feat of visual effects, therefore, the series reduced the entire war to its American and European dimensions. Variations on this perspective are also commonsense in Europe. Related narratives pay little attention to the multiplicity of political symbols, motivations, ideas, and beliefs that drew other regions into that war.

There is a similar thrust to the manners in which IR theorists identify the origins of ideas and attach meanings to practices or institutions; define their teleologies; and determine their relevancies and functions beyond their presumed European points of origination. Disciplinary notions of international existence, morality, and ethics still presume an evolutionary linear movement toward modernity and a diffusion of norms, values, and institutions from Europe (and the West) to other regions of the world. Related accounts depend upon temporal metaphors that posit differentiations among world populations according to spaces and cultures. They interpellate subjects according to anterior but parochial structures of interest which, in turn, serve as basis of a hierarchy of solicitation—West, Rest; Christian, non-Christian, civilized, noncivilized, and so on— that prejudge the value of actions.

Despite disciplinary insistence on objectivity, its accounts of institutional development depend largely on subjective understandings based on regional experiences, cultural idioms, and political imaginaries. Thus, the identity of agents and the political affiliations of actors determine the nature of political institution—that is, whether it is neutral, disinterested, and universal or, alternatively, parochial and particular—and not the other way around. They hold supposed Western values and preferences as necessarily rational and, as such, essential ingredients of international morality and norms. These are thus taken to be indispensable to human franchise and universal advancement. Related accounts are structured around rationalist beliefs in a linear temporality and, within it, a single political rationality and an uneven distribution of human faculties and capabilities across the space.

The present chapter revisits institutionalist perspectives on international developments with the view of broadening or deepening their arguments regarding the nature and forms of certain practices (for instance, solidarity and humanism) and institutions (states and systems of states) and their place in international politics. It focuses on the structure of interests that are implicated in both its accounts and methods of cataloguing ideas and practices as exemplar institutions; of memorializing events as epical; and of retrieving such events at the moment of construction of theory. Of central concern are the intrinsic merits, effects, and teleology of institutional accounts of transnationalism and the related perceptions of theorists of values and preferences of networks at the moments of the spatial instantiations of ideas and institutions.

My goals are threefold. The first is to challenge an implied notion that, due to culture and tradition, time travels outside the West in slow motion until the inhabitants of such spaces are liberated through enlightenment by the West. My second goal is to demonstrate that, although Western inflections on modern political practices and institutions remain pivotal to understanding international relations, their place and significance have been exaggerated. Third, the kinds of morality that flow from modern conditions exist as a common idiom globally to subtend interactions and transactions everywhere, their implementations reflect temporal and spatial concerns, ethos, and languages of politics. These temporal and spatial instantiations are not all Western in origin and their executions have distinct effects and implications for international relations.

With particular regard to World War II, for instance, the conditions of international solidarity and other institutions were the co-contemporaneity, coevalness, and convergence of multiple political rationalities that momentarily overlapped in purpose or teleology. Although the battle lines and symbols of military defeat and victory were state boundaries, the war itself was not solely an interstate phenomenon. Nor the rationalities of all actors European in derivation and focus. Specifically, in the French empire, Armistice led the dissipation of colonial authority, whereupon no single entity dictated the terms of political actions. French defeat opened the door to simultaneous interventions by self-selected agents from all parts of the empire, operating horizontally—that is, free of prior hierarchies. Thus released from colonial structures of authority and identity, colonizer and colonized competed to generate compelling ideas that not only guided resistance but also opened the space for political interventions and institutional innovations. Participants converged on the the necessity of solidarity, human dignity, and racial equality while retaining their distinct cultural/ideological sensibilities and political ideals. They further agreed that the abolition of the Vichy state (on behalf of the republic) was a sine qua non of resistance and political experimentation. These convergences provided the leitmotiv for resistance to Vichy and the dismantlement of prior colonial arrangements. They also provided the symbolic foundation of anti-Vichy and anticolonial networks. Defined as they were subjective perceptions of the effects and implications of the war, these networks determined to coordinate their efforts politically.

As I show later in the chapter, colonial entities engaged their metropolitan counterparts in a politics of "the moment," characterized as it were by the co-constitution of temporal horizons between and amongst contemporaneous actors, agents, and subjects. Specifically in 1940, it was a black colonial administrator, Félix Adolphe Sylvestre Eboué, who gave France its only autonomous and sovereign space; initiated the first officially sanctioned resistance networks; and set the tone for the actions and policies of the Free French Forces in the colonies before their duplication in the Métropole. Eboué also helped to rescue the emergent French resistance from moral and ideological confusion by providing the political impetus toward the clarification of notions of state and republic, and thus patriotism and treason in the contexts of war and colonialism. To be sure, the events following French surrender unfolded at an incredible speed and this allowed for complex, multidimensional, and unprecedented exchanges and dynamics among participants. So, it is not my intention to build up Eboué as a hero, "founding father," and/or miracle maker. Quite the contrary. The fluidity and ebbs and flows of the events provided opportunities for political experimentations. I merely wish to show that, in the earlier phase of defeat and occupation, the évolués were among the key arbiters of fractured metropolitan contestations and deliberations over postwar symbols and institutions: French identity, sovereignty, state, nation (*Patrie*), republic, and empire, on the one hand, and loyalty and patriotism, dissidence and treason, and liberty and democracy, on the other. The concerned évolués also initiated new standards of international morality that defy traditional disciplinary accounts of the trajectory of international institutions and norms.

Dynamics within the French empire defy state-centric and Eurocentric accounts of international developments. Specifically, the collapse of the state and the institutions of empire did not result in anarchy. Rather, the collapse of state and empire created the opportunity for political experimentations by non-state-affiliated entities. The latter assumed sovereignty and, as such, formulated their own political rationality and ideals. Africans who partook in these events had been freed by the collapse of the state. As such, they did not require the caution of any European power or association of powers to participate in ongoing political experimentations. They were moved by political and moral sentiments originating simultaneously from all parts of the world to enact distinct forms of solidarity, dignity, and equality and to join others in related transnational networks. Neither their networks nor their enacted morality were commandeered by the French state or its representatives. Nor were they, strictly speaking, byproducts of Western political alliances or ideological commitments.

Historicism, Institutionalism, and Disciplinary Recollections

Theory and the idea of it are peculiar cultural and historical products: European and modern in their conception and projection. They are founded upon conceptions of the possibility of discovery, truth, and method. The pursuit of theory in the institutional settings of the academy harkens back to a supposed Greek-European science, *theoria* or philosophy, that speaks universally in "thematic forms."[1] As proposed by Edmund Husserl, *theoria* generates "absolute theoretical insights" and, as such, has the unique capacity to serve as foundation for "a praxis" that "elevates mankind through universal scientific reason"[2] Critically, Husserl establishes an indispensable connection between philosophy and a particular historical project: to identify a doctrine of history that explains the progression in time of human societies. Ideas are no longer merely important devices for envisioning the future, they must be logically deduced from historical developments in which the European trajectory thus deduced from Hellenic nostalgia is assumed to reflect nature and the rational progression. Europe thus must serve as a template or model for the course of history everywhere.

In constructing the present as the culmination of the Greco-European past alone, Husserl erases the teleologies of contemporaneous societies. He does so through an unimaginative comparativism in which he privileges theory (the vessel for Western rationality) over other modes of knowledge, particularly those originating elsewhere outside Europe and/or the West. In an illustrative passage, Husserl contrasts philosophy with the more "mythical-religious" Oriental forms of knowledge that have only "practical-universal" applications. Husserl is not much interested in the recovery of truth about the past in its complexity. As it happened, he was interested in constructing a justificatory doctrine of nineteenth-century European hegemony: an ideology that asserts universality, redemption, and progress for Europe while assigning temporal lag, cultural degeneration, and social fixity to non-European societies.[3] This ideology was central to the preoccupations of nineteenth-century natural history. Its themes and theses congealed later into Orientalism[4] and a belief that Orientals (by which Husserl and others often meant Indians and Chinese) and other non-Europeans metaphysically existed somewhere outside of the European present in another time—either lagging in a prehistorical or premodern time or moving against the teleology of the more contemporaneous modern European temporality. In the latter case, the concerned non-Western entities were assumed to exist in an antihistorical and antimodern time.

These contrasts do not simply allow Husserl to ascertain the continued relevance of the intentions, insights, and will of the Greeks and their European progenies for the present. He also cast Europe as the permanent force through which human rationality and development must be understood. Nostalgia becomes science (philosophy) which in turn becomes a politically motivated instrument: historicism. Indeed, Husserl's version of history is as perverse as his understanding of philosophy. Leopold von Ranke disparaged Husserl's kind of epical history, as one teleological narrative constructed in light of "the demands of a philosophical system," a "poeticizing" intended to satisfy parochial fantasies about one's past.[5] Ranke does not dispute that historical events can be meaningfully established through attention to individual sources. He advises nonetheless that such sources be used in comparison with contemporaneous sources pertaining to the same events.[6] More recently, Michel-Rolph Trouillot too has argued that credible historical knowledge must not only consider multiple sources but also the circumstances under which particular historical trajectories become relevant and the conditions of the sources that buttress the related claims.[7] In both Ranke's and Trouillot's views, history is only as important as it is meaningfully related to the present of the narrator; but, to meaningfully recover truth, it is incumbent upon the historian to establish adequate methods and practices. In any case, it is unlikely that meaningful historical truth can be attained on the basis of singular sources.

These concerns about the nature of history, archives, and the possibility of historical truths apply to IR, where historicism survives for various reasons. First, historicism has survived in IR thanks to the influence of the English School and other Anglo-Saxon traditions that have fostered a diffusionist principle according to which most international institutions and standards flow from the West to the Rest.[8] This is to say that there exists today an international society or "world polity" united by political and cultural practices originating in the West and spreading progressively across the globe. Following in the footsteps of the likes of E. H. Carr and Hedley Bull, the so-called English School has maintained that the condition of international society and morality is the diffusion of Western values and institutions through European conquest of other continents and the adoption by others of European norms of diplomacy, law, and commerce. The underlying views are not jaundiced simply because they cast conquest and colonialism benignly as unfortunate instruments of world culture. As I show throughout this book, such views are mistaken also about the role of Western leaders, diplomats, and networks of capitalists, adventurers, activists, and intellectuals among others in the initiation and maintenance of transcontinental and transnational morality.[9]

Across from the Atlantic, in the United States, institutionalists too have embraced historicism, its methods, and assumptions. The latter remains the basis for the categories and concepts through which theorists understand the world, to apprehend intercommunal relations, and to give intelligibility and meanings to collective experiences. As I show later, institutionalists have given new life and sustenance to historicism through intellectual implements that define disciplinary ontology on the basis of conceptions of difference and political subjectivity that are both based on differential time: modern versus nonmodern; civilized versus noncivilized; rogue versus non-rogue states; rational versus nonrational entities. This ontology assigns reasons, causes, and logical relationships to social relations and phenomena prior to any explanation of behavior. Due to historicism, therefore, the mental capacity or ability (but not intuition) to grasp or comprehend reality is *subordinated* to the mastery of temporal categories and concepts that are anterior to explanation. I should hasten to add that, although I link the capacity to explain to a base-ontology, I do not mean to suggest that explanation is always predetermined. The latter is as deliberate and intentional as the techniques of appreciation or methods.

Institutionalism in Disciplinary Perspectives

So-called theories of international regimes, networks and social movements, and epistemic communities give salience to non-state actors. They underscore the importance of ideas and their stabilization through international instruments, associations, and other institutions.[10] Their views are premised on the notion that actors do not always behave instrumentally in pursuit of material self-interest; that they may in fact act on the basis of peculiar logics embedded in ideas rather than immediate material gains.[11] Related views underscore the mediating role of institutions in shaping political conducts and outcomes. This is to say that conventions, regimes of laws or rules, and norms and principles, whether formal or informal, do structure and orient the everyday of political agents and actors. They also guarantee transparency and translation of political intentions. In short, institutions provide a source of political stability, especially during periods of intense political contestations.

Institutional approaches also stress history as determinant of the present as well as inspiration for future possibilities. Because it shapes actors, history provides the context for understanding political dynamics, their timing and sequencing. This structuring effect of history in institutionalist accounts is called path-dependency.[12] Besides providing clues to the teleology and direction of political actions, historical path-dependency ensures the predictability of political systems and systems that at first appear complex and subject to unpredictable dynamics. In sum, history and path-dependency help provide explanations for the large consequences that result from small, contingent, and incremental events.

In the aforesaid regards and others, institutionalist speculations and perspectives have undeniably enlarged the scope of IR. Institutionalism has elucidated previously obscured connections between institutions, ideas, and values, on the one hand, and the nature and constitution of interest and rationality and the conception of policy, on the other. But it is not without criticisms. For instance, it has been criticized for undue attention to endogenous processes (or internal forces) as explanatory factors of actors' behavior and their representations of values and interests. Additionally, institutionalism places an undue premium on the promotion and prescription of their preferred values and preferences *over* meaning, implementation, and perversion of values and preferences. The related accent on certain values and preferences (wealth, skills, enlightenment) leads to the downplaying of the role played by other institutions and values (power, deference, and normativity). As a result, institutional approaches pay little attention to the instruments of institutionalization—diplomacy, ideology, economy, and military—and their application as persuasion, affect, capitalism, and force.[13]

The promises of institutionalism are blunted by the residual effects of historicism and its doctrines of time. Historicism manifests itself at the moment of both the memorialization of events and the assignation of meanings. The first is characterized by an exclusive embrace of Western institutions without due attention to the complexities and contingencies of their materialization as dimensions of political systems. This embrace is followed by taking the purported adoption elsewhere of related norms as indicative of historical consciousness; and the implementations of Western institutions by others as signs of development or progress. The result is the privileging of European and Western imaginaries of politics and political life.[14] This liability exists even when theorists are inclusive in their accounts of political action and subjectivity.[15] Related views of *political action* are inevitably embedded in Western hermeneutics of politics and their notions of progress, freedom, industry, creativity, and culture. So too are institutionalists' conceptions of *political subjectivity* grounded in an ontology of order that depends upon authoritative and formal Western notions of competence, authority, legitimacy, and entitlements.[16] By assuming an institutional void elsewhere, particularly in the postcolonial world, institutionalist accounts reproduce a pathos of power that give the West the authority to legislate and adjudicate while laying on the non-West the burden of moral sociability and conformity.

To paraphrase Aihwa Ong, institutionalist assumptions are culturally but mistakenly Western in their conception and inspiration.[17] While they recognize institutions to reflect historical consciousness, Western theorists are nonetheless liable to assuming that the development of institutions is the result of a progressive movement of values and norms across linear spaces and times. I concur with Ong that political spaces are subject to multiple temporalities and teleologies, reflecting specific relations of power and linguistic technologies. These temporalities and teleologies inherently structure the reception, translation, and intelligibility of institutions in their discreet spatial instantiations. Consistently, non-Western developments cannot be understood solely through analogies. Nor can they be assumed to be inspired from values and teleologies similar to Western ones. As I show later, it is hazardous to conflate the imminence, utility, and appeal of particular institutions with their efficacy, exclusivity, and universality. Further, even developments that concurr and thus coincide politically may still be inspired by different conceptions of political teleology (corresponding to community), subjectivity (inspired by morality), and interest (to be legislated). From this perspective, the identification of agents, contexts, and political actions is but the beginning of a good analysis of institutional developments.

Actors, Contingency, and Political Actions

Institutionalists hold that the present moment is rife with uncertainties, but also possibilities. The uncertainties arise from the sudden collapse of existing social orders, followed by the rise of exclusionary and illiberal forms of nationalism (for instance in the Balkans) or the inability of states to secure the safety and well-being of the citizenry (in the context of so-called failed states in Africa). These events are triggered by nationalists, thugs, and others motivated by hatred and/or greed. At any rate, the political quagmires, violence, and displacements created by ethnic nationalisms and failed states presumably strain the logic of the institutions which once mediated politics both nationally and globally. These include inclusionary democracy, the providential state, and the juridico-political regimes of the international system of states.

The post–cold war era is supposed to have brought about new possibilities as well. The possibilities arise from a different kind of insurgency against state sovereignty. This time, the battle is led by non-state actors whose goal is to broaden and institutionalize certain historical norms as universal. These actors too challenge state monopoly of political morality, but in the direction of collective action across boundaries. They thus operate transnationally thanks in part to new technologies of communications: the internet and satellite telephones and televisions among them. Emphasizing the possibilities, Thomas Risse-Kappen, Peter Haas, Kathryn Sikkink among others have recently highlighted the role of international and/or transnational networks as agents of transformation of the moral compass of the international system.[18] They note accurately that networks of experts (of accountants, lawyers, and financiers); activists (advocating the human rights of farmers, women, children, and prisoners of conscience); corporations (particularly, multinationals); and other nongovernmental organizations (of environmentalists, philanthropists, and humanitarians among others) have recently emerged as purveyors of consciousness regarding agency in determining norms and institutions in international life.[19] Accordingly, transnational networks successfully frame domestic and international agendas often in support of their own issues and causes. Thus, environmentalists, philanthropists, and other humanitarians have pressed for the creation of a variety of international regimes implementing humanitarian assistance (including food aid and refugee protection); enforcing human rights; banning deadly weapons; and criminalizing acts of genocide.

In these regards, institutionalists call into question the ideological hubris of neorealist statism and the complacency of neoliberalism: the one for its confidence that sovereignty and national interest ultimately prevail; the other for its contemplative proclamations of the inevitable victory of finance capital and its brand of market economy.[20] In exchange, institutionalists have given life and meanings to institutions and historical events that could not be explained solely through state rationalities. Non-state actors, particularly liberal and progressive Western groups, have played important roles in the institutionalization of norms that have thus far been overlooked in IR. They contributed greatly to improving international morality and the global ethical environment toward the attaining of uniform standards on human rights and human dignity. For instance, progressive Western coalitions helped to undermine slavery, imperialism, and colonialism by questioning or indicting the underlying political determinants, juridical mechanisms, and ethical imperatives.

Institutionalists do not merely identify the new mechanisms through which the international system might be oriented and transformed.[21] They also seek to foster new collective identities, values, and institutions for the successor orders. Here, it seems, however, institutionalists have exaggerated the transformative possibilities of non-state actors. They have generally overlooked the resilience of affect, ideology, and interest as well as global structures of power and subjectivity. The criticisms here follow two sets of comments made by Stephen Krasner.[22] The first concerns the necessary insufficiency of institutionalist's conceptions, representations, and interpretations of truth and morality. The second comment, which I discuss later, is that the normative biases of liberal institutionalism—particularly its conceptions of governance, rights, and liberties—run counter to the dynamism implied by institutionalism.

In both these regards, Krasner notes, theorists are not simply recorders of international events. They are themselves actors and agents. As such, they help to mold institutions, norms and rules such that they are consistent with their own values and interests.[23] In short, institutional debates are not merely intellectual speculations. Nor can related discussions be meaningfully separated from the intellectual roots, ideological connections, and political situations of theorists themselves. These comments do not apply evenly across theories of transnationalism. For instance, Peter Haas's treatment of epistemic communities confirms a key Krasner insight more than others.[24] In "Knowledge, Power, and International Policy Coordination," Haas sets out to study the manners in which Western-based experts have labored assiduously to direct the flow of knowledge and information toward justifying historic ideological and political ends. He makes his points by omitting the fact that transnational organizations are often more parochial and national than global and disinterested in outlook. Further, transnational liberal epistemic networks maintain distinct and complex relations to the structures and mechanisms of global governance, particularly the interstate system and international institutions. Still, Haas offers a mystifying view of the contribution of epistemic communities in the production and distribution of ideas. This is not the place to explore the institutional context of the academy and the fields of exchange in which these transnational networks operate. Nor is it appropriate in this context to venture views of the relationships between the academy, grant foundations, and national policy makers and their agendas. Still, it would seem significant that such networks have undertaking to shape policy in favor of parochial national interest.

Like yesteryear's abolitionists and today's human rights groups, epistemic communities are engaged in finite processes with definable outcomes. They are not free of political attachment and ideological commitment. It therefore takes a feeble and unimaginative comparativism to argue that transnationalism necessarily advances the common good or that their processes reflect the values and preferences of free, rational, and equally willing agents. It is more likely that interventions by transnational networks have had mixed results. Specifically, epistemic communities with institutional or corporate ties have supported ethically dubious dynamics—including unidirectional injunctions by hegemonic powers and/or corporations to the weaker states and their constituencies; unilateral intrusions by the powerful in the domestic affairs of postcolonial entities, resulting in the disruption of the domestic structures of authority and legitimacy. To borrow an expression from William E. Connolly, liberal institutionalism like Haas's "celebrates common sense and shared understanding too eagerly and too unambiguously" to warrant comfort.[25] This is that they pay little attention to the political contexts of the actualization of institutions. Here, I think especially of the politics of marginalization and/or exclusion contained in the process of institutionalization. Further, institutionalists reach their conclusions on the basis of a limited scope of social interactions and modalities of global politics. They frequently ignore historical forms of politics that originate from the periphery of the international system, particularly in regions other than the West. Related political modalities correspond to normative rationalities (regarding power and interest) and thus manifestations of wills, desires and identities. Their omissions have impoverished many an institutionalist conclusion. Significantly, wholesale exclusions of alternative modalities of politics and their base-imaginaries have helped to justify and privilege a particular political ethos in the form of categorical commands. Such commands, flowing from Western states as universal imperatives directed at other states are thus underwritten by theorists through appeals to the ideas of Aristotle, Kant, Grotius, and others.

Transnationalism: Narratives of Progress and Modernity

Eric Hobsbawn among others has recently shown that non-state agents, and not states, were the early vectors of European notions of liberty and right abroad.[26] As liberalizing agents of the emergent international society, missionary societies, philanthropist organizations, and other progressive networks championed key elements and dimensions of Western morality as humane and therefore universally applicable. Institutionalists have recently rediscovered facts about the activities of such groups and taken them up as evidence of both international society and the positive roles of progressivism within it.

In this vein, Margaret E. Keck and Kathryn Sikkink have ably illustrated the manners in which progressive networks have transported Western institutions beyond their points of origination and helped to implant them elsewhere as basis for transnational action on behalf of the needy.[27] The study "highlights *relationships*" or "connections . . . between activists and their allies and opponents."[28] This perspective is enriched by the identification of "*resources* that make a campaign possible" along with the "kinds of *institutional structures* . . . that encourage or impede particular kinds of transnational activism."[29] The authors aim to show the generative power of networks, focusing particularly on the ability of principled networks to "broaden the scope of practices" through negotiation and transformation of the involved norms.[30] Finally, the authors are interested in "the creative use of information, and the employment . . . of sophisticated political strategies . . ."[31] In short, the study illustrates positive connections between networks (or "groups that seek to channel information leading to alternative visions),[32] practices (or "the act of doing something repeatedly" with the intent of actualizing norms),[33] and norms ("the collective expectations for the proper behavior of actors with a given identity").[34]

Keck and Sikkink begin with two central observations. The first is that the international order is "an arena of struggle, a fragmented and contested area" among groups that have unequal access to states, governments, international organizations, and other politically significant groups.[35] Specifically, they "distinguish three different categories of actors or groups: (1) those with essentially *instrumental goals*, especially transnational corporations and banks; (2) those motivated primarily by *shared causal ideas*, such as scientific groups or epistemic communities; and (3) those motivated primarily by *shared principled ideas or values* (transnational advocacy networks)."[36] The second point is that, once organized as networks, groups can effectively influence "(1) issue creation and agenda setting; (2) influence on discursive positions of states and international organizations; (3) influence on institutional procedures; (4) influence on policy change in 'target actors' which may be states, international organizations like the World Bank, or private actors like the Nestlé Corporation; (5) influence on state behavior."[37]

These distinctions highlight the relative utility of the interpretation and strategic use of information, particularly in regard to the "ability of networks to convince policymakers." This ability, they argue, is as important as the political advantages bestowed by say economic resources and technical expertise.[38] In these regards, Keck and Sikkink leave aside debates about the points of origination of institutions. Instead, they highlight the instrumentalization of ideas and beliefs in political contests, on the one hand, and the rationalities of networks that engage in such practices, on the other. Where others have been reluctant to take note of the multiplicity of voice in international relations, Keck and Sikkink amply demonstrate that state ideology is not the only locus of legitimacy under republican institutions.[39] In this regard, the authors satisfactorily answer their self-assigned questions on the nature of transnational advocacy network; the reasons and manners of their emergence; the manners of their operations; and the conditions under which they are likely to achieve their goals.[40]

Keck and Sikkink poignantly point out that political legitimacy remains grounded in historical and collective sensibilities. Thus, nineteenth-century progressivism brought about sensibilities in stark conflict with the violence and exploitation implicated in slavery and the imperialist project of racial subjugation and exploitation.[41] The desire to reform the domestic and international arenas brought together progressive clergy, suffragists, abolitionists, and philanthropists on behalf of the right of women to vote; the end of the slave trade; the promotion of legitimate trade in lieu of slavery; and the dual mandate of colonization and development in European colonies.

Keck and Sikkink thus highlight the fluidity and openness of international relations. Once again, they note the relative adaptability of groups and networks over states. They show that "committed and knowledgeable actors" can successfully "plead their causes of others or defend a cause or proposition" where states often do not.[42] This adaptability is in evidence in global politics today. Specifically, nongovernmental organizations (NGOs) have recently initiated actions, introduced new ideas, provided, and thus effectively lobbied states for policy changes in multiple arenas, extending from the land mine convention to the creation of the International Court of Justice. To these ends, NGOs have had to establish linkages across space and territories.[43]

The study exudes optimism and rationalism. It takes progress to be the culmination of rationalism and the realization of an unspecified but universal reason. Progress thus construed is the inescapable future of the past, a time-bound, timely, and preordained outcome of the internationalization of public life under Western leadership.[44] The condition of progress is among others the embrace by progressive Western actors of the cause of others and, consequently, the former's determination as agents to advocate on behalf of others, less fortunate, before the politically significant Western governments. In so understanding progress and its conditions, Western norms and institutions emerge as central ingredients of international morality and public life.

As I show later, this confidence in the openness of Western polities or politics and the primacy and the adaptability of Western-derived institutions is an overstretch. So too is the elevation of the teleologies of such institutions as reason and ultimate signs of progress mistaken. To be sure, Western norms and institutions have been central to the internationalization of public morality. They have been the bases of meaningful relationships between the West and the Rest, particularly among leaders, public intellectuals, advocates, and/or activists.[45] But related events did not unfold in a linear fashion and in accordance with institutionalist narratives. As Frederick Cooper has indicated in relation to the end of slavery, slave revolts were its principal catalyst.[46] "The actual unraveling of slavery," according to Cooper, "first occurred in (1804) Haiti via the action of slaves . . . and in Jamaica and Martinique in 1831 and 1848" in slave revolts that preceded the emancipation sought by bourgeois antislave movements.[47] The revolt of slaves too was a transnational movement. Not only was the Haitian revolution a direct rebuke to French and American revolutionaries, it and the Jamaica and Martinique revolts reflected the global circulation of ideas that contradicted core tenets of French and American ideologies of equality, justice, and race. These thoughts and ideas "crossed oceans" and regions even if sometimes in the forms of rumors among illiterate slaves.[48] Related thoughts and ideas were intended to generate practices that rivaled those based on Enlightenment precepts. To recognize such facts is not to diminish the significant historical role of Europe and the West in international developments.

Keck and Sikkink are keenly aware of the multiplicity of historical modes of engagement and the diversity of vocality. It stands to reason, therefore, they would give the impression that international civil society harbors "a medley of . . . social movements, interest groups, indigenous peoples, cultural groups, and global citizens" acting in concert, through knowledge and practice-based networks to "eclipse" prior boundaries.[49] In this regard, Mustapha Kamal Pasha and David L. Blaney have expressed doubt that the world is witnessing a post-Westphalia democratic consciousness of solidarity, human rights, and humanitarianism.[50] They are even skeptical of the self-identification of social movements and networks as emancipatory agents: either as selfless and thus committed to the realization of social solidarity as do social movements and NGOs; or self-seekers and self-interested and thus committed to forwarding particular interests, values, and preferences as do corporations and interest groups; or self-affiliators and thus committed to group affiliation as do indigenous and cultural groups.[51] Pasha and Blaney fear that "the mutually constitutive relationship of civil society, capitalism, and the liberal state" might be lost in the midst.[52] They hope that theorists will not lose sight of the fact that "the aspirations for individual [and collective] self-realizations" have been particularly contradictory in modern life and that the practices of networks have had unconnected goals.[53]

The scope of Pasha's and Blaney's criticism exceeds the particular arguments forwarded by Keck and Sikkink. This is in part because Keck and Sikkink's concept of advocacy network "cannot be [totally] subsumed under notions of transnational social movements or global civil society."[54] The latter are particularly attentive to "issues of agency and political opportunity" in the evolution of new international institutions and relationships. However, there are several questions that arise in their study. They include the following: the manners in which differently situated individuals develop their world views, become acquainted, and remain engaged over long periods; whether political subjectivity has any effect on the power to leverage and what related mechanisms do to social dynamics within networks; whether theorists may assume transparency of motives on the part of individual entities or affiliated groups; and finally, whether charges of cultural imperialism become irrelevant once it is established that the relevant groups voluntarily entered into political association.

Imaginaries of Politics Across Space

The institutionalist presumption that emancipatory ideas and institutions necessarily emanate from the West is highly mistaken.[55] As I intimated in the case of slave revolts, universally recognized institutions and norms have also sprung in other regions. Even from a strictly philosophical standpoint, one must entertain the possibility that societies afflicted by the same historical conditions might independently, autonomously, or collectively envisage institutions and norms with similar rationalities if not forms. Aihwa Ong views the effects of globalization in this light. Like Keck and Sikkink, Ong too argues that globalization has undermined the structures of modern sovereignties and the political affiliations that once mapped the existence and expectations of citizenship—be it within the state, nation, and other communities like universities.[56] But, unlike the former, Ong maintains that the collapse of old dogmas, social knowledge, and political programs has been felt differentially across space.[57] She therefore cautions against the tendency of reformists, including institutionalists, to rely exclusively and unquestionably on Western traditions and institutions. Ong is particularly concerned that transnational and cosmopolitan ideologies that harken back to the Enlightenment both foster philosophical parochialism and promote political and cultural exclusion.[58] She is alarmed that the proponents of such ideologies seldom propose their own ideas as part of a larger ensemble of comparable and/or competing sensibilities. They acknowledge human diversity and the multiplicity of political subjects, but they expect all others to conform to uniform Western ideologies for the sake of universalism.[59] As a rectification, Ong exhorts institutionalists (and cosmopolitans) to aspire to a fuller understanding of international existence by engaging difference, particularly the sensibilities contained in non-Western traditions.

Ong provides strong evidence of the diversity of cultures and traditions of transnational (and by extension cosmopolitan) existence. She forwards a case study of a non-Western transnationalist experiment that simultaneously complements and diverges from those contained in Western modernity. Her subjects belong to the Chinese diaspora in East Asia who practice a distinct form of transnationality. According to Ong, these ethnic Chinese inhabit distinct regimes of power marked by cultural modes of behavior that set them apart from their Western contemporaries, whether counterparts or competitors. Specifically, they entertain discernable patterns of social relations (through networks of family and commercial ties) that are enabled by their ethnic Chinese identity and distinct cultural norms. Significantly, these individuals and groups share their identity and cultural traditions across states with members of like communities, but not with their conationals of different ethnic groups. The principals are aided in their transnational activities by modern commercial institutions which allow the concerned parties to move through and across national sovereign spaces for the purpose of capital accumulation.[60]

By way of elaboration, Ong explores the constitutive order of non-jural regimes of institutions and cultural practices that enable the actions of agents. She finds that the condition of possibility of this particular Chinese transnationality is an arsenal of not-so transparent archives consisting of Chinese traditions, local customs, and the collective memory of the concerned agents. These archives allow the participants to inhabit a symbolic but effective and enforceable moral universe. The related regimes and cultural institutions regulate political projects and markets by shaping the participants' identities, motivations, desires, and struggles.[61] Indeed, these regimes and institutions complement (and may supersede) the more formal constitutional rule of law and alone neither provides the basis for understanding the articulation of power and interest globally.

This case study provides correctives to institutionalist approaches to transnationalism. One correction is that the norms, values, and truths that enable transnational transactions flow horizontally among diverse constituencies across geopolitical and cultural spaces. It is therefore to their peril that institutionalists, particularly cosmopolitans, do not recognize this fact of international existence. According to Ong, cosmopolitans have yet to fully grasp the multiplicity of meanings and implications that may be derived from their own concepts of *immediacy* (or temporal urgency), *greater good* (which is based on an assumed notion of commonsense ontology), and the *political imaginary* (which depend upon epistemology and its base faculties). In a different context, Arundhati Roy has noted that continued attachment to parochial political agendas and intellectual programs often results in ambivalence—and occasionally hostility—toward non-Western political agendas and intellectual traditions, particularly postcolonial ones.[62] Ariel Dorfman adds that moral ambivalence in turn has led to discounting others' experiences, aspirations, and expectations on unavowed grounds of their lesser agencies and the structures, processes, and positions that enable them.[63]

The institutionalist cosmopolitan pledge to establish universally shared values has been more speculative than substantive.[64] Liberal institutionalist and cosmopolitan arguments do not account for the multiplicity of political languages and ethical idioms from which differently situated individuals and communities derive their notions of the common humanity, or social justice. This absence of temporal and spatial diversity of circumstances in cosmopolitan accounts of social justice, for instance, may in fact reveal insensitivity to the unevenness of access to resources necessary to the ennoblement of human existence in given circumstances. It also has implication for understanding violence and its manifestation across time and space. We are reminded here by Bruce Robbins that loyalty and attachment to one's own position or imaginary of social order "can and sometimes does contradict the manifest demands of justice as seen from any extra-national perspective."[65]

One of Ong's central theses deserves close attention: any transcendental ideology requires a credible practice as its counterpart. In other words, transnational and cosmopolitan declarations of intent must be founded not only upon appreciable goodwill, but also moral clarity, ethical consistency, and philosophical openness in order to ensure transparent outcomes. Transposed to the academic context of production of theory, this means that reflections about transnationalism would benefit greatly from practices that also foster reciprocity—and not domination—within the academy and across states.[66] Ong's exposé of the neglect of non-Western experiences shows the uncertainty of scholarly commitment to understanding the complexities of international relations and the actual performance of scholars. It also raises the question of the conditionality of truth in the production of knowledge, for it may well be that the specific experiences valorized in articulating the universal have a lot to do with the historical form it receives operationally.

The intrinsic merit of exploring the cultural dimensions of transnationalism is that it allows for the indexation of an array of related practices and political implements that pertain to the object of institutional analyses. It allows for the restoration of the experiences of the marginalized to the actual repertoire of political imaginaries. Such indexation and restoration are not only ontologically significant. They also exude a generalized ethos that better accommodates those presently marginalized from the political process and the realms of intellectual and cultural production. Indeed, Western advocates of global citizenship would be better justified if they studied from a non-Western perspective the mechanisms and political implements that sustain their own power. Granted, such an opening is not an easy task, but subtle cosmopolitanism itself is a complex and complicated matter. There is a certain wisdom in Ong's argument that the neglect of non-Western traditions hinders the overall capacity of theorists to productively envision different futures. The successes and failures of non-Western institutional experimentations could offer new prospects for global constitutionalism as well point to the difficulties of future political re-ordering.

Conscience, History, and Solidarity

I wish to explore two central themes of Ong's arguments. One is that the disciplinary memorialization of ideas and practices is not neutral and devoid of political agendas. These have bearings on which institutions and ideas are identified and given meanings; which are deemed transportable and suitable in time and space; and which logic, intentions, or rationalities are declared compelling. The other is that the appropriateness and sufficiency of Western institutions are a matter of record, which can only be obtained from comparative analyses of their ethical advantages. They cannot be derived solely from assumptions based on textual or policy makers' propositions of will, motives, and intentions.[67] From these two perspectives, a good institutional approach must have in view the environment actualization of institutions, including their mechanisms and processes as well as the relative values and imports of actualized institutions.

I take up these issues in the context of two general propositions. The first proposition, widely discussed by R. B. J Walker and other postmodernists, is that "sovereignty-as-enclosed-territory" has not been a sufficient condition of global politics.[68] The second interesting proposition is that ideas and institutions that are presented today in IR theory as novel and inspiring have been in existence across space and time in historical projects that remain in competition modern Western ones. To illustrate these points, the present section investigates *human solidarity* in the context of wartime anti-Nazi networks in the French colonial empire. My first objective is to offer evidence that human solidarity and its axiomatic derivations—including humanitarian intervention—are neither essentially modern nor necessarily Western institutions. My second objective is to contest the historicist allusions and illusions of institutional approaches that combine liberal ideological affectations and (realist) partiality to power to appropriate humanitarianism and its manifestations as properties of the West. Indeed, the following case study demonstrates amply that the moral character of African solidarity toward France during World War II far exceeded the modalities (or modes of operations) of French (and Western) solidarity toward Africans for the entirety of their encounters. Specifically, African solidarity toward defeated France lacked instrumentality or instrumentalization, particularly in regard to the principal African concern of the moment: anticolonialism.

States, Empires, and Colonies

It is testimony to the gap between theory and reality that IR holds the state as the most prevalent political institution of the modern era. The terms "state" and "interstate system" have undeniable literal meanings: the former is understood as a historical social form organized as sovereign, without political competitor or moral coeval in its supremacy and autonomy; while the later is said to be an association of like entities based either on mutual accords or necessity. Both the state and the interstate system are modern European institutions. They originated first at the end of the Middle Ages from the rejection by territorial political entities of the authority of the Church before succumbing to the revolutionary aspirations of the enclosed populations for self-government. Throughout, self-declared sovereigns projected themselves into history as inevitable and necessary outcome of progress. From the initial phase of their imperial ambitions, European powers construed the state to refer exclusively to European modes and structures of political organization: a territory, population, and bureaucratic infrastructure as well as the political paramountcy of the governor— monarchs, kings, potentates, and the like. Related representations implied corporeal and constitutive identity, steadfast political autonomy, economic self-reliance, and ethical impermeability to other entities. These organizational modes, structures, and their representations would provide the foundations for the modern systems of states, the international community of states, and similar metaphors.

Assuming anarchy to be the primary condition of the international order, proponents of state sovereignty proposed self-help and the will to power as means to state survival. The basis of legitimacy in such an order depends upon the will, capacity, and power of the state to ward off the ambitions of other states and to provide security to their populations or citizenries. In sum, states are subject to different norms, rules, and laws than other political entities. Unlike them, the state claims for itself the monopoly of violence (euphemistically the use of force) and the means to it.[69]

These arguments proliferated in Europe because of the barbarity of the wars and chaos that blighted the face of that continent over centuries, spanning the crusades and gaining new momentums from the Renaissance to the Reformation and beyond. Since then, major Western canons have pointed to the permanent state of war in Europe as evidence of a permanent state of anarchy worldwide.[70] Upon the conquest of the New World, the slave trade and colonialism, European theorists began to look to Africa, the Americas, the Arab world, and Asia for new evidence of anarchy and lawlessness in the absence of the state.

The underlying Eurocentrism masks key pathologies of modern politics. Colonial entrepreneurs, adventurers, settlers, and their ideological kin instrumentalized the logic of the state of anarchy to parody and comedy. State-centrism made it logically impossible for colonial adventurers to apply coherent ethical judgments to the rationales, mechanisms, and processes of empire building and empire maintenance. It also allowed theorists to envisage modern international institutions and their political economies as properties and proprieties of the West and, thus, to cast the West as the universal entity, speaking and legislating for the rest in the collective interest. Unfortunately, related topoi and tropes have entered the corpus of IR commonsense and international knowledge.[71]

State- and Eurocentrism have obscured the full extent of modern institutional and normative revolutions. Global politics have long unfolded between and across large spaces—regions, empires, and states—on the basis of historically inflected practices instituted by identifiable agents. Related interactions and institutions shaped particular spaces, but they eventually found their way into other areas because of overlapping structures and networks. For instance, the transatlantic slave trade took place between Europe, Africa, and the Americas which may be defined for the purpose as a zone of trade, with its own norms.[72] The consequences of this trade are still under dispute,[73] but it was governed by conventions that generated expectations and practices. The latter were not the same as those applicable within Europe or between Europe and other regions of the world. According to Jane Guyer, Europe spoke of "open trade" during the slave trade while it purposefully instilled devious relationships among participants:[74] viz, "African rulers, European slave traders, merchants in the West Indies, planters in the Americas, and industrialists in England" and elsewhere.[75]

Other spatial organizations commanded their own norms, juridical regimes, and morality. Religious institutions such as the Catholic Church, empires, and parallel organizations and structures have continued to rival the state in foregrounding identity, compelling actions, and eliciting loyalty without leading necessarily to a chaos akin to anarchy. For the better parts of the nineteenth and twentieth centuries, for instance, Great Britain, France, and other colonial powers defined themselves by the expansiveness of their territories and the degree of the integration of such expanses within the métropoles. These zones not only incorporated distinct political units, with detectable base-identities, values, and interests their underlying structures, mechanisms, and processes produced conflicting, contradictory, and complementary effects that cut across empires to allow for distinct bundles of political transactions, moral discourses, and ethical possibilities. The latter in turn created new identities, values, and interests that allowed for different kinds of politics. Specifically, they compelled otherwise unconnected entities to temporally coalesce and to generate alternative values, norms, and institutions, with distinct teleologies, logics, and significations.

Modern empires remain one of the most significant institutional events of recent history, with effects lasting to date. Specifically, empires—not states—gave globality its actuality as large-scale spaces marked "the intersection of [global] institutions, networks, and discourses."[76] As Frederick Cooper has noted, modern empires contained multiple and concurrent structures of power, identity, and interests.[77] These converged, diverged, and crisscrossed simultaneously and differentially to produce the practices, conventions, and political ethos that define modern international morality. Indeed, over time, empires juxtaposed multiple structures and networks that mobilized individuals and collectives around moral discourses.[78] According to Cooper, they comprised multiple spaces—including "zones of settlement," "zones of supervised appropriation," "catchment zones," and "zones of marginal control"—all contingently organized to produce specific effects.[79] At any rate, in nearly all these zones, imperial powers associated so-called natives in some fashion to the functions of administration, security, and production.

Take the French empire. *L'Empire français* brought together disparate territories and regions of the world in a historical republican logic that simultaneously unified and subordinated all others to France under French sovereignty. The underlying logic produced one of the most elaborate territorial, legislative, and bureaucratic organizations of the modern era.[80] By the end of World War II, for instance, the so-called French Union included the métropole or French state, its overseas departments and territories, protectorates, associated states, colonies, and communes that stretched every region of the world. These territorial units laid the foundations of a political system that was inevitably complex and inherently unpredictable. It nonetheless shaped the values, identities, and interests of vast majorities of human entities for a far longer time than states.

The foundations of this colonial empire were concurrent hierarchies of subjectivity (identity), institutions (values), and economies (interests) distributed spatially to both reflect and reproduce the political realities of conquest and colonization. As spaces of enactment of politics, empires were founded upon historical forms of violence that negated social legitimacy, cultural authenticity, and political autonomy. It also bears no repeating that the purposes, rationalities, and actualization of empires constituted an extroversion, perversion, and deviation from notions of sovereignty, political autonomy, and public morality. Imperial institutions defined the positions and roles of the colonized such as to bar them from instigating actions based solely on their wills, desires, and interests. They imposed an order of moral solicitation of subjects, agents, and actors that availed differentiated opportunities and limitations. Under this order, the colonized were not the equal of the colonizers. The latter could not forward their wills, desires, and interests as sources, foundations, or bases of formal and effective political action in some circumstances but their values, institutions, and interests remained complementary or subordinate to those of the colonial Métropole. Nor did imperial institutions permit such actions. This is not to negate that the colonized possessed means with which to alter, negotiate, or even thwart the wills, desires, and interests of the colonizers. It is to posit, however, that colonial subjectivity did not bestow upon the colonized formal primacy of agency.

Defeat, Political Awakening, And Realignment

Before the onset of World War II, the Métropole provided the structures and material and symbolic resources of power, culture, and economy throughout the empire. These gave precedence to the Métropole and kept the colonized at a distance from the formal functions of government beyond their particular locations. French imperialism and colonialism also provided the language, symbols, and values that gave form to the relationships between and among public officials, bureaucrats, missionaries, merchants, teachers, veterans, and "native populations." From related processes, there emerged trans-imperial subjects and identities, all more or less acculturated, transcultured, and/or hybrid in their ethnographic, intellectual, and political backgrounds. These included autochthonous French individuals and collectives; ethnic and religious minorities; French settler groups in the colonies; and other French citizens who inhabited the colonies. They also included national, religious, ethnic, and racial minorities in different subject positions throughout the empire: French-born blacks, Arabs, and Jews; French citizens of

Eastern European origin; North African Jews; and the multitudes of colonized Africans and Arabs among others. Even these categories boasted internal complexities and overlapped in actuality. Still, the political positions and juridical capacities of each subject category were determined not only by state legislation but also by political practices and cultural traditions.

State actions both fostered and hampered trans-imperial solidarity and political action. During his rise to power in the 1930s, Léon Blum for instance assembled a coalition and an agenda open to colonial reform and to inclusion of the colonized in the administration of the empire. A so-called Israelite of Bulgarian descent, Blum earned his humanist credentials during the Dreyfus Affair before his involvement with intellectuals associated with L'humanité. As leader of the Front Populaire, Blum tried and briefly succeeded in uniting liberals, socialists, and communists in actions intended to save France from the depression-era political chaos. As a political movement, the front populaire was also confronted rising Fascism (represented by Francisme), racism, and anti-Semitism, all of which blamed the crisis on foreigners, Jews, and communists.

Even before the depression and, later, the advent of Vichy, colonial populations—black Africans and Arabs among them—and French minorities such as Jews were subjected to insidious systems of racial discrimination, with distinct outcomes. They faced cultural and ideological discourses, lexicons, and structures that set them apart from so-called *Français de souche* (autochthonous French individuals and collectives). But discrimination and its effects were not uniform. Whereas blacks were colonized outright, Jews were merely marginalized in the Métropole and in the colonies through a system of difference based on ethnicity and religion. The latter were the bases for speculations on the moral character of Jews. Related ideologies about the (im)possibility of Jewish loyalty and integration within French society had no parallel for the colonized, as long as the latter remained confined geographically to the colonies.

Blum sought to combat these pathologies as well as bring about social peace through empire-wide social reforms. Specifically, sensing that political repression of "native" anticolonialists would result in political instability throughout the empire, Blum sought out and engaged so-called moderate anticolonialists for the purpose of their co-optation.[81] While repressing protagonists of radical anticolonialism (*anti-colonialisme de fond*), Blum's ruling coalition granted meaningful political roles to representatives of the colonized within imperial institutions, and not just locally.[82] He also appointed progressive metropolitan intellectuals to head public schools in Africa.[83] This solicitation not only encouraged their African partners, it also modified French attitudes toward colonial subjects. Blum's partisans now considered their African partners worthy of moral solicitude and not mere recipients of a civilizing mission. Under Blum, Africans became moral subjects involved in mutual transactions of exchange and cooperation. Subsequently, metropolitan political parties began to extend membership in French political organizations to the colonized and, beyond the related affinities, political goodwill toward individual Africans and organizations.[84]

Blum had hoped that his reforms would better reflect the legitimate interests of the multiple constituencies of France and the empire.[85] However, his reforms angered many French conservatives and liberals who suspected Blum of putting into question French colonial claims among others. They charged that Blum's political and economic reform was unduly influenced by foreign and Jewish concerns. The conservative group, Action Française, even called for Blum's murder.[86] Others were more circumspect and careful in their criticisms of Blum's policies. These included the liberal Radical Party, which represented business interests. Still, Radical Party leaders made an issue of Blum's identity, although many of its members were themselves Jews. One sentiment expressed bluntly in a letter addressed by Réné Mayer to the Jewish community was that Blum's flirtation with colonial elites confirmed popular sentiment of Jewish disloyalty.[87] Mayer, who was competing in an election with Blum, thus declared Blum untrustworthy to lead the state. In actuality, Mayer was upset about Blum's economic reform laws.[88]

Mayer's reaction was emblematic of French society, where racism and anti-Semitism elicited different and often contradictory responses even among the victims. French defeat, Vichy collaboration with the Nazi regime, and French deportation of Jews momentarily changed this situation. The reactions of the colonized also vindicated Blum. Apart from Jews, therefore, no corporate entity was as liable to negatively react to the racist ideology of the Nazis and Fascists as colonial populations. Indeed, all colonial reports show that blacks were fearful that a victory of Vichy and the Nazis would be a victory of racism and the return of days worse than slavery. To underscore this point, a 1940–1941 Vichy administration report on the Muslim world found that German and Vichy propaganda had failed to woo Arabs away from Britain and the United States even though Nazi propaganda had played up British support for Jewish immigration to Palestine.[89] The stated reason was Arab fear of Nazi racial ideology.

While the anti-Vichy coalition blended the political left and right, the aversion among French minorities and colonial populations to the ideology of Nazism created more dependable bonds during the years of dissidence and resistance.[90] Colonial entities recognized the immorality of anti-Semitism and for this reason empathized with (and in many cases supported) progressive Jewish groups and their activities against the Vichy state.[91] The memories of the presumed and actual accomplishment of Léon Blum's Popular Front played an important role in mobilizing Africans to the French cause.[92] Although Léon Blum's governing Front Populaire was short-lived, it set into motion a new course in the relationship between the Métropole and the colonies. Specifically, Blum's policies brought about new insights into the life of empire, particularly in regard to its pathologies. Among other things, they sensitized progressive metropolitan and colonial groups of the rising tide of anti-Semitism and racism in Germany, France, and elsewhere.

Blum's policies left a legacy of optimism and cooperation between colonized and colonizers that set the context for some African goodwill and empathy after defeat and occupation. The experiences of the war also lent credence to Blum's wisdom and African demands for equality and representation in French politics. Now seeking and looking forward to African support for defeated France, most all French politicians within the resistance entertained the idea of the franchise as reward for African loyalty and military service as well as democratic representation to counter Nazi and communist propaganda. In these regards as others, the institutions and structures of communication charted by Blum allowed anti-Vichy intellectuals, communists, and socialists to set up resistance networks in colonial Africa in association with African elites (évolués).

The memories of camaraderie across racial and national lines among post–World War I veterans also played a crucial role in mobilizing Africans.[93] Residing in the far reaches of the empire, and away from German surveillance and the reach of the instruments of the Vichy state, World War I veterans remembered the stakes of the war and, therefore, could easily relate to the pathos of the present war. They felt particularly betrayed when the Vichy government, upon the Armistice, abandoned thousands of African draftees to Germans. This betrayal also awoke fear of the return of antiquated claims of white supremacy and perhaps even harsher colonial policies. As I show later, these veterans would not only volunteer for the Free French movement, they pressed for radical reform of French colonial policies in return.

Beyond Allies and Axis Powers: A War of Networks

German occupation and the Franco-German Armistice invalidated the institutions that had sustained public and civic life in France and the empire. They caused the disintegration of the French state, the momentary disappearance of bureaucratic oversight in the colonies, and the breakdown of traditional political alignments, both metropolitan and colonial. Nowhere were the ensuing confusions more obvious than the French colonial federations of Equatorial, West, and North Africa. They offered spaces for political opportunism to both sides of the divide created by the advent of the Vichy regime and its ascent to the German Armistice. Both sides had to contend with the collapse of the colonial administration and the virtual cessation of bureaucratic oversight. These events freed colonial administrators and settlers of colonial protocols and allowed them to engage one another as well as other political actors on new terms.

Vichy first sought support for its policies from military officers, colonial administrators, cultural conservatives (including Catholic groups), and other *Français de souche*. It is to these groups that Pétain often addressed himself to justify capitulation under the Armistice and his decision to set up a government in Vichy under German control. In a speech commemorating Joan of Ark in Limoges, for instance, Pétain compared that heroine's era to the one in which France found itself in order to extol French citizens to be self-reliant and place their trust in his judgment and Vichy.[94] Just as in Joan of Ark's times, Pétain explained, France was in a moment of "weakness, division, and self-doubt." Such a moment exposed "internal squabbles that worsened the tragic consequences of a foreign war."[95] As the French head of state explained it, a foreign war was forced upon France by the English who now supported an important political party of desperate French citizens who, in turn, wished to place the salvation of France in the hands of foreigners.[96] Under the circumstances, Pétain boasted that the Armistice was a lesser humiliation than outright German rule and the loss of empire to foreign rivals. The Armistice was thus a temporary and immediate means for preserving French unity and sovereignty at a time of weakness. In his concluding statement, Pétain extolled the conservative traditions, values, and personal attributes that enabled Joan of Ark to save France: first, love of family and nation; second, faith in God, country, and oneself; and, third, selflessness and unity around the leader.[97]

Pétain frequently made allusions to foreigners and foreign threat that demanded a French response. In this one case, the "foreign" was ethnic, viz. English. At other times, however, the figure of the foreign stood for progressive ideologies, including socialism and communism, and French constituencies mistakenly associated with them, including Jews. Léon Blum and his supporters were frequently singled out by Pétain and his followers. The former were blamed for weakening the French nation, family, and character a well as fracturing French public life and undermining national security. Blum took the blame also for the breakdown of traditional political alliances, undermining preparation for the war, and thus creating the condition for the rapid defeat of France at the hands of the Germans. These accusations led to an insidious system of discrimination, confiscation of property, and interdiction of public functions to so-called Israelites under Vichy.[98]

While many military officers and colonial administrators were troubled by Vichy's anti-Semitism, Pétain's bid to restore France to its past glory got their attention. Pierre-François Boisson, the governor of the federation of French West Africa was among them.[99] Positioning himself strictly as an official of the state, this governor was committed to the preservation of the unity of French sovereignty, the defense of the French state, and the protection of the *Patrie*. In so doing, he accepted the indivisibility of French sovereignty and the claim of the Vichy government to be the sole representative of the French state. He also accepted Pétain as head of state and sole sovereign of France on the same grounds.[100] Boisson pledged to defend the state represented by Pétain, as its head, but he would not pledge to preserve the Vichy government. Boisson's commitment to the preservation of the empire followed the same logic. Thus, Boisson continued to receive his directives from Vichy, but he implemented only those that accorded with his own estimation of the interests of the French state.[101]

As proponent of French Grandeur (France as world power), he objected to the surrender of France to Germany and conceded that the Armistice undermined France's world standing.[102] As a result, Boisson was sympathetic to those who entered into dissidence to oppose the Armistice and its terms. Indeed, he was favorable to the need to end German occupation of French territory, a need most forcefully expressed by Charles de Gaulle and represented by his free French movement and the Council for the Defense of the Empire. Yet—at least initially—Boisson ardently opposed the dissidents whom he regarded as engendering disunity and weakening France before its competitors: in particular, Britain and the United States. In the end, Boisson held the paradoxical position of pledging to defend the French state, even if this meant Pétain, against dissidents with whom he agreed in principle on the need to remove German occupation.

Vichy loyalists and their sympathizers were not alone in their predicament. The dissidents also faced predicaments of their own. Their pledge to defend the institutions of the state proved more problematic than they had anticipated. It gained them short-term in "middle France," but it initially cast the emergent resistance in unfavorable light among French progressives and minorities and the colonized. Indeed, lacking state instruments and support of the colonial administration, particularly in West and North Africa, the dissidents had to turn to sympathetic colonial functionaries, soldiers, merchants, and clergymen. The new situation called for horizontal alliances and relations between military commanders (for instance, General de Gaulle and admirals Giraud and François Darlan), their subordinates (the like of Colonel Edgar de Larminat), colonial administrators (Pierre Olivier Lapie, Réné Pleven, and Félix Adolphe Sylvestre Eboué), French businessmen, bankers, academics, and researchers (including professors Robert Laffont, Camille Fidel, and Monod), and the évolués (including local colonial chiefs and intellectuals). In regard to the évolués and colonial populations, the tasks of the dissidents were complicated by a changed political environment in which the old symbolic lines that once distinguished the colonizer from the colonized had now been blurred by the conjoined experience of the humiliation of defeat and political oppression. The dissidents now had to de-emphasize national origin, ethnicity, and race as bases of political and organizational affiliations.

For many in the dissidence, the new approach to political alliance and coalition building reflected a new pragmatism, born of the ambition to reverse the political fortunes of the Métropole, rather than an ideological conviction. In practice, however, the incompleteness and paradoxes of the colonial project proved more salutary than even the most optimistic of dissidents had anticipated. The tenuousness of colonial control compelled colonial administrators and others to espouse open solicitation of the colonized and tolerance for political deliberations. Such solicitation and political debates were facilitated by the convergence of views, ideological sentiments, political outlook, moral orientations, and political interests between some dissidents and progressive colonial entities. These convergences rendered French and African agendas and their premises mutually intelligible, even if they remained at odds.

The collaboration between the dissidence and the colonized, particularly the évolués, laid the foundation for the initial anti-Vichy and anti-Nazi coalitions in the French empire. The political opportunity arose in French Equatorial Africa and was seized by an évolué whose initiative found immediate support among a group of black and white veterans of World War I. Indeed, while General Charles de Gaulle appealed for resistance from the safety offered by the British, it was the black colonial administrator of Chad, Félix Eboué, who took the strategically crucial step of placing his colonial territory under the symbols of the French republic and "the dissidence," the movement opposing Vichy. For nearly a year and a half, de Gaulle and other metropolitan officials merely followed in Eboué's footsteps, replicating every one of his actions on the larger scale of the republic and empire. Indeed, Eboué's political acts and the networks that he helped to set up served as models for others to follow.[103]

On August 26, 1940, Eboué invited a group of French citizens and colonial subjects in Fort Lamy, Chad, for consultation over developments in the war: the defeat and surrender of France to Germany. The governor of the colony was to inform participants, which included black and white veterans of World War I, of the June 1940 decision by Maréchal Pétain to end all resistance to Germany and to cooperate with Germany during the war. The news that Pétain had pledged to end hostility toward Germany prompted riots among the veterans that lasted three days. The riots that turned to revolt against Vichy ended on August 28, 1940, only after Governor Eboué pledged to defy Vichy, suspend cooperation with the authority (or French state), and restore the sovereignty of France in the colonies after the restoration of the French republic and republican institutions.[104] Consistently, Eboué placed the colony under the authority of the budding Free French movement—until then only a symbolic entity that lacked military and bureaucratic, as well as infrastructure, in the colonies.[105]

Following his dissent, Eboué led the way in providing the rationales and justifications for resistance to Nazism and solidarity toward France. The lone black governor of a colony, Eboué called on other governors and colonial administrators in Africa (Gabon, Niger, and Cameroon among them) to join the dissidence.[106] His most ardent supporter in this enterprise was another Antillean évolué, Raphael Saller, who rallied Cameroon to Free France.[107] Both directly confronted their superiors in the echelon of the colonial administration to attain their goal: the heads of the colonial federations of North Africa (Admiral Darlan) and West Africa (Pierre Boisson). The latter did not rally the resistance until the end of 1943, when de Gaulle's partisans prevailed in North Africa.[108] With words of Eboué's successful defiance spreading throughout Greater France, the colonial administrators of Gabon, Niger, and Cameroon overcame traditions and institutional loyalty to adhere to the cause of the resistance in defiance of the instructions of the state, represented by Vichy.[109] Everywhere, even in West Africa, the partisans of the resistance could count on networks of African intellectuals who, upon graduating from public and parochial schools, formed cultural and sports associations as well as trade organizations—foyers, associations, amicales, mutuelles.[110]

Eboué's action also set the pace for others around de Gaulle. On August 29, 1940, following in the footsteps of Eboué, de Gaulle's representative in East Africa, Colonel Rene-Marie-Edgard de Larminat enacted the *Acte Organique No. 1* that constituted a government of Free France for the entire East African Federation.[111] As in Chad under Eboué, de Larminat's Act laid the foundation for a parallel federation-wide bureaucratic infrastructure to channel dissident activities and African solidarity. These actions laid the foundation for de Gaulle's decision to establish the Council for the Defense of the Empire in Brazzaville, the capital of French East Africa on October 27, 1940.[112] Significantly, these events in the colonies added to the credibility of the resistance. They and events in North Africa weighed heavily in the December 1941 decision by Great Britain and the United States to endorse de Gaulle as leader and spokesman for all of France.[113]

In sum, Eboué's political innovations and the ensuing transformations illustrate not only the complexity of identities and values within empire, but also the shifting nature of power and interest upon the collapse of the old colonial order. This évolué black colonial administrator and his Chadian followers gave comfort and legitimacy to the resistance based in London. Chad also defined earlier French strategy. This is where de Gaulle sent his most charismatic and brave commander General Phillipe François Maire de Hautecloque, also General Jacques Leclerc. Eager to impress his Western allies, de Gaulle needed a presence on the field and Chad provided the basis for that presence. Leclerc, who was burning for revenge against the Germans and their Axis allies, was de Gaulle's man for the task. From Chad, Leclerc raised a column of troops, took them to Lybia, and routed Italian soldiers at Koufra.[114] Upon this victory, probably among the most specular performances of the Free French forces, Leclerc joined General Bernard L. Montgomery's British Eighth Army "and fought on its desert flank."[115] By 1943, when Leclerc was instructed by de Gaulle to form the second French Armored Division, Leclerc could pull together a "mosaic of peoples and races, religions, and political convictions: Free French from the United Kingdom and Syria, French North Africa and Equatorial Africa, Catholics, Jews, Moslems, and animists, communists, social-ists, radicals, free thinkers, militant Christians, and Quakers, all min-gled in friendship."[116] The author of these quotes, Martin Blumenson, mistakenly attributes the formation of this great mosaic of peoples, faith, and ideologies to "the hatred of the Germans, love of France, and the spirit of Leclerc."[117] The driving force of this network was hatred of Nazism (not Germany), love of republicanism (but not the French state), and the spirit of human solidarity (but not French grandeur).

Conclusion: Remembering to Forget

No account of international relations can be expected to include all international events in their narratives and assignation of meanings. Nor are theory and international knowledge ever complete invento-ries of available data. Nor should they aspire to be so. Like recalling or remembering, theory and knowledge select from incomplete archives; but meaning-assignation is of the utmost importance. This is why it is noteworthy that institutionalists assign meaning-creation only to a limited range of events, their symbols, and metaphors. It is this context too that omissions and silences recover their own meanings.

Silence therefore is not without effects. Charles de Gaulle's postwar campaign to "whiten" the French image began an enforceable edit of erasure or silence on key wartime events. This edict was issued on the day of the liberation of Paris in August 1944.[118] De Gaulle could not bar Americans from the spotlight, but he did manage to outmaneuver French communists by robbing them of the credit of liberating Paris. He also ordered the confinement of African troops to barracks away from Paris. This action was followed by an official policy of whitening—or *blanchissement*—of the ranks of the Free French forces and the national army[119] as well as an unofficial but equally potent policy of whitening the national memory and image. Since this original event, French officials began to instrumentalize Africans' contributions to the resistance and to limit related references only to the domestic context of French reconstruction and colonial reforms.

The postwar whitening of history has not been limited to France. Successive postwar French-ruling coalitions revised their views and representations of the role of Africa in the war in order to accommodate Americans and U.S. influence in postwar reconstruction. The United States encouraged the marginalization of Africa and thus the *whitening of history inter alia* for practical political reasons. On the day of the liberation of Paris, American officials worried that the sight of Africans among the liberators of France might complicate race relations, already made tense in the American South by President Harry Truman's decision to integrate the U.S. army during the war. Indeed, black veterans of the war were already filling the ranks of the nascent civil rights movement. Beyond this point, the United States worried that the Franco-African Union dream of the French left (and of the right, too) might dilute the impact of the Marshall Plan, particularly if funds allocated to French reconstruction were diverted to its African colonies. As I show in chapters 4 and 5, with each passing moment and French parliamentary debate about European reconstruction, French officials and intellectuals substituted Occidentalism and the need for Western supremacy to humanism and solidarity and thus necessarily felt compelled to tell a new story of the self, the war, and the requirements of the future—all whitened.

To be sure, few institutionalists would intentionally commit to Charles de Gaulle's campaign to "whiten" history in order to sooth the national ego. Still institutionalist accounts of international events inevitably lead to upholding belief in the uniqueness of the West as initiator of the ethos of global politics and legislator of international morality. Specifically, theorists continue to assume that the colonized, even when they acted independently, conformed to the desire and will of their colonizers as well as to their imaginaries of society, order, and morality. Thus is the implication of Myron Eckenberg's thesis that "African contribution [to World War II] became larger than at any other time in colonial relations only because of 'accidents of war and French policy.' "[120] One is to understand that occupation and the Armistice only broadened the supportive role of the colonized in an event whose primary object was the freedom of the Métropole. While the colonized were thus elevated from their subordinate role into independent actors, they still lacked autonomous agency as subjects with autonomous will, valid desires, and meaningful interests. As framed by Eckenberg, the argument is a backhanded slight in the form of a compliment. It mistakes the generosity and humanist spirit of the colonized for mere opportunism in a game long cast for them. Both renditions of history lacks vision and consideration of the motivations of the évolués and the black populations that they led. The war did not merely position the colonized as the primary arbiters of metropolitan contestations and deliberations over the nature and place of French institutions and symbols, particularly the state, sovereignty, nation, republic, and loyalty. That it did not was indeed an accident of history. But, as an observant Vichy official noted, the colonized had been left to their own devices for a considerable time and could have abandoned France in a time of defeat and occupation. They did not. One may speculate today about what might have happened if they did or whether Great Britain and the United States would have allowed a generalized movement of decolonization at this point.

The most charitable explanation for continued silence on the role, agency, and imaginaries of the colonized is an unquestioned deference to "Europe," the modern state, the interstate system, and their structures of subjectivity. This deference and the structures upon which it is built, more than politics or ideology, provide the reasons for which some histories, institutions, paths (or trajectories) matter more than others. The importance of the figure of Europe in IR accounts cannot be overstated. They are the central axes of the colonial ontology, and its metaphors of human agency and subjectivity, which abided faith, racial identity, and location: Christians and heathens, whites and blacks, Europeans and natives, settlers and colonized. The underlying mystic of Western culture (or civilization) has been redeployed throughout the modern era.

This mystic of Europe is buttressed by another central mystic of IR, that of the state. After the state, all acts of national and international remembrances conformed to its political rationality and related intellectual, cultural, and political arsenals. Since the advent of the state, to paraphrase Benjamin Stora, the conjectures of remembrance have varied according to temporal and spatial dimensions, but they have always been stimulated by political rationality.[121] The conjectures of remembrance include in any case political circumstances that necessitate political agendas and corresponding discourses. The stimuli of remembrance too have spatial and temporal dimensions. In any case, they manifest themselves as political will and ideology which avail themselves to such agents as nationalists and imperialists. Both conjunctures and stimuli are productive only when supported by intellectual, cultural, and psychological and political arsenals.[122] The latter set the context for probable discourses, the construction and translation of values, and their significations. In short, the these arsenals give form to what is remembered. Stimuli are therefore never a complete inventory but merely that which may be revealed through the available arsenals, their structures, and forms.

By the nineteenth century, the production of international knowledge was no longer a hobby for the intellectually curious. Nationalists and imperialists now committed the collective memory and knowledge to hegemonic purposes. Henceforth, memory and knowledge had to be united in the past (history) and a putative destiny (national grandeur, national interest, manifest destiny, self-determination, and the like). This nationalization of memory and knowledge occurred even though particular representations or fragments of memory or history had never been fixed or uniform and, by implication, had been open to variations and contestations. This process was aided by emergent national political cultures and power dynamics resulting from a world organized geo-spatially as nation-states.[123] From this moment onward, national imperatives—or the domestic and international interests of the sovereign—dictated the cataloguing of historical (and after the nineteenth century, scientific data) about self (including those made through archeological excavations); the arts of rediscovery, erasure, or forgetting (poetics of narcissism or imperialism); and the act of preservation of memory (monuments, museums, official archives, and so on). In short, modern historical representations, their symbols and metaphors, became outcomes of hegemonic and othering processes.

These processes continued beyond the era of modern nationalism and imperialism. Thus, during the cold war, policy makers, funding foundations, and the agents of intellectual production (including academics) converged to defend the national interest, understood as geopolitical imperatives. The underlying identities and sense of purpose were signs of moral stakes in the promotion of the moral status of the national state in the international order. Related differentiations in national and international civil society translated into differences of interests and rationalities. Then too, individual scholars and epistemic communities were driven by national imperatives, particularly geopolitical ones, to construe appropriate justificatory narratives as necessary and sufficient accounts of international relations. Then as now, deference to the idea of "Europe" or "The West," the state, nation, and their associations promotes a general lack of sensitivity to, or absence of recognition of, other constituencies—actors, agents, and subjects—of the moral order; their structures and processes; and the effects of the latter on global relations. Then, as now, developments and trajectories such as those that happened in Chad threaten to inject discordant notes into the process of recollection and thus disrupt the justificatory narratives that shape the geopolitical claims of our time.

Chapter 3

Félix Adolphe Sylvestre Eboué: Republicanism, Humanism, and their Modulations

If we realize that the individuals who comprise our communities, whether eternal victims or eternal villains, deserve better than the images with which we have branded them, we might just overcome the dangerous gaps that separate us.

—Estèbe, *Annales de L'Assemblée de L'Union Française, 1948*

Since the end the cold war, there has emerged a disquieting phenomenon today among some Western powers of instrumentally refurbishing the Western self-image. The reasons are many, but a few countries have invested time and resources in this effort in order to reclaim moral authority, lost during decolonization, and to project their power as legitimate guardians of international morality. The construction of this self-image depends upon purposefully embellished traditions and false representations of the concerned states' intentions and actions throughout the modern era. France, for instance, boasts "honorable traditions" of humanism and democratic rule of law that afford liberty, equality, fraternity for all as well as solidarity and protection to the persecuted regardless of their origins.[1] The European Union and the United States frequently make similar representations of themselves as the incipient model of civilization and the principal producer and guarantor of the public good.

For these reasons, the European Union and the United States nearly demand that other entities or regions defer to their moral authority or economic and military power, or both. In politics, this has meant that the West can intervene elsewhere, by reason and experience, to instill essential values, norms, and institutions. This presumption has been endorsed by activists and advocates who favor unilateral Western military interventions to enforce universal values: human rights, refugees rights, rights of the internally displaced, rights of children and other victims of war, and the like.

The academy too has rediscovered the mystic of the West as dispenser of values, norms, and institutions. This is particularly the case with constructivist approaches that explore the reproducibility of social identity and practices as source of normative behavior. The rationalists among them argued that the adaptability of global politics can be attributed to the Western genesis of norms, the acquiescence upon decolonization of the formerly colonized to their universal applicability, and their utility and uses in the context of contemporary struggles. Accordingly, Western ideas, norms, and practices have revealed themselves self-evidently by reason and interest to all modern or modernizing entities as essential values and institutions. These beliefs have theoretical implications as well as practical consequences. In the ideological instance, they lead to the expectation that rational or modernizing non-Western entities should necessarily desire to reproduce and/or complement Western institutions as foundation of their own states, societies, and morals. In the political instance, these expectations feed into political agendas and programs that mandate or condone political pressures or interventions elsewhere by the West.

There is a great deal of confusion in constructivism about the place of Western canons in the intellectual lives and political actions of non-Western entities. These confusions arise from the lack of sufficient attention to the structures of global politics, the social forces sustaining identity and interests, or the motivations of political actions. Indeed, constructivist notions of sociability are frequently based upon mistaken views of international developments that erroneously assume that the use of Western-inflected idioms for purposes of communication necessarily signifies conversion by their non-Western users to their base-Western values. Indeed, by generally overlooking the conditions and implications of adoption, constructivists have mistaken the worldwide use of Western languages of politics and their idioms for a general acceptance of their original or historic base-imaginaries, values, and interests of the cultures of origin of the used languages.

This chapter revisits two key operative concepts of constructivism: first, sociability as constitutive dimension of universalization of Western values, norms, and institutions; and, second, the co-constitution of temporal horizons between and amongst contemporaneous subjects and agents. Once again, I arrive at my conclusion by revisiting the French context of empire and colonialism. It is that constructivists have consistently paid inadequate attention to the global contexts of production of ideas and, as such, are mistaken in their understandings of the utilities and flows of ideas and their adoption and circulation as institutions away from their points of origination. As Alice L. Conklin has recently shown, the colonies provided spaces "of conflict and negotiation between colonizer and colonized, where French assumptions about the ability of Africans to evolve, and of France to civilize them, were contested."[2] In French colonial Africa, where speakers had no alternative but to communicate in the available Western idioms, anti- and postcolonial critics did not merely model their borrowed idioms on their uses. Speakers and users used their borrowed idioms as imperfect substitutes to incommunicable African ones while making their views and intentions clear through their own referents and teleologies. These are reflected in distinct modes of thoughts, imaginaries, and visions of society, morality, and order.

Anticolonial thoughts appear in distinct constellations as historical languages of politics among coherent constituencies or epistemic communities. Specifically, after French defeat and occupation by Germany, metropolitan elites were compelled to confront the distinctiveness of the ideological representations, political experimentations, and cultural practices of the évolués. This conjuncture allowed the évolués to significantly reshape, along with their French counterparts in dissidence, the intellectual, cultural, and political landscape of not only the Métropole, but also the empire. In this context, while they used post-Enlightenment French idioms as vehicular languages, Eboué and other évolués elaborated their own visions of solidarity, reciprocity and mutual solicitation, which they opposed to those of other constituencies of the French empire, including metropolitan France. They also operated on the basis of a moral imaginary and political ethos that complemented and yet differed markedly from official French ones.

Unfortunately, the relevant languages—embodied by postcolonial declarations, speeches, and reflections on international relations—have either been discounted or, when they do not conform with Western notions of normativity, debased as rhetoric, catharsis, or worse.[3] However, as J. G. A. Pocock has shown, the language of politics includes public speeches, which as political operant, performs a paradigmatic function within a political community.[4] Like theory, political speeches may forward consistent views of politics and the moral order and, as such, encompass symbolic apparatuses with discursive as well as nondiscursive referents. Political speeches necessarily belong to conceptual worlds and, as such, are founded upon detectable structures of authority, identity, and interests.[5]

It follows that the international order is a monolingual universe and that modern political ideas, practices, and their languages have not flown unidirectionally from a mythical Western center to equally mythical non-Western peripheries. This is not to dismiss international sociability and the co-constitution of temporal horizons. As will be evident later, anti- and postcolonial discourses often had deliberate, autonomous, and complex purposes, but their objects and meanings were sufficiently commensurate with global wartime sensibilities to envisage their translation and adoption elsewhere as an acceptable base of international morality. The condition of the latter is that multiple and distinct languages temporarily converge in their objects across nations, states, regions, and cultures. In sum, theorists cannot simply assume the origin of ideas and practices or deduce the convergence of moral horizons. In the event that particular ideas and practices are adopted, the purposes for which they are adopted must be demonstrated prior to the determination of the related temporal horizons. The overlap of such horizons form the basis of sociability.

Constructivism in Disciplinary Perspectives

John G. Ruggie,[6] Alexander Wendt,[7] and others have described social constructivism at once as a theory, an approach or method, and a practice. The label applies to theorists and practitioners engaged with broad methodological issues. They converge on the notion that ideas, culture, and identity are central to the articulation of interests by actors and are thus related to the meanings that they attach to the material world and the decisions that they make. Constructivists also converge on the need to investigate the ideational embodiments of politics and related contestations. Contestations are said to be the means by which political entities from different spatial constructs formulate norms and rules and "settle them down" before they are sedimented in practice as institutions.

Constructivism comes in many forms and shapes and from a variety of intellectual traditions. Wendt for instance distinguishes modernist constructivists from feminist and postmodernist. He associates each category with a number of precursors and/or pioneers: John Ruggie and Friedrich Kratochwil for modernists; Richard K. Ashley and Rob Walker for postmodernists; and V. Spike Peterson and J. Ann Tickner for feminists.[8] In establishing these categories, Wendt seeks to cast their adepts as hard constructivists who take as mere human artifices social structures and institutions such as the state and the international system. Again, although significantly at odds in many regards, these individual theories and theorists are said to adhere to the assumption that political action is predicated primarily upon *ideas* and *identities* and that *interest* is conditioned by the former to a greater extent than they are by exogenous material forces and nature.

Wendt sets himself apart from these hard constructivists on the ground that the endogenous factors of politics (ideas, culture, and identity) are often subordinate to external material forces and structures. Accordingly, the constructiveness of human institutions and their structures must always be weighted against material factors and material interests as subordinate if not secondary. In this regard, Wendt agrees with neorealists on the materiality of anarchy and power as the principle structures of international relations. But his attempts to chart a philosophical middle way between ideational and structuralist approaches has been roundly criticized.[9] David Campbell sums up the criticism when he says that Wendt's *via media* is really driven by a logic of conciliation with neorealism and a commitment to "a social science concerned principally with the states system."[10]

If there is one way in which his theory might be called soft, it is in the manner in which the author outlines the international environment and its opportunities and constraints. Relatedly, Ronen Palan dismisses Wendt's distinction between constructivism and materialism, which associates the one with "the politics of norms and law" and the other with "politics of self-help and coercion, on the other."[11] Palan also argues that Wendt's materialism merely allows him to avoid a number of "materialist questions" about the manners in which societies, including the international society, "erect and sustain mechanisms that ensure the appropriation of one human's labor by another; and second, whether such mechanisms are . . . at the heart of human history."[12] Indeed, this appeal to history is highly problematic. As David Campbell shows, history cannot be reduced merely to ill-conceived notions of the reality of international life, of "facts," and their representations.[13] Michael Shapiro makes similar points in regard to state, violence, and interest.[14] According to Shapiro "people" everywhere are not "determined to kill and conquer" in the same manner. Nor has warfare been approached in the same manner by all people. Further, the differences across time and space are not material, that is, a function of distribution of capabilities, external constraints, or unequal access to the means of violence.[15] They reside in local, regional, and international cultures, identities, and their values.

The causes, nature, and persistence of anarchy are in fact historical and cultural "events." To the extent that the state and its relation to violence may be likened to a "project," as Wendt does,[16] international relations lend themselves to ethnographic analyses as products of culture and identitarian claims. Antonio Gramsci, who is Wendt's reference in this regard, was an Italian Marxist and an ideologue with great interest in culture and identity. Both culture and identity played a central role in Gramsci's articulations of the hegemonic process, alongside other social processes.[17] Accordingly, the modern European state is also a set of duplicable rituals, rites of identification, and mental habits that can only be obtained in time and place according to historical conjunctures and regional or local stimuli.[18]

From this point of view, the writings of Thomas Hobbes, John Locke, Niccolo Machiavelli, Baruch Spinoza, and others are interesting temporal and spatial narratives, even if very systematic and compelling ones, about the nature of politics. This is not to say that general lessons or wisdom cannot be drawn from their conclusions by similarly situated entities. Such writings would not be compelling if they did not resonate with our times. But, philosophically speaking, the circumstances upon which these authors reflected cannot be conflated with the human condition. Theirs are only provisionally constitutive of dimensions of the human condition. Nor are the behaviors and actions of their times fully constitutive of human nature. Again, related conduct can only be ascertained hypothetically as a provisional dimension of human nature. Thus, the imaginary of anarchy in the ideas of Hobbes and Locke is respectfully English and, to the extent that it implicates the world outside of Europe, invented.[19] This is not to devalue the authors of *The Leviathan* or *Treatises on Government*. It is to reproach constructivists and other IR theorists of a tendency to confuse the authority of the speaker (for instance, that Hobbes is a great thinker) with the grounds of knowledge (that his ideas are trans-spatial and trans-temporal). In the event, Hobbes's authority may be derived from his representativeness (based on the historical or cultural embeddedness of his knowledge) and his qualifications to speak for or against. The grounds of knowledge, in this instance, is envisaged in relation to the base-symbolic and linguistic systems and the methods through which knowledge is both generated and acquires its validity.

This is to say that international politics cannot be properly grasped through theoretical answers to ontological and epistemological questions (first order). Such answers must be verified in the empirical domains of history, anthropology, and/or culture. As Wendt himself admits, IR is inconceivable without powerful assumptions about the kinds of things that are to be found in state life. While I do not uphold any implications that may emanate from the distinctions of theory from philosophy and anthropology, it seems an odd dictum to say that "the state-systemic project" is about the ontology of the states system and that, as such, "is more about international *theory* than about international politics as such." Without much history and ethnography, theory runs the risk of naturalizing its own context and thereby elevating its own pathos into either human nature (reduced to the instrumentalization of rationality) or human condition (framed as transition from passion to reason), or both. This is in fact where Wendt's social theory leads: he combines the worst dimensions of neorealism, by assuming the European state to be historically given, and neoliberalism, by assuming that interest and the benefits of power and authority are the same everywhere.

There is much value to the brands of constructivism so impudently dismissed by Wendt—viz., modernist, postmodernist, and feminist. These offer better understanding of the co-constitution of international relations; the nature of belief or commonsense; and the temporality and spatiality of historical consciousness, all of which figure prominently in shaping ideas, norms, and institutions.[20] In sum, so-called hard constructivists highlight the boundaries and possibilities of modern structures of governance and their regimes of morality. They do so by underscoring the importance of institutions and ideas and identity (and sometimes gender, class, and culture). The more cautious champion a reexamination of the current structures of power, wealth, and military power in a bid to create the conditions for an alternative moral order. They would ground the latter in ethos of reciprocity, moral solicitude, or solidarity, but not power or coercion. As illustrated by Jutta Weldes and Mark Laffey, the co-constitution of identities and interests involves uniform processes of identity (and thus will) and mechanisms of enactment and implementation of values that require the inevitable desirability of otherwise spatially contingent values and institutions. In other words, co-constitution occurs within singular time frames of multiple movements of consciousness across spaces. This very revolutionary idea has yet to be translated into an IR research agenda.

The Res Publica In Question

In *World of Our Making*, Nicholas Greenwood Onuf implores IR theorists to broaden their understanding of the international by looking at the facts: "deeds done; acts taken; and words spoken."[21] Several years later, in *The Republican Legacy in International Thought*, Onuf proposes evidence of the enduring legacy of the "republican way of thinking about law, politics and society in the context of international thought."[22] He highlights this phenomenon through two parallel stories: of the multiple trajectories of the thoughts of Emerich de Vattel and other seventeenth- and eighteenth-century thinkers; the other of the legacies of Immanuel Kant. Neither of these books can be adequately summarized in this space and it is not my intention to do so. I wish merely to highlight two contrasting wisdoms that emerge from *World of Our Making* (or *World*) and *The Republican Legacy* (*The Republican*) because they have equivalencies in constructivist theory and practice.

World is advisory in thrust if not substance. It recommends that scholars look everywhere for evidence of constructed life and the dimensions of the co-constitution of social life and international relations. Onuf contributes to this endeavor by elucidating the relationships between history, theory, and politics. Onuf conducts his historical analysis purely in the realm of the history of ideas. Onuf combines this reflection with a moral appeal to others to heed the world "out there." This turn toward the "world out there" is one of Onuf's greatest insights. This latter gesture has been mistakenly derided by critics, including Ronen Palan, as a feeble attempt to find material bases outside of theory upon which to reconstruct international relations.[23] But, the appeal remains an ethical imperative of sort, even if reflection is mistakenly "presented as the ultimate cause of history."[24]

The Republican may be read as Onuf's attempt to advance international knowledge along the lines set forth in *World*:[25] to substantiate the enduring patterns of thought, and legal and ethical principles, that give form to international morality. *The Republican* is an expository exploration of a tradition in international thought that focuses on the evolution of republican ideas and, according to the author, with an exclusive European eye and with a European-inflected accent. It puts forth a uniform historical movement of transformation toward modernity in which Europe successfully grapples with three dimensions of politics: politics, law, and ethics. There is no need to repeat the outcomes. In the domains of law, Onuf reaches to "the transitional period from the medieval to the modern world" to find the beginning of the modern international imagination. Logically, Francisco de Vitoria (1486–1546) and Francisco Suarez (1548–1617) are credited to have brought "Catholic theology face to face with Spanish practices in the new world."[26] Then, Onuf turns his gaze "to Northern Europe and the towering presence of Hugo Grotius (1583–1645)" who sets much of the context for nineteenth-century scholarly debates.[27] Thus was born the English myth that Grotius was the father of international law although he never used the term "international law" and Jeremy Bentham (1748–1832) clearly did.

The period between Grotius and the nineteenth century is occupied primarily by naturalists and their philosophical kin: Pufendorf (1632–1694); Christian Wolff (1679–1754); Emerich Vattel (1714–1767); and Immanuel Kant (1724–1804). These figures combined the concerns of Roman law, from which they derived *jus gentium* as the law of nations, with the requirements of the *balance of power* in European diplomacy. Roman law played an important function after the Reformation as European intellectuals sought to bring a multiplicity of peoples and traditions under one identifiable law. This emphasis of one identifiable body of law emerged concurrently with a temporal consciousness about the commonality of Europe. It also necessitated reflection on society and the common good (*res publica*).

Emerich Vattel first connected legal thought to the republican tradition by postulating a stable republic of Europe governed through legitimate power and international law.[28] Vattel imagined Europe as the Greek republic, held together as community by a state under the rule of law. The purpose of the state and law was to create and serve the common good (*res publica*) of the community, or political collectives linked principally by history, fate, and geography. Such an order rested on notions of representative bodies, public liberty, protected rights, and clearly defined public institutions (which gave form later to the constitutional separation of powers). Without such an order, European publicists and international lawyers could not envisage the embodied *res publica*: political society, state, the family of nations, and, after imperialism and decolonization, the international community.

As Onuf specifies, seventeenth-century theorists had no more expansive conceptions of political society than the current state-centered notion of international society would suggest.[29] Even eighteenth-century-Enlightenment movements and intellectuals reached out to Greece and Rome for models of society. From French humanists to British utilitarians to later day liberals, European (and Western) theorists present genealogical accounts with monovalent referents to Rome and Greece, religion and state, diplomacy and war, and law and morality (or ethics) within multiple but intertwined symbolic associations to modern political metaphors and allegories of republic, rule of law, order, liberty, and justice. These referents are the stuff of European self-representations. The metaphors and allegories are unspecific as to their origins and configurations and yet all undistinguishable from public and self-serving ideological representation of the purposes and rationales of European politics, cultures, and foreign policies.

Onuf is justified to propose reflection as the very foundation of "inter-subjectivity" even if at times the latter conjures up a messy process of reconciling bundles of subjective meanings across spaces and cultures. The stories presented in *The Republican* are compelling. Europe legitimately emerges a key contributor to international institutions and morality. From the Thirty Year war, Napoleonic wars, and the two world wars, Europe produced epic treaties (for instance, of Augsburg, Westphalia, and Osnabruck), international entities (including the Council of Europe and the League of Nations). These events were properly the actions of political giants, emperors, kings, and statesmen; inspired partly by intellectual giants (including Emerich de Vattel and Immanuel Kant); and motivated by cultural giants (countless poets, artists, and humanists).

Unfortunately, *The Republican* did not heed the wisdom of *World*: to investigate more broadly into like concepts and categories, thought processes, and political actions. *The Republican* leaves out the manners in which politics rendered the examined concepts and categories intelligible across time and space. The gap between *World* and *The Republican* in these regards is emblematic of a tension in constructivism between the postulated open-endedness of science and the deliberative narrowness of research agendas.[30] Onuf succumbs to a general problem in constructivism whereby the act of mentally grasping or apprehending general relationships between concepts, categories, and events is limited to giving reasons, causes, or relationships. This means that explanations are based purely on linguistic and other analytical techniques that leave aside facts and their appreciations or interpretations.

Onuf of *The Republican* has no inclination to inventory, to paraphrase the author of *World*, all modern republican deeds done; republican actions taken; and republican thoughts and words spoken everywhere. There are a number of possible reactions to this choice. The one, more charitable, is that Onuf honestly presents *Republican* as a story of the self, Europe. Everyone else, he argues, must assume "that they are the natural custodians of thought." But Onuf is not interested merely in telling a story or his story. Although he generously offers that "any story about the way we all think is [a] story to tell,"[31] he projects his own as exemplar of the "the way we all think."[32] Thus, the postulated "we" refers temporally in the collective present, but it metaphysically harkens back to a narrowly conceived thinking subject: one that is European (or culturally European), inheritor of Greek traditions mediated by medieval Rome, and a modern subject imbued in post-Renaissance philosophy and legal theory.

Even so, European publicists presented contrasting views of Europe, particularly at the time of European conquest and colonization of the rest of the world. Early into that process, Antonio de Montesinos and Bartolome Las Casas, for instance, presented views of the actions of the historical and imperial Europe that contrasted widely with those of the mythical spatialized Europe projected by their jurist contemporaries: Vitoria and Suarez.[33] The Enlightenment too provided contrasting views of Europe. France, for instance, developed a reputable critical tradition in both the humanist traditions that looked askance at European self-representations, particularly those forwarded by orthodox or conservative elements.[34] Critics, whether humanists like Voltaire or relativists like Diderot, were particularly skeptical of social norms, politics, law, and religion in the everyday. In these regards, they described contemporary French and European Christians and their societies in near uncomplimentary terms. They also abhorred European behavior during its conquest, enslavement, and colonization of other people's lands. All these events set the context within which critical theorists and publicists appreciated the relationships between philosophy and political ideas, on the one hand, and governance and practice, on the other. I return to these themes later.

Two provisional conclusions impose themselves. The first, already fleshed out earlier, is that the idea of a unified and timeless Europe (or West) with authentic and coherent traditions is fiction. Europe and the West have never been factually singular, except as interpellated subjects. The other is that natural law theorists and their successors have not consistently called forth a singular world subject to a singular morality. In the earlier period of conquest, the likes of Montesinos and Las Casas, and not natural theorists and/or republicans, were the champions of the humanity of the other. By contrast, naturalists forwarded different systems of laws and institutions for Indians and other heathens. They assumed the inapplicability of European morality to others on the assumption of the absence among them of value, norms, and institutions parallel to those of Europe.

This assumption of absence of coevalness between Europe and the Rest was the basis for conquest and colonization—and for many of today's so-called humanitarian interventions. John Locke and his contemporaries in fact created "phantom facts," many contradicted by reality, on the assumption of institutional void where Europe had implanted itself.[35] International law and modern international thought too were devoid of history and politics as they projected a mythical Europe in an "encounter" with the Rest.[36] The proposed image of Europe (and the West) was constituted merely through ideas, values, and institutions, which are both timeless (or transcendental) and timely (universal) for politics today. Europe thus envisioned is fully formed and constantly predictably as rights-bearing, value-creating, enlightened, progressive and regenerative. Such narratives of Europe pass off centuries of civil wars, interstate wars, pograms, enslavement, and genocide merely as testing moments of Europe's resilient march to progress. They also strip off instances of solidarity, cooperation, negotiation, and empathy between Europe and others of their more profound meanings and significations.

Although the textual image of Europe was less than accurate, the related reflections had two powerful legacies. One is the belief that the encounters between Europe and others left the former unadulterated by the experience. The other is the assumption of void or absence of generalizeable institutions and norms outside of Europe. Onuf endorses the one proposition without directly venturing opinion on the other. As I show later, Onuf is mistaken in not looking closely at the world of Europe and republican ideas during Europe's "encounters" with regions, its rise to hegemony, and imperialism. It is equally a mistake to not look around the world for evidence or not of republican practices before concluding that republican ideas and thoughts are the exclusive gift of Europe, which it bestows upon the world. At least, Onuf should have entertained the idea that the production of republican ideas and their circulation as international thought during the modern era occurred through complex processes and practices and few republican in inspiration. These include the political instantiations of ideas as institutions or their furtherance through foreign policy as capacities, resources, and technologies for all within the moral order.[37] Onuf might not disagree with this latter point.

Felicity, Self-Understanding, and Concealment

The story of modern philosophy, Jurgen Habermas has stated, "is an important part of the story of the democratic societies' attempts at self-reassurance."[38] At its best, this enterprise channels the expectations and demands of civic and civil communities for a public culture and social norms that correspond to the collective aspirations and their structures of identity, interest, and value.[39] Viewed in this light, international *Theory* is a particular mode of knowledge or form of communication that a historical community has used to narrate its identity, role, and national and global aspirations. Theory is not only one mode of signification among many others, it arrives at its findings teleologically without necessary attention to facts. Hence, for instance, Hugo Grotius, John Locke, David Hume, Baron de Montesquieu, Immanuel Kant, and G.W. F. Hegel posited the unity of Europe during historical periods marked by intra-European conflicts—competition abroad. A good component of these authors' enterprise was therefore to buttress the battered image of Europe and, also, to justify conquest and colonization. These authors and others also helped to screen off the dynamism, fungibility, and fluidity of the modern world. They thus naturalized the hegemony-seeking behavior of Europe and the attendant violence.[40]

In their times, Grotius and others projected the idea of Europe as a civilizational sphere only upon negating Europe's connections with and debts to other regions. The post-Renaissance negation of the hybridity of historical processes of production, distribution, and consumption of ideas and goods reflected Europe's new sense of self, resulting from unprecedented scientific and technological advances. But, the underlying processes were at once compelling, perverse, and disturbing!

The refusal to recognize the intellectual debts of Europe to other regions was merely emblematic of larger political trends and their collective psychology processes.[41] Francis Bacon best captivated the nascent European ambivalence toward the world: the desire to maintain Europe both as a special province of the world, with special gifts and providential rights, and the core of a modern and integrated global order bound by a uniform international morality.[42] To reach its potential, Bacon advised, Europe had to built its achievements solely on its culture, institutions, and science.[43] Bacon was not alone. From the Renaissance onward, European narrations of their "encounters" with others expunged the roles of non-European intellectuals, politicians, humanists, and others from their records.[44]

These are some of the reasons that self-understanding must be undertaken with care. From Michel Foucault, one takes that any perception of the world is obtained from "genealogies of time and space—of histories, of movements, of past encounters, of that whole plenitude of being that go into the background conditions of every contemporary encounter."[45] According to Sankara Krishna, the ordinary feat of self-representation is frequently froth with a desire to "escape history and to efface the violence" marked the expansion of Europe.[46] Even as they assemble whole worlds in spatial and temporal terms of space and time, discourses such as Onuf's must present their objects as encompassing the most relevant experiences and aspirations of the greater majority of the relevant political entities.[47] Another reason for humility in presenting self-stories is that, in international relations particularly, policy and political trajectories are seldom grounded in the theoretical formulations that seek to justify them. Not only is not policy always inspired by philosophical knowledge, theory often makes sense of policy only after the fact. Tradition is thus born of retrospection.

This is not to say that the ideas, thoughts, and thought patterns contained in theory are less relevant than ones outside of it. It does suggest, however, that international theory is ill by the assumption that international thought and morality emanate exclusively from geographical Europe.[48] In this belief, international theory dispenses with others' experiences and representations of the larger world, even when such representations and their referents remained central to European reflections, deliberations, and actions.[49] This obstinate quest for a uniform genealogy of a world modeled on a exorcized Europe has been decried by Sankaran Krishna among others.[50] Krishna appropriately notes that this insistence is a paradox because of the hybrid and polymorphous nature of the diasporic world that emanates from modernity. In such a world, one would expect, theorists would take it for granted that the origins of ideas as the forms of identities, cultures, and values are inevitably multiple and if not uncertain at least unpredictable in their manifestations.[51]

Traditions, Languages, and Commitments

Onuf finds support from John Pocock for his belief that Europe may claim authentic traditions.[52] Pocock classifies traditions into two categories, authentic and invented, on the basis of the degrees of continuity and self-consciousness from their adherents.[53] Writing about Niccolo Machiavelli, Pocock suggests that the Italian statesman and philosopher was inspired by longstanding traditions that continued long after him,[54] presumably reaching the present. Accordingly, the fragments of thought linking Machiavelli to his present day adepts are constitutive of an authentic tradition, one that has an element of continuity which still inspire its adherents.[55] Pocock opposes such authentic traditions to "invented" ones—those that "import self-consciousness at a late date and impose continuity." This distinction has echos in African historiography where Terrence Ranger proposes that so-called African traditions were mostly invented through the instrumentalization of real or imagined local cultural practices.[56] If Ranger is to be believed, perfectly practical institutions were discarded in favor of other less compelling practices.

Reading Pocock and Ranger together, it appears that the political effects of so-called traditions do not depend on whether they are authentic or invented but because they find adherents who uphold them. Onuf understands the underlying processes emotively but resists their implementation in theory. For instance, quoting Vattel, Onuf argues that voluntary relations among nations could be derived from the actual conditions in which nations find themselves: "from the natural liberty of Nations, from considerations of their common welfare, from the nature of their mutual intercourse," and from a proper understanding of the spheres of conscience and public life.[57] But the rules upon which Onuf grounds international decision making suggest commands: instruction rules, directive rules, and commitment rules. These emanate from distinct speech acts, identified by the author as assertive, directive, and commissive which, in turn, proceed from rules of recognition and conclusive identification that set the context for rules of change.[58]

No matter how one describes their teleology, the rules of instruction, direction, and commitment frequently emanate from the West and are based on authoritative and command-like speech acts that seek to direct others to adopt them as institutional facts. These appear as political fiats disguised as ethical necessities and hence nonnegotiable, with practical consequences. One consequence often overlooked is the entrenchment in thought of the expectation that, on account of reason and tradition, Western powers must be obeyed by others. This expectation has been met, in postcolonial contexts, by retrenchment and defiance on accounts of cultural relativism and the non-authenticity of Western values and norms. The result is a particular configuration of politics in which one side, the West, believes that it has power and moral rectitude behind it; while the other, constituted of so-called third world nationalists, believes that it has history and culture behind it. It is evident that this configuration of politics is ill-suited to a more complex world that concurrently accommodates incommensurable differences and incongruous desires together with willful cultivation, mutual solicitation, linguistic polyvalency, and moral forbearance.

Other constructivists have taken a different approach. For instance, Friedrich Kratochwil accepts emotively the need to look outside of Western canons for institutional facts and processes.[59] In *Rules, Norms, and Decisions*, Kratochwil favors the abandonment of entrenched positions while highlighting "the necessity and virtue of debates" and of the "arduous give-and-take." He opposes both to the more negative ethos of "the monologue of instruction."[60] Earlier in *Rules*, Kratochwil rejects the hierarchy implied in the literature of regime theory between "*principles* (which are 'beliefs of fact, causation, and rectitude'), *norms* (which are standards of behavior defined in terms of rights and obligations), and *rules* (which are prescriptions or proscriptions for actions)."[61] He rightly argues that "regimes are usually the result of accretion and incremental choices" and do not depend on "deliberate design or consensual knowledge." Second, "even when regimes are explicitly negotiated," they may ultimately serve several purposes, some of which may lie outside of the purview of the legislator.[62] Kratochwil's approach invites one to consider multiple possibilities or directions in institutional developments, most due to historical conjuncture and the available political practices. He thus recognizes the principle of open engagement as a democratic right and thus incorporates it in theory as essential fundament of international morality.[63] As such, he elects observations, intentions, and available practices as foundations for institutional engineering and decency, justice, and goodness as their ultimate end.[64]

The contrast between Onuf and Kratochwil suggests that there is a certain aura of indulgence in the insistence of constructivists that actors, agents, and subjects recognize the European origin of certain values and norms and in so doing accept their historical instantiations as universal institutions. This is the lesson that one must take from Onuf's history of ideas and the incorporation of such ideas as institutions of governance. Machiavelli is not so interesting because he says or not that communities are thrust together by the virtue of the few—through their power, essential properties, or the moral goodness of their actions—or fortuna, that is contingency. The most important point for the moment is to figure out whether power is in fact wielded in the collective interest and whether the personal traits of those wielding (or wishing to wield power) have any bearing on good governance. The moral character or goodness of the citizenries of states wielding force matters in the same vein when fortune unites different communities together in a moment of violence. This is why Machiavelli's admonitions that "extraordinary virtue is not enough" and the "prince must institute a republic" also matter. Finally, republicanism matters heuristically because it was among the first sets of ideas to contemplate a world of politics without reference to the state. This is to say the validity of republicanism rests in its historical appeal and not in the fact that it may be traced back to Aristotle. Nor is it because Aristotle initiated a compelling distinction between nature and conventions for the purposes of politics: "that justice belongs to the city (naturally) where it is administered (conventionally)."[65]

A more solicitous republican doctrine looks "at the real world" for mechanisms and processes that protect the interest of the majority, without creating permanent minorities. Thus, a committed republican cannot ignore either institutional or historical facts. Unfortunately, constructivists have not given enough attention to the facts of non-Western political analyses, political criticisms, political languages, and political programs. As a result, constructivism adds new layers to international theory that merely render politics less intelligible.

Humanism, Republicanism, and Mission Civilisatrice

The French republic has at its core entrenched ideas of democracy and solidarity as well as emancipation from oppression, bondage, and false beliefs. Its foundation was laid during the eighteenth century by men of letters and philosophers who objected to existing orthodoxies of rule by customs exclusively determined and applied by the monarchy, aided by nobles and the clergy. Philosophers and Men of Letters such as Voltaire and Denis Diderot found in universal history[66] and natural law[67] the foundation of the unity of humanity. From this conviction and others, they helped to shape the values of the republic and to promote what became humanist notions of entitlements and obligations. At first, French revolutionaries converged on the ideas of self-government through representation, toleration of religious and racial differences; relief from the poor through a proper allocation of property; the abolition of Negro slavery; the accession of women to professions reserved to men; and the like. French politics retrenched later due to counter-revolutionary surge from its initial promises. This later move defined the contours of republicanism and, within it, self-government, political society, liberty, rule of law, justice, and the common good.

The *philosophers* and revolutionaries did not defend the rights of all with equal vigor or conviction.[68] To be sure, many philosophers (e.g., Voltaire and Condorcet) and revolutionaries (Robespierre among them) did not support these institutions. But a great deal of ambiguities remained, for instance, in the views of the applicability and extension of the humanism and its embedded political subjectivity to the colonies and their nonmetropolitan subjects: slaves and natives. Indeed, the Enlightenment only "exacerbated the fundamental ambiguity that dominated the encounter between ontological discourse and colonial practice."[69] Many French philosophers who, like John Locke in England, envisaged slavery as the preferred trope for an intolerable and illegitimate exercise of power also found the actual institution of European enslavement of others to be "a legitimate form of property."[70] The slippage denoted a calculated ambivalence that reflects a colonial strategy of power and knowledge: the double articulation implements a "reform, regulation, and discipline, which 'appropriates' the Other as it visualizes power."[71]

Michel-Rolph Trouillot notes that in eighteenth-century France, England, and elsewhere in Europe, "colonialism, pro-slavery rhetoric, and racism intermingled and supported one another without ever becoming totally confused."[72] Anticolonialism, antislavery, and racism mingled in the same fashion. According to Trouillot, this fluidity "allowed much room for multiple positions."[73] Trouillot remarks for instance that Diderot and Raynal advocated the abolition of slavery "but only in the long term, and as part of a process that aimed at the better control of the colonies."[74] Mirabeau too was confronted with the ambivalences of the revolutionary era when he tried to have "the French Assembly to reconcile the philosophical positions explicit in the Declaration of Rights of Man and its political stance on the colonies." As happened, the constitutive revolutionary declaration spoke of "the Rights of Man and Citizen."[75] It appears, therefore, that French republicanism, humanism, and universalism were calibrated to endorse slavery and colonialism.

While the eighteenth century was ambivalent toward the institution of slavery, the nineteenth introduced scientific racism as common currency of European thought and political debates. Henceforth, the successors to the philosophes produced a taxonomy of subjects based on notions of society, industriousness, creativity, culture, and teleology. These ascribed rational proprieties and ends to the action and labor of metropolitan subjects who, it was understood, deserved rights and privileges measured by their values in the political economy. Scientific racism also determined the extent of recognition and solicitation to be extended to the colonized. Through it, colonial rationality provided that the colonized created lesser value and therefore had fewer faculties to protect. The rights of non-European, therefore, were to correspond the value of their labor and moral expectations supposedly derived from their customs and traditions.

The republic (also commonwealth) actualized in the nineteenth century produced its own affective economy upon supposed civilizational achievements, the truthfulness of faith, and mental endowments. Accordingly, the colonizer was a rational (a condition likened to adulthood), godfearing believer, civilized, and modernizer. In contrast, the colonized lacked proper reason (a condition likened to childhood), heathens for the most part, uncivilized, and held back by traditions and customs. To supporters of the institutions of slavery and colonialism, therefore, humanism and its universal values were at the core of the colonial enterprise. Hence "Mission Civilisatrice": a mission to civilize. This meant that slaves and the colonized could still be recipient of humanist values, although they were not properly speaking individuals (for lack of reason and property) or citizens (due to political distance and local customs).

Modular and Nonmodular Humanism

Acting on the basis of the aforesaid ontology, French colonialism created a cast of elites who owed their status and privileges through loyalty to the colonial administration (e.g., "customary chiefs"); their associations with the colonial enterprise and its civilizing mission (veterans of colonial wars), and French education (*assimilés*).[76] These were all assembled under the heading of the évolués. The basic idea of the *évolués* was that black and other colored men—they were mostly men—endowed with the requisite affect, privilege, and knowledge would desire to be associated with the colonial enterprise: the civilizing mission. It was believed that most colored men who cohabitated with the French or were properly educated would want to either play a supportive role in the French mission to civilize or replicate French values and ideals in their everyday. They would become if not white men, at least culturally French. Thus, from the Third Republic onward, France created a panoply of colonial schools from Indochina to Madagascar to Senegal.[77] Their purpose was to ensure a superior (if not hegemonic) status to the French language, to promote French culture, and to cultivate learning and science in such a manner as to provide sustenance to French colonial rule.[78] The colonial school curriculum focused on providing pupils with functional if practical skills: clerkship, secretariate, nursing, teaching, handcraft, and the like. Yet, the expectation was that the colonized absorb metropolitan and republican ideas about man, morals, and society.

The initiators of this agenda and their defenders argued that the civilizing mission benefitted greatly by exposing the colonized to the utility of French humanism and universalism.[79] Thus, according to Albert Sarraut, colonialism might have begun "a primitive act of force," but it developed into "an admirable act of law" and generosity.[80] In this light, colonialism not only ended "a tragic condition of war, massacre, and slavery among the natives," but in addition it brought them progress, rationality, and modernity.[81] These views were doubled by the arguments that the native subjects thus created would not only gladly convert to but would also wholeheartedly imbue themselves in Enlightenment ideologies along with their temporal and spatial metaphors.[82]

A conclusion and two deductions can be obtained from what has just been mentioned. The conclusion is central to the colonial ideology. It is that the *évolués*—literally the evolved—were educated by their metropolitan masters to logically submit to the latters' culture as means to becoming ("*formés par des maîtres de la Métropole, soumis à notre culture, des jeunes écrivains noirs*").[83] From this conclusion, theorists and historians deduced that the évolués always took guidance from French ideologues, politicians, intellectuals, and cultural elites. They also held that the terms of metropolitan contestations provided the necessary languages and political imaginary for the colonized's own struggles.[84]

This idea of the modularity of French humanism and thought appears in different contexts.[85] It holds that French thought charted all the necessary philosophies about Man, morals, and society for the colonized.[86] The French system of education has greatly contributed to the persistence of this belief. But the expectation created by the colonial ideology has had greater effect for its endurance.[87] For some, French education merely allowed the *évolués* to move up and around the structures of empire. Accordingly, thoughts and their categories necessarily imposed themselves because there was no other available language that was acceptable to colonial authorities as media of communication. In this situation, the évolués were obligated to grapple with Enlightenment views of rationality, science, and progress, whether they accepted related propositions and metaphors or rejected them.

Others have made much of the contingency of colonial education by arguing that French language, cultural sensibilities, and moral philosophies also enabled anticolonial and postcolonial emancipatory discourses. This modular view of anticolonialism and decolonization was recently popularized by Benedict Anderson.[88] Accordingly, the West set the model for the imaginary of political futures around the world, particularly in the colonial and postcolonial contexts. This argument received a mild rebuke from Craig Calhoun who insisted that Anderson would be "more precise to say that the discourse of nationalism was available as an international discourse, and new groups of people could take it up, could participate in it, and could in varying degrees innovate with it."[89]

Frederick Cooper is closer to the views of Calhoun than Anderson. Cooper has argued that French humanism and humanist discourses availed themselves after World War II as questions about "the equivalence of human beings" arose in the colonies[90] A condition for the availability of the language of equality, for instance, was that the war had been fought in name of liberty and against Nazism and Fascism. Decolonization was also triggered by the fact that empires had become "possibly too big, too hard to control, too ambiguous in its moral constitution to be immune from widespread mobilization" for freedom.[91] Cooper's arguments constitute a significant corrective to the notion that decolonization arose in the natural course of the evolution of Western institutions. He has argued that "colonized people and slaves certainly played crucial roles in their own liberation, [and] not simply by acting their categories."[92] He has also insisted that in these moments the oppressed were joined by "intersections of different sorts of [metropolitan] people with different motivations and interests, whose overlapping viewpoints crystalized around particular ways of framing an issue."[93]

Cooper has said that his remarks coincide with those of Partha Chatterjee on the derivativeness of nationalism.[94] Accordingly, French ideologies and languages of politics set the context for colonial perceptions and understandings of their own political possibilities: political autonomy, sovereignty, and universal rights. Additionally, "nationalist discourse," now a reference to the totality of anticolonial discourses, was itself a "European extraction" and it "excluded a wide variety of forms of political action" to focus solely on the political rationality of the state.[95] But these remarks are an incomplete reading of the derivativeness of nationalist thought.

Alice L. Conklin, for instance, has noted that the struggles between colonizers and colonized often arose from fissures in the colonial system, signified not only by differences in cultural claims and political aspirations, but also political contingencies.[96] Conklin's position is affirmed by events surrounding the surrender of Vichy, the advent of the resistance in France, and the mobilization of the colonized on behalf of the French republic.[97] These events fundamentally altered the system of difference upon which both colonialism and the French civilizing mission were founded.[98] The war not only altered existing relationships, it transformed them.

Once again, Chad, the French Federation of East Africa, North Africa, and later West Africa emerged as the most important sites "of conflict and negotiation between colonizer and colonized" within conditions under which "French assumptions about the ability of Africans to evolve, and of France to civilize them, were contested."[99] The terms of these contestations were not set by the colonial system of difference, principally because the empire had been physically severed from the Métropole. At this moment of severance, the fate of the French republic and Greater France (or France and the empire) rested equally in the hands of colonized elites, or *évolués*. As I show later, the *évolués* took control in Africa in reimagining the symbols and institutions of empire toward a vision of a postcolonial future. Specifically, it was Eboué, and not de Gaulle's autochthonous representatives to the colonies, who defined the concepts of political identity, sovereignty, state, nation (*Patrie*), republic, and empire that allowed for the mobilization of Africans and other colonial entities. Eboué also provided the operative language to the French resistance with which it redefined loyalty and patriotism, dissidence and treason, and liberty and democracy.

Cooper also insists that colonial processes of "translation and negotiation did not define a dialectic; science did not negate tradition and produce a new and higher unity."[100] One is to understand that colonial entities based their collective claims to equality on the ontological grounds of post-Enlightenment ideologies of "citizenship, equality, or participation."[101] Given that colonial peoples formulated the same desires at the time of colonial penetration, it is hard to maintain that the new claims aimed to obtain such rights as they were formulated by Enlightenment ideologies. It is more precise to say that humanism and other Enlightenment-era idioms resonated extensively with many local idioms that both entertained the idea of the human and the generality of the human condition. "A human does not fit in someone else's hand," a thousand-year-old Mande adage begins, "even if the hand must necessarily be trained by another it cannot indefinitely be held by another. The only thing that is suited to be held in a person's hand for ever is dirt."[102] Is it not why one washes one's hand permanently? Is not why the struggle for freedom is constant?

This adage has been passed down from generation to generation by West African griots even prior to the advent of Sundiata Kéita and the Mali empire. Mande griots also tell us that "it is difficult to guard against the language of the country of one's birth."[103] This is not, echoing Chatterjee, to hold that each culture should have its own "categorical scheme for ordering reality and its own distinctive system of logic."[104] It is an argument against the kind of cultural essentialism germanc to the Enlightenment according to which "rational knowledge" and its view of the world assume a very definite form, not attainable in other cultural contexts.[105] After all, the Mande code of wisdom advises that the only three essential human faculties are: "to see what it desires to see"; "to do what it desires to do"; and "to say what it desires to say."[106] It does matter what language it is.

By claiming that humanism found resonance in non-European locales, I am not assuming perfect alignments of the metaphors or tropes of equivalent African idioms on the former's. The transfer of one particular object of thought from its point of origination to different locales often intervenes within the context of contestations involving claims to power and agency. The appreciation of the product requires linguistic and symbolic "points of entry" into equivalencies, similarities, adjacencies, substitutions, and the like.[107] At any rate, new knowledge, when if new at all, attach themselves always to prior ones. This means that outcomes may differ particularly in regard to their "objects, modalities of enunciation, concept-formation, and in the thematic choices."[108] Regrettably, Chatterjee concludes, the underlying processes do not necessarily lead to new and higher unity.[109]

Rationality, Republicanism, and their Replication

Theorists of the modularity of Western idioms mistakenly view their own sites as exclusively authentic fields of cultural production, leading to redemption, regeneration, and progress. In the Métropole, cultural appropriation is tantamount to destiny, essential and inevitable. It is assumed, for instance, that the Métropole gains much from the colonized. The process of transculturation is mediated discretely and rationally as means to new knowledge and institutions. The experience of transculturation therefore amounts only to cultural enrichment manifested by various forms of bourgeois existence, including cosmopolitanism. An opposite process of transculturation presumably occurs in the colonies where life (or becoming) begins upon acculturation, by conversion and/or assimilation, an imperial sign of native sociability. This alternation of the soul and conscience is viewed accordingly as the beginning of salvation, either by graft of new knowledge (or practice) onto existing ones or by adoption of the new forms as a higher standard. The first results in hybridity while the second gives birth to mimicry.

Alberto Moreiras contests the contrasting views of cultural exchanges that assume either enrichment-preservation (in the West) or infusion-deformation (in the Rest).[110] He notes that the metropolitan theater associated with cosmopolitanism is not a field of unfettered mediation of diverse influences with rational preferences for best practices. It is also a field of selection guided by parochial interests and values. Nor is the non-Western theater a culturally empty space of unimaginative and impressionable entities waiting on cue for the latest idioms of salvation. What Moreiras concedes as inevitable is that the outcomes of processes of encounter differ according to location, object, and relations power.[111] Traditionally, all sides, even the more powerful ones, have been affected by such encounters. All sides absorb external influences and incorporate new values and insights effectively affecting the integrity of the body. Moreiras correctly rejects both scenarios, particularly the impression that transculturation and acculturation are not equal forms of cultural enrichment and the latter is a sign of cultural inferiority.[112] The implication that acculturation does not lead to rejuvenation or regeneration, but a sign of cultural death, is unfortunate.[113]

The views of cultural processes in the French empire conform to views contested by Moreiras. Here, the commonsense is that the *évolués* are alien to their former selves due to their conversion to French philosophy (if not religion), and their adoption of Western ideas, values, and institutions. This commonsense is nonsense. France's imperial adventures altered its identity, culture, or political subjectivity more profoundly than suggested by assumptions of benign transculturation. In the first instance, colonial conquests and political and commercial expansions gave France a sense of cultural and intellectual vigor as well as political indispensability. Related views congealed in notions of Métropole, empire, and *grandeur Française*, all linked to a sense of moral and scientific superiority. Together, they implied that France was a great power with a central role to play in the world commensurate with its achievements and standing among "civilized nations."

As Enlightenment-era debates showed, French intellectuals mistook material endowment as confirmation for superior moral attributes. From the Enlightenment onward, France viewed its technical and political "achievements" (which include its advances against other Europeans powers during intra-European wars) to justify its place in the world and support its claim to conquest (imperialism) presumably to regenerate and elevate the indigènes from their social inertia and moral bankruptcy.[114] This motif provided the background to both conservative and liberal ideologies that supported France's Mission Civilisatrice. It set the contexts for metropolitan approaches to colonial territories, particularly in regard to the colonial order of subjectivity. The latter included citizenship and the status of the native or *indigène* (juridically defined as indigenat). It also included particular statuses that applied to the évolués and other natives who proved themselves culturally or politically worthy due to acculturation into French ways and habits of mind.[115]

The imputation throughout was that (1) France was a "democratic rule-of-law state" that affords protection and dignity to the individual, citizen, and subject; (2) the French state and nation may legitimately position themselves as dispensers of lessons to Africans and others regarding human solidarity and humanitarianism toward afflicted populations, groups, and individuals; (3) French civilization and humanist traditions provided ideological, ethical, and cultural compasses to native and former colonial subjects; and (4) assimilated or socialized colonial subjects and their followers constructed better moral orders, ones that exhibit Western civilizational import.[116] These views posit(ed) the French (and the West) necessarily as cultural and moral teachers of natives who were henceforth learners (if not pupils), to be socialized and, preferably, to be assimilated. This view of the place and role of the two sides of the colonial divide, the colonizer and the colonized, entered constitutively into French colonial strategies of power and agency as a crucial dimension of the practices associated with French grandeur.

Viewed in light of political rationality, the colonial order placed an emphasis on the identity and subjectivity of participants such that one side, the colonizer, was identified duly as sovereign, autonomous, and knowledgeable and, thus, legislator and teacher with will, desire, and interest, all deducible from intentionality. In contrast, the agency of the colonized depended upon their subordinate status, their inability to will, their lack of intentionality, and thus their capacities for moral learning and sociability. One was thus to expect unidirectional flows of values, norms, and institutions from France to the colonies, whose task laid in exercises of appropriation (and not simple translation), interpretation, and assimilation.

This colonial rationality and the institutional context of imperial France vanished upon the 1940 defeat and occupation. So too did the myth of French cultural and intellectual superiority. The "reality of the defeat" and "submission" revealed the fragility of the institutions of state, republic, national autonomy, and sovereignty. They revealed the fragility of the republican order. With no credible central authority, the empire itself was in great danger of imminent collapse. In short, the institutions of governance in France and Greater France, imperial and colonial languages of politics, and their political ideologies had all fallen into practical irrelevancy. France and Greater France were in need of new institutions, new languages, and ideologies of man (community), morals (political languages), and society (ideologies).

The task of summarizing metropolitan French reactions to the these events would be daunting under any circumstance. France was ultimately an amalgamation of individuals and communities, and cultures and institutions. These entities naturally entertained inclusive as well as exclusive relations. They asked conflicting as well as complementary questions about the future according to cross-imperial political and ideological alignments uniting French citizens and noncitizens. The emergent debates took place along existing lines of fissure in the imperial and colonial ontology. Biology per se, that is ethnic and linguistic descent, did not determine political sensibilities. But individual and collective biographies, owing to history and political conjunctures, helped to shape the views of French collectives toward the empire. As noted in chapter 2, both de Gaulle's resistance movement and Vichy's government targeted these so-called *français de souche* (or autochthonous French) because they were more sensible to its associated symbols of Franks, Gauls, Joan of Ark, the Marianne, and the like. Both camps imagined these groups of French citizens to be responsive to notions of French grandeur on the basis of their faith in the essential value of French culture and civilization.

Some of the participants were more immediately connected to the empire. Such were colonial administrators, professionals, military personnel, merchants, and missionaries who served in the Métropole or the colonies in official or nonofficial capacities. The vast majorities existed along distinct spatial alignment, mostly horizontal and trans-empire, that linked colonizers and colonized according to ideology, politics, professional occupation, religion, and race. These alignments had palpable effects. While French minorities and colonial subjects collectively opposed Nazism and Fascism, the first could be found to favor the elimination of political and cultural intolerance as policy objectives. Significant colonial constituencies, however, radically opposed all forms of racial and ethnic discrimination, or the very foundations of the colonial order, as their postwar goals.

Above all individuals played a crucial role, particularly those interested in the restoration of grandeur and empire. As self-proclaimed chief of the resistance, for instance, Charles de Gaulle aspired to restore French grandeur: the traditional place of France as a great power implicated in the determination of the destiny of the world. The most important corollary of this restoration would be the defense of the empire. Indeed, one of his earlier acts was to appoint himself as chief of the Council for the Defense of the Empire.[117] In this regard, de Gaulle reflected the views of the majority of the French population and, paradoxically, even the Vichy government.[118] Other French citizens had more ambivalent relationships with French symbols and cultures and thus greater ambivalence toward the full restoration of empire. Among them were French citizens of racially mixed or African, Arab, Eastern European, Jewish, and slave ancestries. A century of natural history, colonial ontology, pogroms, the Dreyfus affair, and now Nazism and Fascism had made them wary of overt racial and ethnocentric appeals.

Solidarity, Humanism and Loyalty to the Republic

French officials contemplated their post-defeat dilemmas in practical terms and through languages that were tailored to receive support from the colonized. They also weighed the price of support by the colonized in protecting the republic and its institutions. Related contemplations focused on visions of postwar society (connected to postcoloniality) and its institutional foundations: liberty (associated with humanism) and morals (associated with politics). Gone were assertions of French grandeur and civilizational superiority. Instead, the central concern of the resistance was to restore French sovereignty and republican institutions, both of which required the restructuring of the state and empire in light of the new realities.

For French dissidents, the visions of the future were necessarily anchored in postrevolutionary symbols and representations of public institutions: popular sovereignty, republican state, a *Patrie* of equals, and representative democracy. They set to redefine political identity and rationality, encompassing the values of loyalty, patriotism, and sacrifice. In this regard, Charles de Gaulle and his loyalists faced a complicated task: to wrest legitimacy from Pétain without appearing to undermine the state and its republican institutions. As head of state, Pétain could claim to embody French sovereignty and project the dissidence as initiating disunity and weakening France before its competitors, viz., Great Britain and the United States. The argument in favor of the indivisibility of French sovereignty was compelling to many. Again, Pierre-François Boisson, the governor of the French Federation of West Africa, many metropolitan and colonial officials sought alternative ways to resist German occupation while serving the state, preserving French sovereignty, and defending the *Patrie*. As stated in chapter 2, Boisson held the paradoxical position of pledging to defend the French state, even if this meant Pétain, against dissidents with whom he agreed in principle on the need to remove German occupation.

De Gaulle's task was complicated by the fact that the dissidence did not control state machinery and, therefore, lacked sovereign authority to speak in its behalf. The dissidence was also vilified by Vichy as aiming to dismember the empire in favor of Britain and the United States in exchange for their support. Facing charges of disloyalty, treason, and irresponsibility, de Gaulle and his loyalists had to establish a political ontology that reconciled their rebellion against the state with their vow to restore the republic and republican institutions. Put differently, the dissidence had to demonstrate that one could oppose the state without being disloyal and committing a treasonous act. Finally, they had to appeal to the colonized for support and in so doing reconcile the latter's desire for postwar reform with some of the dissidents's ambition to preserve the colonial order of subjectivity and morals in the interest of French grandeur.

To the dissidents, Vichy lacked philosophical and jurisprudential rejoinder to the argument that surrender effectively undermined French sovereignty. They founded their arguments upon the illegitimacy of the state under Vichy due the absence of popular support. In a postrevolutionary tradition, many argued that the only legitimate form of government was independent and republican. Vichy was neither. It had abdicated its historic republican responsibility. It had also abandoned the French humanist vision of the world and its mission to civilize the peoples whose destiny it controlled: colonial populations. In sum, the dissidents' reflections gravitated toward the nature of the republic, *Patrie*, state, and empire and their relations to loyalty, humanism, and republicanism.

The Imperial Republic

The Chad events of August 1940 (and later the 1942 rally of Algeria to the resistance) provided the earliest context for dissidents' views on society (community and citizenship), order (including state and empire), and law (or morality). On the political right, Charles de Gaulle led in exploiting the Chad events as evidence of the loyalty of the colonized to France and the need to restore the empire under a republican form of government. This ideological accommodation of republic and empire was first and foremost a bid to justify resistance to the state led by Vichy. It was also an attempt to reconcile imperial designs with the aspirations of colonial populations for freedom. In the first instance, it was the patriotic duty of French citizens, whether in the Métropole or the colonies, to heed the bravery of the colonized and to join the dissidence in its aim of restoring the republic—now the undisputable basis of French grandeur. The related ambition to "recover the moral authority" of France and its "place among the great powers" was the greatest moral calling of the citizenry.

De Gaulle was comforted in his position by autochthonous colonial administrators invested in the preservation of the empire. In Equatorial Africa, they included Pierre Olivier Lapie (deputy governor, then governor of Chad, 1940–1942) and Colonel Rene-Marie-Edgard de Larminat (delegate for the Resistance and chief of East Africa Government, August 28,1940 to August 11, 1941). These loyalists supported de Gaulle's dream of instituting a republic that was imperial and thus reflected the ontological colonial order of differentiated subjects under new guises. Any call to Africans for assistance and any resulting change in colonial relations had to be mitigated by these ambitions.

De Gaulle and his loyalists, particularly those in the colonial administration, hoped to encourage African participation in the liberation of France, without any commitment to colonial reform. They would stress the war against Nazism and Fascism as war against racism without any engagement to implement republican equality and justice among the involved communities. No one made this ambivalence toward African coequality in citizenship clearer than Pierre Olivier Lapie. Lapie was an ideologue and committed race supremacist who bristled at any intimation that Africans deserved equality. His objection was founded upon an anthropology according to which Africans lacked reason, science, and the institutions required for citizenship. Specifically, Lapie saw much to applaud in the actions of Chadians. Accordingly, he agreed with de Gaulle that the days of August 26, 27, and 28 "augured a new era of selflessness that will restore life and nobility to our country."[119] But Lapie reacted with disbelief at Eboué's implied notion that Chadians could have been motivated by high ideals amounting to political rationality.[120] In *Notes Sur Mon Passage Au Tchad*, Lapie argued that Africans joined the resistance because they were impressed by de Gaulle and not because of any inherent humanism or political rationality. Quoting an old veteran on the border of Cameroon, he attributes African loyalty to France to an aversion to German rule, which they witnessed next door in Cameroon, and a certain myth of De Gaulle: "the strong man who does not eat and leans on a fetish called the Cross of Lorraine"[121]

In a related message sent to de Gaulle, Lapie wished to acknowledge that "the natives possess the essential requisites of generosity that characterizes humanity."[122] However, he insisted that French policy must recognize "the nature of things African, particularly in regard to the internal differences within humanity: degrees of civilization, the existence of irrefutable ancestral customs, and the presence of traditional commandments."[123] In forwarding his "political testimony on Chad" to de Gaulle, Lapie reassured his commander that the view expressed in his memo were not his alone but that they transpired during deliberations with his advisors: "administrators, soldiers, a priest, and merchants."[124] According to handwritten notes accompanying this message, de Gaulle shared the substance and principle enunciated in Lapie's message. But de Gaulle was annoyed about the timing of such a note from a colonial administrator. De Gaulle feared that, if leaked to Africans, the document would inflame an otherwise tense ideological standoff between conservative colonial administrators and progressive French elements, who supported Eboué. Worse, the memo could demoralize Africans and undermine their resolve to defend France and the empire.

Other de Gaulle loyalists feared negative fallouts from Lapie's indiscretions and wished to discourage other colonial administrators and resistance officials from repeating them. Upon his appointment as governor general of French Equatorial Africa, Larminat advised all colonial administrators against speculations about the after-war.[125] The impression of one of his principal assistants was that he was "unconcerned by philosophical and ethical considerations of wartime relations, particularly in regard to their implications for postwar French responsibilities and obligations toward the natives."[126] The man who reported Larminat's private thoughts, M. Parr, warned against public reflections on the future of the colonial order. Such reflections, he argued, would not only adversely affect African moral, but they would run counter to "the other side of public opinion." That side of French opinion was equally faithful to the *Patrie* but remained hostile to the dismantlement of the empire.[127] In other words, M. Parr made the argument that the conservative side of French opinion, equally "authentic" and integral to French traditions and institutional practices, had to be taken into later consideration of the future of the empire. But for now, and in the interest of managing African sentiments, M. Parr and like-minded colonial officials on the political right wished to harness African assistance without causing excitement among them by taking on issues better left alone. What M. Parr did not say in this particular memo was that de Gaulle and his loyalists had good reasons to be uninterested in imagining a new order or reconsidering the philosophical and moral foundations of global politics.[128] Their desire to restore French grandeur had received a boost from Winston Churchill who assured them of the support of Britain and other Western powers for "the rights and Grandeur of France."[129] In short, the reform contemplated by the political right brought republic and empire together as bases of duty, responsibility, and entitlement.

Muddled Republic

The political French left played a disproportionate role in these debates because it was then the most significant political force in French society. Now humbled by defeat and a devastating war, progressive intellectuals, including but not limited to politicians and philosophers, contemplated new questions about the international order, its geopolitical foundations, and base-political economy. They did so through universal humanist and socialist sentiments that paid heed to the ontological status of the other: the colonized and minorities. These values gained the French left the sympathies of the great majority of the évolués and, as a result, extensive relations and networks in the colonies.

The French left was divided on the extent of colonial reform—and their faith in an inherent African humanism. A segment of the French left—among them Christian and social democrats and socialists—was interested in restoring "the moral authority of France in the world" as matter of pragmatism. This position brought its views closer to de Gaulle's on the republic, duty, citizenship, and empire. Within other quarters of the left, the colonial question was frequently weighed against French republican ideals. Specifically, public intellectuals were keen on setting the republican agenda apart from Nazi and Fascist ideologies of racial superiority. As a result, they favored a modicum of emancipation for the colonized to underscore the contrast. This desire was manifest in the 1946 Constitution that devolved considerable power and responsibility to new entities, no longer to be labeled colonies.

Réné Pléven best exemplified this desire to combine French liberalism with the restoration of French grandeur and political emancipation of the colonized. A onetime commissar of the resistance for the colonies and president of the French Council, Pléven envisaged postwar colonial reform as a reward to the colonized for their support of the Métropole in times of need. This idea of reward contrasted with a republican entitlement to liberty, equality, and fraternity. Pléven began by cultivating the spirit of "The faithful of Chad, Cameroun, and French West Africa who bound their lot in with the destiny of France."[130] These were among "the strong who never surrendered to fear, the brave who gave their all to an apparently lost cause."[131] This cultivation of the spirit of Chad was a calculated bid to win further support among the colonized. But the solidarity showed by the colonized was also evoked to elicit support for a reformed colonial empire and French grandeur. These sentiments culminated in messages sent by Pléven to colonial administrators on the day of the liberation of Paris: "Among those of Fort Lamy, Douala, Brazzaville, Bangui, from the bushes to the combatants of the hinterlands, there formed a community of faith whose end rested in action and in success. These are the children of the same people guided by the same instinct in Africa and in the maquis who pulled France from the worse nightmares to restore it to enlightenment and grandeur."[132]

Even as Pléven was extolling the virtues of African solidarity and the exemplary courage of the human mosaic that brought about the Chad events, he was creating an emotional distance between the colonizers and the colonized. Thus, upon recognition of humanism, solidarity, and "deliverance of the French people" by others, Pléven quickly reverted the imperial modes of celebration "of re-conquered cities," manifested by the "virile joy" "at the irresistible victory of the French people and its allies."[133] That virile joy was generated by the American-aided spectacle of "Leclerc entering Paris at the head of a glorious French division" on August 24, 1944.[134] In one moment, Pléven had absorbed and adapted to the new mood in France. African war efforts were integral to the liberation of France, but the reborn imperial France was now ready to move on and to assume its role in global politics.

Pléven labored later to refurbish the restored empire with a humanist face by accentuating the theme of solidarity and by promoting new modes of engagements with the colonized. He personally enlisted a number of politicians and intellectuals to help design new relations with the colonies.[135] He also helped to set up study groups to look into postwar questions, particularly questions that arose from the empire.[136] One such group functioned as an unofficial advisory body to the commissars of the resistance and, after liberation, to successive French governments. It comprised scientists, ethnographers, merchants, industrialists, and others with professional and personal attachments to the colonies. As a result, its members were dedicated to reforming the empire while ensuring French control over the colonies. This and like groups contributed to laying the groundwork for the neocolonial arrangements that would characterize France's relations to the colonies, from 1946 to 1958, and later, from 1960 onward to postcolonial Francophone states.

Progressive Republic

A group of French progressives, represented by Professor Robert Laffont, envisaged ideological reflexivity and political reformation as recipes for a new form of French grandeur. Laffont was president of the Union of Overseas French, a group of resident French citizens in the colonies known for its "native" sensibilities. Many factors shaped Laffont's own sensibilities. The first was happenstance: his birth in North Africa. North Africa boasted French nationals and minorities whose personal, familial, and collective circumstances and experiences mediated their political convictions. They were ambivalent toward colonialism and the privileges associated with their own identity within it. These factors pushed countless toward a certain skepticism if not suspicion of French discourses of reason (rationalism), humanism, and republicanism.[137] Laffont therefore belonged to a group that was committed to the realization of French ideals for all.

Laffont's reputed attentiveness to the need of the colonized made him a valuable asset to the resistance. It earned him a position in the resistance's propaganda efforts, where he frequently helped to draft radio messages destined to the colonies. His propaganda messages often encouraged the colonized to endure the sacrifices of the war for a better future no longer favorable to racial privilege. In conjunction, Laffont proposed an idealized view of French republicanism, organized around the core values of universalism and emancipation; self-help and solidarity; reason, science and progress; and patriotism by loyal, disciplined, and enlightened citizenry.[138] In one notable address, Laffont opened with the theme of community and love, which he believed had been established between the colonizers and the colonized during the course of wartime events. "I myself who is one of you," he stated, I was "born like you in overseas France where my family has lived for over a century."[139] "The war of 1914," Laffont continued, had already brought us "closer." It "caused us to better familiarize with one another and to love one another."[140] Now, Laffont persisted, whether "you are from Africa or Asia, from America or Oceania . . . you are brothers as soon as you enter French territories."[141] Laffont insisted that the Métropole was in total communion with "all of the inhabitants of overseas France regardless of their race, color, or religion."[142] Indeed, we "all [belong] without exceptions to the same family."[143]

As an advocate of freedom and political liberties, Laffont also believed that the war should cause "subjects and slaves" to "pull together as free men and citizens."[144] He was convinced that "the French spirit [had] never been so committed to eradicating religious barriers and all prejudices that still separated humans beings from one another."[145] Finally, Laffont had faith "that true Republican

France never established distinctions among its overseas children, whether they were Muslims, Buddhists, Christians, or Jews, Brahmans or Animists."[146] This faith was vindicated by the fact that "France . . . deemed us all capable of taking up arms on behalf of the country of Liberty, Equality, and Fraternity."[147]

While Laffont's connections to "Africa" made him an invaluable propagandist for the resistance, his vision of the future was more extensive than most of his contemporaries were willing to entertain. To one of his superiors, Laffont's proclamation sounded more revolutionary than ordinary. A certain M. Perret explained that Laffont's views represented an "unfortunate specimen of bad literature for the republic."[148] Referring specifically to the text of the message quoted in this section, M. Perret argued that Laffont was not only misguided but outright dangerous. For these reasons, Perret advised against the broadcast of Laffont's message by Radio-France in Algiers, also the voice of the resistance. In his remarks, Perret noted that his immediate superiors, including M. Laurentie, a prominent member of the resistance, had advised that the commissar for propaganda muzzle Laffont until such times when the professor abandons his views or at least modifies the manner in which he wished to convey them in print to the natives.[149]

Individuals like Laffont were sincere in their commitment to humanism and the republic. Jean-Pierre Biondi and Giles Morin cite Laffont among anticolonial French intellectuals whose humanism was rooted in a revolutionary tradition that is shaped by bourgeois virtue and popular notions of fairness, decency, and good intentions.[150] During and after the war, many such intellectuals attempted to lay down the foundations of a new kind of politics: one that favored not only human solidarity, but also a republicanism that fostered democracy, humanism, human dignity, and political autonomy. In this manner, Laffont's views represented those of a significant number of progressive intellectuals who, in the course of the war, grew sensitive to the fact that the colonized's perceptions of France had undergone crucial transformations and that France needed to accommodate such changes. Like them, Laffont wished to transform colonial relations to implement a postcolonial order founded upon a new humanism. These sentiments were out of tune with the vast majority of the resistance. In desiring to transform (and not merely alter) French institutions to make room for new subjects, Laffont was particularly mistaken about the depth of political openness and cultural transformations in French society. The war had not fundamentally dented the ideologies of French Grandeur and imperial ambitions. These still outweighed the republican and humanist convictions of too many of his compatriots.

On the other hand, even Laffont's personal credibility and moral fortitude could not make up for the limitations in his own ideas and political imaginary. While he spoke of the need to reform the republic and the mental habits and political reflexes of "its children," Laffont sadly could not free himself from the spell of French parochialism. This was particularly true in regard to the colonial metaphors of "France as the Motherland," "the colonized as children," and "emancipation as the completion of France's mission of civilization." Even his conceptions of patriotic duty and treason were sketched in familial and imperial metaphors. Hence, patriotic duty befell the emancipated colonized who, now "grown children," could not skirt their responsibility to "take up arms" in defense of Mother. It was thus morally unthinkable and indeed real moral tragedy and political treason on the part of the colonized to not answer such a call.

In sum, Laffont's vision of postwar reform was circumscribed by fixed cartographies of France, French North Africa, Equatorial Africa, West Africa, Indochina, Madagascar, and the like inhabited by subjects with fixed identities; however, many—Africans, Animists, Arabs, Catholics, French, Jews, Protestants—but none with mingled and/or trans-spatial identities. Invariably, even the likes of Laffont were constrained by longstanding French traditions that fixed the meanings of the available idioms of rights, justice, and liberty such as to burden the imaginary of their users. As it happened, linguistic appropriations by others and attempted innovations were blunted by juridical mechanisms and constitutional resources with limited malleability.

A Republic of Sincere Humanism

French public life was highly fragmented during the war. Its partisan politics produced public inertia, brought about by coalitions that spoke from perspectives that approximated their combined political positions: conservative, liberal, and progressive, right, left, communists, anarchists, libertarians, free thinkers, and the like. This situation brought into relief new subjects who were united by a desire for self-realization. Among them, the *évolués* maintained personal, political, and institutional relations with other metropolitan and colonial entities, organizations, and individuals that varied according to ideology and political ambitions. To be sure, the so-called évolués had inhibitions of their own, which emanated from their own contexts and traditions. They approached political issues from their subject position as colonized. They also spoke from various positions with diverse intellectual, cultural, and political sensibilities. But they confronted the existential questions of the day with more openness, with few of the considerations due to power, privilege, and cultural hegemony. Yet, once freed by metropolitan defeat from the political and social constraints of the colonial order, the évolués implicated themselves in the war, with clear ideas and expectations of the terms of its resolutions.

Eboué was among those who approached the war with clear views of global pathologies as well as precise expectations of the future. An évolué who had fought for the franchise and colonial dispensation, Eboué argued that the "sclerosis" of the international system was not limited to Nazism, Fascism, and totalitarianism. The global pathology encompassed larger crises of the spirit and body, state and empire, and values and institutions. This crisis engulfed everyone and thus everyone needed to be emancipated from their mental habits, political culture, and material proclivities. It included the pursuit of grandeur by the autochthonous political elites. The ambition to grandeur also laid the seeds for future discord, hostility, and insecurity. It not only undermined French humanist and republican claims, it sapped African faith in the Free French movement.

Eboué also had an expansive view of a postwar republic that required equal responsibility and provided equal privileges to all who inhabited it and sacrificed for its preservation. This republicanism was founded upon solidarity, generosity, and justice to account for the sacrifice and collective spirit of colonized and colonizers alike. In this regard, Eboué dismissed much of the dissidents' views of republicanism, humanism, and postcolonial reform as reflecting "petit bourgeois sensibility," "arrogance," "self-centeredness," and "wanton individualism." To him, the betterment of Man required that everyone transcend their own positions and interests. He was convinced that French elites and populations had to be sensitized or reasoned into the sentiment and knowledge that they are not free until such a time when they can will equality and justice for others. The full measure of humanism was therefore justice for those who had been "enslaved."[151] Nor was Eboué confident in the conversion of the French public to humanism and republicanism. "[Colonial] opinion is an amalgamation of contradictions," Eboué noted, but there existed within it an "obstinate hostility to change."[152] In this and other regards, Eboué found that French opinion makers and politicians never "rewarded merit."[153] He was particularly miffed that some politicians sought support from public opinion for policies destined to "keep Blacks in their place" and/or to destroy native societies without proper attention to their cultures and resources. He warned that such actions, mistakenly undertaken to provide security to the colonizer, were in fact detrimental to security and the colonizers' "own peace of mind."[154]

In place of the republicanism proposed by French dissidents, Eboué envisaged a different kind of society, a new republic with its own form of humanism. In the spatial instance, his republic was not limited to metropolitan France, with territorial appendages elsewhere. The postwar republic was to reflect territorial diversity as well as philosophical openness to multiple political and cultural processes as well as diverse intellectual and moral sources. The republic was to countenance political change, meaningful citizenship, meritocracy, and security for all. It was also to be based on new values. Specifically, Eboué expressed faith in the existence of an African humanism, fully garnished with its own political lexicon and grammar of engagements (or ethics). In short, it emerged from his arguments with autochthonous colonial officers that Eboué envisaged a different ontology of humanity. This vision of humanity had distinct intellectual, political, cultural, and ideological dimensions, themselves the results of realizations of the erroneousness of French colonial policies and personal understandings of "Africa" and "Africans."

Eboué understood the African mood more than his peers in the colonial administration.[155] An Antillean by birth, he was encouraged as a young man by one of his seniors to attend school in order to help transform the Antilles.[156] He confessed to fellow Antilleans that he hoped to help remove all institutional and cultural barriers to humanism, including racism and parochialism.[157] He also meant to engage in struggles intended to dispense with the intellectual and ideological justifications of colonialism.[158] But it was colonialism that most offended Eboué and, according to him, it was only as a colonial officer that he could help restore humanism and republican ideals to the actions of France.

This choice of career initially baffled many contemporary Antilleans.[159] But Eboué was convinced and, in hindsight, right that French colonialism had caused republicans to lose their humanist ideals. As fate would have it, Eboué's application to the upper echelon of the colonial administration was twice rejected before he was admitted to the position of deputy governor in Mali, West Africa. French officials had initially rejected his application because many doubted the wisdom of appointing a black colonial administrator. Such an appointment, it was feared, would undermine the thesis that Africa needed white colonial rulers. It proved even more difficult to elevate Eboué to the position of chief of territory. He was appointed to the post of governor of Chad only after an autochthonous Frenchman had turned down the position. It was only after his successful defiance of Vichy upon the Chad events and his rally to the cause of the dissidence that he was elevated to the rank governor general of East Africa—his last post.

Eboué's trajectory can be encapsulated by his commitment to PanAfricanism[160] and what Gaston de Monnerville, called sincere humanism.[161] His inspirations were many, but Eboué understood that two successive world wars had drastically altered African perceptions of France, its post-Enlightenment ideologies, and therefore African visions of the future of France and empire. He was aware that African expectations of Franco–African relations had shifted drastically and that the war offered an opportunity to replace empire and colonialism with new institutions. His messages to his peers and, later, to subordinate colonial administrators reflected these sentiments. Thus, in his first message as governor general to the chiefs of territories, Eboué enjoined that pride and conscience "forbid me to contemplate the implantation of a foreign race in Africa that would substitute itself to the natives."[162] "We will not bring happiness in these lands," he admonished others, by imposing upon natives "the principles of the French revolution," "the Napoleon Code," or our "colonial functionaries." These are ours and for our sake alone.[163]

Africans are humans, he continued, and as such are "not isolated and interchangeable individuals." They have traditions, family, villages, and are capable of progress.[164] On this point Eboué called on fellow colonial officials to hear him correctly (*Qu'on m'entende bien*), "it is not that we must consider political custom here as rigid, immutable, and destined to furnish museums."[165] "Yes, they have their chiefs, notables, and bourgeois. But I advise you to look at the foundations of local traditions and note that they are unlikely to be traded in for wanton individualism."[166] Eboué not only advised fellow officials to pay attention to the foundations and meaning of native institutions, but he also admonished them to consider the disruptions caused by colonialism among natives.[167]

Eboué believed in what he and his contemporaries called sincere humanism (*humanisme sincère*), one that aspired to give humanism new foundations. Among PanAfricanists of the day, this meant removing all structures and barriers that emptied French humanism and republicanism of any meanings. It meant ridding the world of certain modern conceptions of power and subjectivity, particularly imperialism and colonialism and their base political economy. The latter was believed to be based on narrow rationalism and materialism, their mechanisms of distribution and consumption, and their modes of valuation and social consequences. Eboué thus sought to rid the emergent republic of values and structures of interests that created complicities between humanism, on the one hand, and slavery, imperialism, and colonialism, on the other.

Related observations and deductions gave form and substance to Eboué's deliberations on freedom, political autonomy, sovereignty, and self-determination. They also enabled him to ask questions and propose solutions that were unavailable to the French left. Specifically, he favored political pluralism and multicultural fluency over the reigning liberal orthodoxy and post-Enlightenment faith in political rationality, the unity of political morality, and their origins in Western texts. While versed in European rationalism, he understood that the "divergent thought patterns" of the "different religious and philosophic doctrines" of the French empire were a source of strength rather than discord. "Nobody amongst us," he insisted, "can be reproached for their philosophical or religious opinions for they find in such opinions the keys to the problems that confront the conscience of the French."[168] In this latter regard, Eboué was expressing an idea that had great currency in the colonial world: the barbarism of the war and the role of science and rationality in it, confirmed flaws in European values, institutions, and science. Accordingly, the latter were no longer to be viewed as the sole source of morality, ethics, and order. Consistently, in his *Programme*,[169] Eboué offered subtle accounts of the inclusive language prevalent in African culture. "If we were able to deliberate together and reach conclusions," he opined, "it is because we share common national and cultural dispositions that allow us, despite our rhetorical and representational differences, to make the same appeal."[170]

Eboué believed that even French chauvinists could be reasoned to envisage others' points of view and positions and to associate them with the greater struggle for equality and justice. Finally, the greater measure of humanism is the attainment of justice and dignity by the racially, culturally, economically, socially marginalized, and oppressed. He introduced the program with de Gaulle's own words that French citizens and subjects must recognize that the war was a true revolution with profound effects for the spirit of community, sacrifices, and the habits of men.[171] To Eboué, the crisis of consciousness was both real and serious and all who ignored it did so at their own peril. The greatest lesson of the war was that this crisis could generate a positive movement toward the republic.[172] Without explicitly saying it, Eboué also hinted that the crisis of consciousness could take different forms and lead to different directions than concord, solidarity, and the advent of a new form of humanism.

Related observations and deductions gave form and substance to Eboué's deliberations on freedom, political autonomy, sovereignty, and self-determination. They enabled the évolués everywhere to both ask questions and propose solutions to global dysfunctions that were unavailable to the French left. In fact, the ideas of a new humanism, republic, and multiplicity of sources offended many colonial administrators who associated French authority and power with one civilization, rationalism, and capitalism. French republicans supported imperialism because their humanism hinged on metaphors of ascension and progress viewed through a linear movement of tone-deaf multitudes imbued in Enlightenment-era rationalism and verities. That humanism was essentialist and grounded in a fundamentalism of sort. It is the kind of humanism that could be enlisted in imperialist and colonialist crusades. In the event, French republican practices developed a political lexicon, languages, and a grammar of engagements (or ethics) that reflected the above tendencies.

Conclusion: The Modular Image Inverted

I do not wish to dispute the idea that Western European states are to a considerable extent democratic and pluralist, capitalist, and prosperous. Nor do I wish to dispute that Europe, mythical or real, has developed institutions of democracy, market economies, human rights, for instance, that deserve emulation elsewhere.[173] However, I do dispute the modular precept of republicanism and the sufficiency of Western institutions and the presumption that they have been *consistently* applied at home and abroad. Modular republicanism supposes the West to incipient and ascendent society, with fully coherent civilizations, ideational, or ideological paradigms. This proposition would not be problematic were it not for the second part of the proposition: that recipient societies were either stationary or would be so if had they not accept the particular words (religions or ideologies), institutions (e.g., the rule of law), or practices (democracy) brought to them by the West. This view does not account for the conditions of replication of institutions and practices. In fact, other regions contributed greatly to modern institutional developments in ways yet to be explored.

The story of the évolués and of French politics during the war contrasts sharply with the commonsense that poses France and the West as initiators and teachers of the values and institutions necessary to social and political reproduction elsewhere. Eboué entered politics not by fiat, but as an expression of concern for the fate of the world. His own horizons include a range of political imaginaries and engagements as well as responses to them that better illustrate the promises and limits of republicanism in global politics. Indeed, French republicanism was suffused with colonial and historicist views of others, their cultures, traditions, and habits. Consistently, French politicians held the expectations that France (or the West) would set the stage for political deliberations and define the parameters of postwar institutions. They did lay down the foundations of the actualized republic, empire, and international system. Even this outcome, however, was the result of an exercise in power and not moral suasion. In contrast, Eboué and other anticolonialists revealed different philosophies and politics that dispensed with historicism, the actualized order, and their structures of subjectivity, morality, and agency. That this new imaginary was illustrated in the language of republicanism is not only a function of power on the part of the colonizer, but also of wisdom and generosity on the part of the colonized. The important point however is that republicanism has endured in international politics as vehicular languages to multiple communities often seeking complementary political goals. The reasons for this endurance are varied, but they are not self-evident. As Eboué clearly demonstrates, visions of republicanism came in different shapes and in line with complex and multiple circumstances.

If constructivists are to help shape the destiny of global politics, they must lay to rest the tropes of "initiation" and "moral teaching," on the one hand, and socialization and "moral learning," on the other. These tropes invariably elect the West as initiator, teacher, if not legislator, of ideas, norms, and institutions and the rest as "pupils" and "students." The latter show evidence of learning only through "conversion," "assimilation," and/or "imitation." If nothing else, these tropes or approximate ones only show that Western reflections pertaining to the moral order and to others depend strictly on self-perceptions, their texts, methods, and outward applications. Constructivists ought to include in their goals the attainment of a picture of the world and humankind that is alert to the values, morals, and interests of the constituent elements of the international order. This may be a tall order given the expanse of the international order. But I do not mean that theorists burden their collective memory with facts of the exploits of all societies and entities at all times. However, they can catalogue, and then call to attention when needed, instances when particular practices and institutions contributed to successful resolutions of conflict, exemplary devolution of solidarity, equitable adjudication of justice, and—to stay au courant—enviable attainment of happiness. To this end, no one needs to clutter memory with endless examples, but no fact is in itself a burden to memory. In the reverse, it would be disingenuous to consistently cast some societies outside of memory (and history) in order to memorize only the presumed exploits of select few. Such approaches are more egregious when they relate their chosen exploits without attention to the relationships between their initiators and others in time and space.

Such accounts would still be liable to errors, aporias, and silences. Further, in the event that they engage in the aforesaid enterprise, theorists will undoubtedly discover that institutions circulate across time and space through goodwill, reservations, and qualifications. They will also discover that transculturation, acculturation, and hybridity persist everywhere despite efforts by some to deny cultural equality and adaptability and by others to counterpose cultural autonomy and authenticity. There will also be difficulties in mapping out all the flows. Such difficulties may or may not be surmountable. But it is better to confront them than allow systematic exclusions of certain places, political entities, families, or genres of events from theory. Otherwise, theory, even promising ones like constructivism, becomes an accomplice to erasure of the wills, desires, and interests of others.

CHAPTER 4

GABRIEL D'ARBOUSSIER: DEMOCRACY IS NOT A MAGNIFICENTLY ADORNED HALL

Never has any country under a Republican constitution been so democratic as to permit the election of representatives of its overseas territories to its own legislative bodies.

— *Centre des Archives d'Outre-Mer*

I find the government's attitude toward this assembly extremely disconcerting. It approaches our views merely as formal opinions . . . The government would let us debate ad nauseam for days, even exceeding our allotted times and budgets, as long as we do not trample upon issues that it considers important . . . [We are witnessing the birth of] a certain autocratic federalism whereby we are admitted to these great magnificently adorned halls, with gold trims, without the power or the right to ask ourselves about our purpose, the source of authority, and the extent of our powers, all living sources of the raison d'être of these assemblies.

— *République Française, Annales de l'Assemblée de l'Union Française,*
June 10, 1948

Francis Fukuyama best captured the mood following the disintegration of the Soviet Union when he forecast the coming realization of Hegel's dream of *the end of history*: the final victory of liberalism and the impending advent of a global liberal order.[1] This mood was one of optimism[2] that the new moment would "ensure in one go political forms of justice and economic forms of production of wealth, as well as setting up interests and optimizing gains for all."[3] It was also believed that liberal democracies would "deliver" peace and good governance everywhere, including where they had not taken roots. This basic idea was given a boost by President George H. W. Bush who, upon waging a war to reverse the 1990 Iraq's invasion of Kuwait, proclaimed the advent of a new world order based on multilateral and peaceful resolutions of international conflicts; prohibition of territorial occupations; preventive interventions in destabilizing nationalist disputes. Caught up in the exuberance, Michael W. Doyle envisaged the emerging union of the great classical doctrines of democracy and liberal forms as legitimating devices of both internal and foreign policies.[4] The democratic peace theory was intended to not only supplant realist commonsense about the nature and telos of international relations, it was to dispense with the tenets of state Marxism and so-called third world structuralism—embodied *inter alia* by the theories of neocolonialism, dependency, and imperialism.

The objective of this chapter is to revisit a number of perspectives that celebrate the advent of liberal peace as well as extol the virtues of Western traditions and institutions of democracy as their point of departure. The relevant perspectives include so-called democratic peace theory and cosmopolitan theories of democracy. Although they do not necessarily share common genealogies and trajectories, these theories uphold as legitimate the goal of institutionalizing democracy. This chapter shares the goal of institutionalizing democracy. But it rejects crucial dimensions of democratic peace and cosmopolitan theories on the grounds that they do not sufficiently examine structures, mechanisms, and processes of the emergent global order that institutionalize the hegemony of particular states, along with corresponding political and ideological traditions. The latter result from historical views of sovereignty according to which powerful states maintain themselves as final arbiters of international morality and, then, construe morality to underwrite their particular political ethos. This drive to combine reason and morality in support of interest had been central to the colonial project. The face of this project reflects cultural and national differences—the British dual mandate;[5] the French Jules Ferry principle;[6] and the Monroe doctrines[7]—but its thrust remains the same everywhere: to rationalize great acts of repression against others which strip them of dignity and property while justifying such actions through the simple and well-meaning ideological tropes of civilizing mission, securing peace, and/or advancing the greater good and values of humanism, republicanism, and/or liberalism. In this sense, the perceived failures of past "international orders" to bring about lasting peace, justice, and reconciliation did not result merely from momentary deviations from loadable national goals, liberal or republican traditions, or universal humanism.

In what follows, I outline several objections to the democratic peace theory as well as to the adequacy and sufficiency of Western values and institutions. To this end, the present chapter orients research and discovery toward a comparative analysis of the ontological bases of politics: the imaginaries that guide actions and social relations; the patterns of behaviors that they elicit; and the norms embedded in them. This approach focuses on the temporal and spatial enactments and implementations of global institutions, international morality, and their processes. It is also cognizant of the multiplicity of languages and practices of democracy and their implications for international relations. Specifically, the question of democracy arises within the context of overlapping spatial and temporal structures and processes, including the state system and empire; the dismantlement of empire or decolonization; and finally the advent of the global liberal order spearheaded by the United States.

Returning to the 1939–1950 period, I revisit debates over postwar reconstruction in the context of political experimentation in the French empire. My goal is to examine comparatively different approaches to and interpretations of global democracy, particularly as it relates to the questions of peace, justice, equality, and security. In this context of multiple political ideas and agendas, I focus on the perspectives of emergent African political subjects and agents. This chapter focuses particularly on Gabriel d'Arboussier who, while agreeing that totalitarianism was the greatest threat to peace, understood that the two superpowers and their allies were equally hostile to the democratization and the pluralization of global politics. This hostility extended beyond skepticism and ill-will toward political experimentations and innovations. It was manifested as a clash of political objectives, coupled with an unwillingness on the part of imperial powers to consider modern anticolonial imaginaries of global democracy and the democratic peace.

Peace, Democracy, and Liveable Futures

Democratic peace theory, cosmopolitanism, and like ideologies frequently undermine the very principles of inclusion, interdependence, pluralism, and justice that they purport to promote. They have scant bearing on the rationalities, cultural prejudices, and institutional arrangements of the foreign policies of the extant liberal democratic states, particularly those aspiring to hegemony. These dimensions of foreign policy are the causes of the disrepute that has befallen the rules, norms, and principles of the international order elsewhere. First, these determinants of foreign policy and their orientations deserve examination by theories seeking to promote democracy globally. Second, the metaphors, imaginaries, and referents of the concerned theory leave out multiple and compelling ethical orientations. Their tendency is to conflate the capacity to think with the capacity to theorize and then to assume that only Europe has shown the capacity to think beyond its immediate environment, to generate universal norms, or to fully participate in the production of international reality.[8] "Europe" or the West thus appears as socializing agent and teacher of other regions and communities, who must accept socialization as "trustees," students, or otherwise. The result is that, although proponents of democracy appeal to the universal will of the governed, they seldom engage non-Western projects or envisage their initiators as allies with shared languages, interests, and values.

One explanation for the disinterest is belief in the indivisibility of modernity and the inevitable progression of social developments elsewhere toward Western models. This belief is sustained by certain historiographies and ethnographies according to which all contemporary political aspirations, forms, and orientations are grounded in Western-induced modernity. The continued insistence on the fixity of ideological and linguistic canons leads either to indifference to cultural and historical differences or ill-disposition toward non-Western thoughts, including ones that have comparative likenesses in the West. The diffidence is symptomatic of the kind of comparative studies prevalent in IR. The discipline discursively interpellates the international community and its constituent entities and, correspondingly, is heavily vested in anthropology and historiography. IR theorists frequently engage in contrasts and comparisons without explicitly embracing comparativism as a project. To the extent that the discipline embraces comparative analysis, it exports its political perspectives from its companion discipline of comparative politics where analyses are heuristic and/or positivist, but seldom hermeneutic. It is a kind of comparativism that is principally indebted either to Emile Durkheim's positive constructive approach[9] or Max Webber's heuristic social theory.[10] It is only secondarily indebted to Marxism and other social theoretical approaches to government, social actors, and their objects: politics.[11]

Although related views reflect contrasting ideologies and approaches to comparative analysis, adepts understand the process of translation in a manner that approximates Clifford Geertz's proposition that translation involves mental and linguistic conversions of the unfamiliar into the familiar through the proper (scientific or ideological) frames of reference.[12] Such views as Geertz's erroneously assume the existence everywhere of parallel ideological processes and practices, even if particular comparativists recognize historical and cultural differences of values and interests. They also defy historical and cultural differences of values and interests by erroneously assuming the existence everywhere of the same ideological processes and practices.

Marcel Detienne argues that "traditional" comparative studies severely limit the purpose of comparison: to transmit information that allows oneself to partake in "value judgements with good sense."[13] Accordingly, the aim of comparison is to develop reliable appreciation. The means are the "furtive analogies", "perceived resemblances," and acute differences that give confidence to the observer.[14] The interpretation or translation of the unfamiliar through methodological rapprochement with the familiar presents some danger. One is that it seldom questions the truths, rationales, and authority of the familiar. Also, adepts may be unable or unwilling to attach multiple valencies to familiar concepts and political languages in time and space.[15]

Detienne's arguments follow Walter Benjamin's admonition to translators that conceptual kinship does not necessarily amount to likeness.[16] According to Benjamin, translation is a mode that must conform to its own internal law, but these laws are both contingent and apodictic. In our discipline, however, translation does not proceed from the original work, that is, the new and unfamiliar. It proceeds from the familiar, often assuming the absence of originality to the unfamiliar. Such approaches, according to Benjamin, lead to "superficial thinking" that denies the independent meaning of the unfamiliar concept, language, or work of art.[17] To overcome such dangers of misreading, Detienne advocates a comparative approach that involves the reconstitution of the familiar, original setup and language in order to make them receptive to novel or unfamiliar mental and linguistic categories.[18] This approach takes it for granted that concepts and languages may have kinship in time while maintaining different valences in various regions and cultural contexts. These questions of comparativeness and translation are discussed in the second half of this chapter.

The polyvalency sought by Detienne is readily available to comparativists[19], but it has long been a necessary commodity of life among postcolonial subjects. By necessity or choice, these entities used European languages as official instruments of communication. They thus functioned positively within contrasting and opposing structures of meanings and significations of political languages, thoughts, idioms, and concepts, whose mastery was essential to survival. The proficiency attained by the colonized in comprehending these languages and their referents was the result of necessity, but also cultures of receptivity and cultivation. However, the desire for mastery also arose from the need by anti- and postcolonial entities to adequately convey their own thoughts through concepts and idioms whose meanings and structures of signification emanated from different historical circumstances and specific social and political ends.

The appreciation of the singularity of anticolonial and postcolonial thoughts can be particularly arduous because of their perceived affinities with metropolitan ones. Historians, anthropologists, and literary critics now readily admit the existence in European-language-speaking non-Western spheres of positive imaginaries and distinct cultures and values. The temporal and spatial diversity of planetary existence also accounts for the plurality and contrast of human resources. It is thus impossible to appreciate moral discourses, or the localized imaginings of the terms of global coexistence, without due consideration of the political contexts of particular linguistic artifices. These arise historically from linguistic and philosophical transmutations that account for the multiplicity of political languages and ethical idioms. The related transmutations produce identifiable intellectual artifices that are mere means to specific referents and moral ambitions.

IR has been slow to come to this understanding, that is to conceive of the existence outside of the West and Western canons of formal, but non-formalized or institutional thoughts with unitary sets of meanings that can transcend their spaces of origination. By imagining the world through mere generalizations of "Western" experiences, Occidentalists particularly entertain the fantasy that universal norms and institutions arise solely from Western philosophical systems and ontological categories. They also harbor the illusion that others outside the West lack the political will, moral faculty, and mental capacity to envisage political agency beyond the state or native communities.

The Imperial Peace: Neither Liberal Nor Democratic

The ideas behind the democratic peace theory are often attributed to Immanuel Kant, Friedrich Hegel, and, occasionally, Woodrow Wilson. They are said to understand the pacifying effect of a liberal regime on international relations. Based on their ideas, theorists predict the impending union of the foreign policy practices of liberal states with liberal ideals. Liberal democracies are thus not only inherently peace-enacting, they are culturally and structurally war adverse. Two key assumptions flow from these views. One is that liberal democracies are more respectful of difference and therefore more tolerant than other regimes. The other assumption is that, even when failing the tolerance test, democratic procedures place limits on the proclivity of decision makers to opt for war of aggression.[20] Consistently, liberal theorists hold that liberal states protect individual liberties at home and human rights for the weak, the dislocated, and victims of human-induced and natural disasters.[21] This belief in the normativity of the foreign rationales of liberal states has led to wholehearted endorsements of so-called *humanitarian interventions*, without due regard to the role of the intervening powers, the adequacy of the means of intervention, and their outcomes.[22]

By Doyle's and others' accounts, democratic liberal states may commit "impudent vehemence" or "careless and supine complaisance,"[23] but they are often justified in their actions against illiberal states and other entities. For them, it is only matter of pragmatism that the democratic peace theory insists on the peaceful and progressive nature of liberal democracy and the crucial role that Western democracies have played in promoting peace and global prosperity. By the same token, the theory envisages to promote democracy elsewhere as means to international stability. Finally, it identifies values and institutions around the world that are antithetical (or inimical) to democracy for the purpose of corrective or remedial foreign policy interventions.

The democratic peace theory takes on ontological and epistemological status in analytical methods, discursive categories, and their conclusions. Its adepts favorably contrast liberal democracy with other political forms by assuming rationalism and civil and political society for the one but not for the others. Rival political forms are assumed to lack these and to function on the basis of immutable cultural and/or religious traditions. Such contrasts further affirm the superiority of Western values and institutions as well as to posit their desirability in other contexts.[24] They show that the danger to the international order rests in the nature of opposite political systems whose orientations, values, institutions, and wisdom are inadequacy to peaceful coexistence.

The related arguments can be summarized as follows: (1) democratic states behave differently toward each other than they do toward non-democracies;[25] (2) liberalism causes democratic decision makers to place emphasis on the protection of the life and property of the citizenries, and therefore to be wary of warmongering;[26] (3) finally, liberalism will eventually triumph over rival ideologies because of its rationality and ethos of tolerance and recognition of difference.[27] The first argument is at once affective and cultural. It is based on the assumption that political societies that share liberal traditions and histories are adverse to fighting wars with one another. This adversity is grounded in their shared traditions and perceived interest in promoting the values and institutions of political negotiation, legal adjudication, and moral pragmatism leading to compromise toward those who are likewise inclined. The second argument is structural. Where leaders of the executive and legislative branches of government are elected, the argument goes, key decision makers are subject to mechanisms of accountability that compel them to heed popular sentiments. The inclination and liberal preferences of such policy makers are imbued in liberal constitutional compacts and traditions: respect for individual freedom, rule of law and property rights; collective and transparent government through elected representation; and checks and balances and independent judiciary.[28] The most important of these institutions is the right of citizens to free expression signified by free speech, free media, and free associations.[29] According to John M. Owen and others, related expectation of transparency and accountability compels the liberal state to reconcile or harmonize the national interest with individual freedom and liberties.[30]

The third argument of the democratic peace theory is ontological. It is based on the identity of democratic states, moral superiority, and inherent goodness. According to this argument, liberal states inherently exert positive influences in international relations. In these regards, rationalists establish a direct correlation between the respect and recognition that liberals presumably extend to others with moral superiority.[31] Some theorists may recognize the limits of liberal recognition and toleration,[32] particularly as it relates to affect and prejudice,[33] but the majority asserts the positivity of mutual recognition. They link the cultural and structural arguments and the processes of identity construction to political relations globally: the concerns of international relations theory at the systemic level. Hence, Michael C. Williams, maintains that liberal processes "play essential constitutive and disciplining roles in the development between liberals and in the evolution of liberal security communities."[34] This argument goes beyond diffusionism by force to posit the co-constitution of the liberal "peace zone" as model for the co-constitution of an incipient global peace zone.

These arguments have serious flaws. It is not clear whether the global liberal regime is effected because of attractiveness of liberalism as political practice and culture or through coercion of illiberal or nonliberal entities by liberal polities through political, economic, cultural, and military measures.[35] Second, democratic control over foreign policy is seldom complete and the *demos* can be as aggressive and war-prone as the subjects of totalitarian and authoritarian orders.[36] As Edward D. Mansfield and Jack Snyder have shown, so-called incipient democracies can be particularly adventuresome and, worse, they can be so moved by small segments of their populations.[37] Thus in Bosnia, Serbia, and Rwanda for instance, policy makers were pushed by bellicose segments of their citizenries to wage wars on ethnic rivals. American reactions to 9/11/2001 suggest that even democratic decision makers may abide bellicose popular sentiments and easily abdicate moral authority and political wisdom in favor of the expediency of constitutional *war powers* on behalf of a *demos* determined to exact revenge.

The democratic peace theory docs not comparatively explore the orientations of liberal states toward the international order. It also overtly resists opposing accounts of the orientations and ethos, motives and interests, and modes of recognition and identity. Williams notes, for instance, that "democracies to a large degree create their enemies and their friends—by inferring aggressive and defensive motives" from their actions.[38] The destabilization by Western states of postcolonial democratic states (say in Congo under Patrice Lumumba; Guatemala under Jacobo Arbenz; and Chile under Salvador Allende) suggests the identification process of "enemies" is less than rational and transparent. From the eras of colonialism to the present, today's liberal democracies implemented varying regimes of recognition to coincide with self-generated views of the subjects (and thus identity) of the moral order. In the nineteenth century, for instance, James Lorimer, president of the Royal British Society of Geography, firmly stipulated as legal institutions the four kinds of recognition due to the various regions and identities of the world.[39] These ranged from full recognition to European and Christian nations to simple human recognition to Africans and the heathens of the New World.[40] To these multiple forms of recognition corresponded regimes of morality: one applicable to Christian powers in their relationships in Europe or within Western Christendom; another regime of norms, moral principles, institutions bearing on the relationships of Christians operating outside of Europe; and a third regime applicable to Christians' relations with non-Christians. These differentiated regimes formed the basis of classical international law.

Liberal democracies have not just been as belligerent as other states. According to Robert Latham, "they have also been responsible for—and are uniquely successful at generating—high levels of global [instability]."[41] These states have purposefully spearheaded militarism and promoted conflicts among weak states, including democratic and nondemocratic ones. As per Latham, related moves "help undermine the successful spread of liberal democracy in the long term."[42] In short, the democratic peace theory is predicated upon the universalization of the extant liberal democratic regime; but the virtues of the system are abstracted from conveniently arranged facts to eliminate all possible objections. Consistently, Williams[43] and Tarak Barkawi and Mark Laffey[44] have suggested the historicization of the concepts of democracy, liberalism, and war so as to reflect their incorporation in global strategies of either "security community" or "imperial order."

The democratic peace theory does not confront the rationales and organizing principles of the foreign policies of hegemonic powers. Indeed, liberal constitutions do not sufficiently inhibit the executive branch in the areas of security and war. Nor, as we find out post–9/11, liberal constitutional guarantees may be abundant domestically but, in time of conflict, they apply only partially to noncitizen residents and seldom to nonresident aliens. Nor does the theory substantively examine the reactions and imaginaries of social relations of those who would oppose hegemonic liberal states. As Uday S. Mehta opines, the constitutional inadequacies of the liberal democratic state, are compounded by cultural and intellectual traditions that orient institutions in directions far removed from the historical drive of former colonial populations to self-determination.[45]

The democratic peace theory actually supports a status quo that is inimical to the institutionalization of democracy globally. It takes existing political structures, forms, and processes of international governance as evidence of political possibility, joining in this regard political realists in their assumptions on the nature of the international order. If it is to envisage new kinds or forms of politics, adepts must take into account the role, responsibility, and policy rationalities of incumbent liberal states in international conflicts and instability. They must also be open to the imaginaries—or mental pictures of social relations—of others, including those that oppose liberal states.

Cosmopolitanism, the Moral Order, and Democracy

Cosmopolitans offer productive avenues for envisaging new forms of politics. Cosmopolitanism originates from the Stoics and "calls for a primary allegiance to the worldwide community of human beings."[46] Taking humanity itself as the primary source of value, cosmopolitans insist on the unity of the human species and aspire to foster a global community. Again, many relate cosmopolitan views to Immanuel Kant and other post-Enlightenment theorists who command "categorical moral principles," moral solicitude, cultivation, and forbearance of other individuals, persons, and communities as basis of politics.[47] The relevant moral discourses are based on inclusive notions of humanity, society, morals, and the relationships among them that collectively challenge and transcend modern political rationalities. Specifically, cosmopolitans reject moral indifference, relativism, and associated notions of incongruities of desire and the inevitability of conflict.

The cosmopolitan project is ambitious and complex. It promotes global coexistence despite or because of the diverse cultures, religions, races, and "civilizations" and their divergent political, ideological, and economic interests. The grounds of cosmopolitan theorizing vary considerably. But cosmopolitans contemplate conditions for working together around practical interests in common enterprises. The cosmopolitan position privileges the institution of a global moral order over the imperatives of loyalty to lesser entities (nations, for instance) and their institutional expressions (including the state). It presupposes the capacity of individuals to assume detachment from political or ideological partisanship and, consistently, to transcend parochial interests for the collective good. It also seeks to foster civil society (domestically) and an international society (globally) on the basis of shared international institutions, norms, and values.[48] Finally, cosmopolitans variably believe in the desirability of moral teaching and learning, based on mutual respect, fair exchange, and the communication of ideal values by their holders to others.[49]

Cosmopolitanism advocates autonomy from the state without necessarily disavowing political allegiance or rejecting political power. Its ambition is to enfranchise individuals from national political power and rationality for purposes of moral autonomy and judgment. This means that no political actor escapes moral assessment.[50] Censure for political violence should not obey political affinity or rationality; nor should it matter that violence originates from the state or that it is vulgarized in the hands of paramilitaries, guerrillas, mobs, or persons. In outlining universal principles and the essential attributes of international society, cosmopolitans thus hope to situate distant and extra-national communities in the same affective spheres as intimate and national entities for the purposes of moral actions. This does not necessarily mean the full rejection of "sovereignty-as-enclosed-territories." It says however that state-dependent political agency is no longer a sufficient basis for international actions.

Martha Nussbaum has recently articulated a cosmopolitan view that is guided by empathy and principles of solidarity and moral solicitude, all founded upon longstanding philosophical and moral traditions.[51] Nussbaum traces the roots of her ideas as far back as ancient Greece (particularly with Aristotle), although her immediate inspiration comes from Kant's moral principles and imperatives bearing on human subjects, the ends of political action, and the forms of community. These are themselves founded upon specific conceptions of human nature, the nature of rights, and the function of morality. These sources do not cause Nussbaum to dismiss the relevancy of primary (if not primordial) relationships to parents, ancestors, family, race, religion, heritage, history, culture, tradition, community, and nation. Yet, she believes in a common humanity and the possibility of a commitment to it through an unending quest for social justice.[52]

Sissela Bok agrees that cosmopolitanism does not compel one "to ignore the intimate bonds to relatives, family members, friend, neighbor, and fellow citizen."[53] It commands that one recognizes that human needs differ according to contexts, immediacy, and urgency so that one is guided by commonsense to "prefer" the greater good at all times, even "another's greater good" when it competes with one's own "lesser good."[54] The determination of the good is intimately linked to the capacity to imagine other people. Elaine Scarry notes that any difficulties of identification are easily overcome through social contract and constitutional guarantees.[55] Scarry argues that social contracts like constitutions provide rules and norms for moral solicitation, negotiation, and adjudication under conditions of instability, contingency, and conflict. They provide the moral foundations and ethical bases for political principles and actions.[56] They also form the vehicular language for social interactions and meanings creation among otherwise mutually unintelligible entities.

David Held has given extensive thought to the constitution and constitutionalization of cosmopolitan democracy.[57] Held's concern for cosmopolitan democracy arises from the context of the "different power systems which constitute the interconnections of different peoples and nations" and the "multiple and overlapping networks of power" that mediate their welfare, culture, and civic associations. The resulting clusters of power are "subsumed under the categories . . . of health, social, cultural, civic, economic, pacific, and political."[58] Held's aim is to rethink "the nature, form and content of democratic politics" around these issues[59] through global solutions. He ostensibly privileges international morality and norms over local, national, and regional or cultural loyalty.[60] Indeed, he presupposes that socialization allows individuals to detach themselves from their own particular circumstances and to transcend political or ideological partisanship and parochial interests in favor of the greater common good.

This enterprise is sketched out in *Theory of Democratic Politics* where Held proposes ways to eliminate global "pathologies" that threaten universal rights: the condition for democracy. The source of pathologies involves "the system of nation-states, international legal regulations, and the world political economy,"[61] all of which undermine social justice and human dignity. His solution entails a constitutional order that ensures a generalized consensus among the governed, when necessary.[62] Due to his commitment to the "principle of autonomy," he embraces a political ethos that takes "account of the place of the polity within the geopolitical and market processes" as essential to creating "empowering rights and obligations." These would cut across multiple "sites of power . . . rooted in politics, economics or culture."[63]

Held finds his resources in the ideas of the likes of Kant, Locke, Marx, Mill, and Rousseau. This focus allows him to demonstrate that Western juridical constructs have been pertinent to the creation and implementation of a generalized culture of citizenship everywhere. He is able to explore concrete transnational and/or cosmopolitan traditions and the political instruments of political actions beyond the state. He also applies a uniform regime of law to complex and nonuniform political, economic, and cultural conditions. His desire to circumvent the state system and its structures and modes of subjectivity leads by to a case against nationality, citizenship, and nationalism, or loyalty to the sovereign. In their place, he would institute a cosmopolitanism based upon universal norms. His cosmopolitan subjects would function within a "public space" regulated by a unified "public law" based on "a division of powers and competences" according to "different levels of political interactions and interconnectedness."[64]

Held is justified that the form and telos of politics have not been fixed historically and that they may be altered once again to correspond to the demands of a new era. He is equally right that historically states have not held an absolute monopoly over power and that it is advisable to redeploy the matrices of politics and power away from states and state control. In fact, there already exist forms of power and therefore politics that necessarily reside outside state boundaries. Specifically, transnational agents of capital investment, production, distribution, and exploitation of resources not only possess inordinate power within states, their spheres of activity exceed individual state boundaries, legislation, and norms. It is thus tempting to agree with Held that the activities of transnational agents and their forms provide inspiration for the forms of changes to come, particularly in regard to the manners in which they escape state hierarchies of values and state control of resources.

In proposing these solutions, Held is particularly conscious of the difficulties posed by colonial encounters and past uses of moral and universal discourses to parochial ends. Related experiences still militate against the credibility of Western institutions of global governance. It comes as a surprise, therefore, that he remains so wedded to liberalism and liberal traditions and that he does not investigate how other traditions and perspectives might inform contemporary approaches to global democracy. By insisting on the transhistorical validity of Western institutions, Held brackets off from debates the many deficiencies of liberal constitutional models and thus fails to anticipate the limits of Western political and cultural paradigms.

There are two sets of criticisms that may be leveled against Held that go to the heart of cosmopolitan views of the moral order. The first is that he willfully ignores these difficulties: for instance, that constitutional entitlements and idioms of liberty and property occupied a central place in imperialism. As a result of his silence in these regards, Held's vision ultimately affirms the desires, interests, and identities of hegemonic power and their base-constituencies—capitalists, financiers, nongovernmental organizations, and even philanthropic groups. Indeed, his proposals are partial to Western power and parochial interests. His proposed reform reproduces the structures and institutions that either excludes non-Western cosmopolitan advocates from the essential political processes of the moral order or places special constraints on their participation in such processes.

Second, Held fails to broaden or countenance other constitutional traditions, modes of inquiry, and ethical possibilities. His exclusive reliance on Western canons and political trajectories and experiments leaves the impression that international life so far provides no evidence elsewhere of political experimentation that may support a positive global ethos. The belief in the singular capacity of the West to imagine and develop ethics implicitly negates the experiences, thoughts, and beliefs of others as points of reference for political imagination. Africa, Asia, the Middle East, and the rest emerge as repositories of centuries-old customs, mysticism, and heathenism, all liable to affect and social pathology. As appears in the writings of Nussbaum, the latter's traditions and modes of thought are localized and particularized so that Europe or the West may emerge as the realm of reason, science, rationality, theology, moral thought, and humanism.[65]

Related epistemological grids create an ontology with practical consequences for the possibility of moral exchange, mutual learning, and communication.[66] By imagining the world as a mere extension of their own experiences, cosmopolitans entertain the illusion that universalism arises necessarily from Western philosophical systems and ontological categories[67] on account of their superiority.[68] The West thus appears as surrogate for international community and global consensus and assumes the requisite moral properties of humanity.[69] Such commonplaces blunt cosmopolitan attempts at envisaging new ethics and/or political forms. As happens, they frequently condone unidirectional injunctions (in lieu of teaching and learning) and paternalism (instead of mutual solicitation and fairness). They hold appealing moral sentiments, but their loyalties "can and sometimes [do] contradict the manifest demands of justice as seen from [other] perspectives."[70] As such, arguments favoring the promotion of democracy and humanitarian interventions often favor the activation of state-dependent political agency, including the will and military of Western powers to intervene in the far corners of the world.[71] They also require that others relinquish spatial and political dimensions of sovereignty for the purpose of humanitarian actions by others.[72]

Postwar Programs and Democratic Reforms

The theories of democratic peace and cosmopolitanism do not live up to their ambition, and not simply because of moral ambiguities, ethical dilemmas, and philosophical contradictions. Their arguments do not account for the multiplicity of political languages and ethical idioms from which differently situated individuals and communities derive their notions of common humanity and social justice. This absence of temporal and spatial diversity of circumstances in cosmopolitan accounts of social justice, for instance, may in fact reveal insensitivity to the unevenness of access to resources necessary for the ennoblement of human existence in given circumstances. It also has implications for understanding violence and its manifestation across time and space. We are reminded here by Bruce Robbins that loyalty and attachment to one's own position or imaginary of social order "can and sometimes does contradict the manifest demands of justice as seen from any extra-national perspective."[73]

The politicization of the questions of democracy, accountability, and justice has resulted in suspicions, accusations, counteraccusations, and hyperboles at global fora. This situation troubled many,[74] not least because after the 1960s the so-called third world begun to oppose the "power of numbers" to the "power of veto" detained by hegemonic powers at the United Nations and other global organizations. Remarking on the situation at the end of the 1980s, Chris Brown noted that mutual incomprehension had become the norms in international fora instead of "real moral conversation."[75] While some castigated the so-called third world for its intransigence in international debates and negotiations,[76] Brown insisted on the need for IR "to produce a coherent understanding of the moral underpinnings of North–South relations."[77]

The rise of the third world began in 1955 in Bandung when postcolonial leaders led by China's Zhu En Lai, Indonesia's Sukarno, India's Nehru, Ghana's N'Krumah, and Egypt's Nasser assembled to envisage an alternative model of development suitable to the needs of the formerly colonized. The 1954 UN Conference on Trade and Development provided the immediate tonus for Bandung. The emergent postcolonial movement soon centered on changing the rules of international relations after the 1956 Suez Canal crisis with the creation in 1961 in Belgrade, Yugoslavia, of the Non-Alignment Movement (or NAM). Although steered by the like of Marshall Tito, Fidel Castro, and Nehru, NAM included prominent nonsocialist members. All resisted alignment along cold war lines separating the U.S.-inspired Trans-Atlantic Alliance from the Soviet bloc countries of the Warsaw Pact. They believed that the related political contests and militarism diverted resources away from the crucial needs of the world.

By design and circumstance, NAM became an advocate of General Assembly (GA) assertiveness on matters of peace, justice, and demilitarization. Its insistence on strict procedural democracy heightened the value of numbers, which was on its side, over compromise, by which the permanent members of the Security Council (SC) sought the surrender of the international community to their own wills and desires. In the 1970s, NAM sought to institute a New International Economic Order. Its members also supported a wave of nationalization of extractive industries of raw materials. These actions and others established the property right of the formerly colonized to their natural resources, thereby reversing centuries-old traditions and Western practices.

Leaving outcomes aside, these policies corresponded to a dialectic of power in which the West sought to perpetuate colonial policies through neocolonial means. Specifically, the United States and its Western allies had come to depend on the veto power to subvert global democracy. (The Soviets did too.) They also sought to marginalize the GA and other UN organs. For instance, they progressively transferred the attributions of the UN Economic and Social Council to Bretton Woods institutions (the World Bank and the International Monetary Funds), the Organization of Economic Cooperation and Development (OECD), the Group of Seven, and their incorporated instruments. The United States and its allies also joined their cold war antagonists of the Soviet bloc in dismissing calls for demilitarization. So too did the General Agreement on Trade and Tariffs give way to the World Trade Organization. Western states also preferred partial enforcement of the Nuclear Non-Proliferation Treaty, focusing on horizontal proliferation, instead of pursuing demilitarization debates at the GA.

Western powers also deserted or withdrew financial support from international organizations that afforded greater participation to third world countries. For instance, in the 1980s, the administrations of Margaret Thatcher (Britain) and Ronald Regan (United States) were offended that the UN Education, Scientific, and Cultural Organization, or UNESCO, then under the directorship of the Senegalese Ahmadou Mathar Mbow, took decisions on controversial issues without due deference to and reverence for Western concerns. These issues included the determination of world cultural heritage, the production and distribution of global intellectual resources, and the redefinition of the common good in the context of scientific and cultural activities. The United States and Britain have preempted international mediation in international conflicts, from Namibia to Palestine, in order to advance parochial interests. Lately too, the Bush-*fils* administration has sought to subvert international legality by opting out of the International Criminal Court and by bribing individual members of the community of states into consenting to special dispensations for U.S. citizens. Still, the Western tendency to issue moral injunction in lieu of solicitation has raised more concern among former colonial entities to others.

The formula by which Chris Brown defined the situation was the "Requirement,"[78] referring to the imperial injunction that "was read aloud to the Indians in the Americas before hostilities were begun against them."[79] It did not matter then what the Indians made of it because the lecture was intended only to provide "moral justification" and "legal" basis for the use of force if Indians did not allow the new-comers to promote the Christian faith under "the overlordship of the crown of Castile."[80] Of papal inspiration, the Requirement was a per-verse way of initiating normative discourse. The *conquistadores* "clearly felt the need to say something . . . to express their thoughts . . . [and to establish] the rightness of their actions at least to their own satisfac-tion."[81] A likeness of the Requirement became the metanorm for select Western states in their communications with others within postwar international institutions. Not only were the former colonial powers scornful of the arguments and imaginaries of the formerly colonized, they resented the notion of egalitarian reciprocity. Today, Requirement-like injunctions have had pernicious and intractable effects, including permissiveness, naked militarism, and imperial autocracy.

By the 1990s, these attitudes led to Western denunciations of global democracy. These denunciations added to third world discon-tent with the procedures and rules of international organizations. The end of the cold war seemed to offer a window of opportunity to recast global communications on new terms. The reform agenda first emanated from the halls of the United Nations. As UN secretary gen-eral, the Egyptian Boutros Boutros-Ghali proposed *An Agenda for Peace* (1992) and *An Agenda for Democratization* (1996) that largely reflected the reform agenda pursued by postcolonial states and middle powers in Latin America, Asia, and Northern Europe.[82] Boutros-Ghali's successor, the Ghanian Kofi Annan added his own *Agenda for Development* (1997) and a later one for *Renewing the United Nations: A Programme for Reform*. These agendas set to strengthen the office of the UN secretariat; increase the role of the GA; redefine the responsibilities of member states; broaden the SC and redistribute its permanent membership to reflect regional and political realities around the world; strengthen regional organizations; and grant greater role to non-state actors particularly nongovernmental organizations to reflect the views of parliamentarians, academics, local authorities, businesses and the media worldwide. They were also to "improve UN ability to deploy peacekeeping and other field operations" as well as "capacity for post-conflict peace-building missions."[83]

These agendas were selected supported by states, but dismissed outright by others. As happened in 2003 during the second U.S. war on Iraq, the U.S. administration underscored the official American attitude toward multilateralism and UN dispute settlement mechanisms when it determined that it may consult others but would accept no opposite opinion; that it may give advice but receive none; that it may get corroborating SC resolutions for its actions but would suffer no obstructing debates. Unlike yesterday when the Western alliance, with a few exceptions, scorned third world call for legality and legitimacy, the United States today faces middle powers as diverse as France and Germany in Europe; Mexico and Brazil in Latin America; India and China in Asia; and South Africa in Africa who now stand where NAM once stood. On issues ranging from the Kyoto accords to the Treaty of Rome on the International Criminal Court to the settlements of conflicts, the United States is more likely to be rebuked by its traditional European allies[84] as well as third world states.

Pluralism, Democracy and Empire

Africanists and IR theorists have generally entertained the view that Francophone African political visions and conceptions of politics, particularly democracy, approximate French ones. They found this belief in the presumed widespread use of French idioms by their former colonial subjects. The difficulties with this analysis is that it does not leave room for the possibility of distinct anticolonial imaginaries, referents, and teleologies. Against this background, two studies have recently made the point that it might be mistaken to view African uses of French or modern political idioms as signs of acculturation and conversion to related Western referents or political forms.

One by Frederick Cooper, stresses the strategic uses of the universalist languages of justice (particularly in regard to wages and social benefits) and emancipation (encompassing the sharing of power) by postwar African nationalists.[85] Although he did not intend a treatise on decolonization, Cooper elaborated two central issues connected to African demands for equal rights. The first is that the initial imperial belief of controlled modernization was mistaken, particularly the notion that colonial powers could manage social change by setting Africans on the course of not merely modernization but one that could sustain "imperial demands for higher colonial production (and lower colonial consumption)."[86] Relatedly, labor questions quickly devolved into questions of racial equality and political autonomy.[87] African radicalization then led to the collapse of European confidence that African society could become the likeness of the industrial democratic West.[88] In framing the labor question, Cooper argues that the meanings that Western notions "took on in Africa were not attributes of the 'west' but products of struggle."[89] The nature of that struggle is dubious however when Cooper characterizes it as one opposing Western attempt to instill and manage developmentalism in the face of African autonomy-seeking strategies. It is not clear that the two sides aimed to implement contrasting orders, based on both commensurable and incommensurable imaginaries of politics and society.

Frederic C. Schaffer too shows that the idiom of democracy varies considerably across cultures by looking at its instantiation in Africa (Senegal).[90] In *Democracy in Translation*, Schaffer argues that the universal spread of democracy has seen the Greek *demokratia* transmutate into something called *demokaraasi* in Senegal with profound implications for the manners in which social scientists understand political regimes; their causes and effects; and processes of democratic consolidation.[91] For Schaffer, the distance between ancient Greece and contemporary Senegal is reason enough to not rely on specific procedures of election and/or mechanisms of decision making as baseline for assessing democracy everywhere.[92] He favors a "conceptual analysis" derived from a "language-centered" approach that takes into account the structure of concepts associated with democracy; their use in ordinary contexts; their place in semantic fields of related concepts; the evolution of their meanings over time; and, finally, issues that arise in translating.[93]

Schaffer's goal is to establish "rough equivalencies" between democracy and associated concepts in order to gain access to equivalent standards of democratic responsibility acceptable to all who use the same language.[94] On these scores, Senegal must be understood as functioning, and not merely functional, democracy. Senegalese democracy is healthy despite the lack of formal education of the electorate, peculiar voting behavior of the electorate, the dependence of political parties on formal and informal networks controlled by religious brotherhood and associations, and the convenient mix of "pre-democratic" traditions and modern politics.

Both Cooper and Schaffer highlight the difficulties of comparative studies and translation. Their focus on thoughts, concepts, and their boundaries represents a departure from the sort of diffusionism that takes Europe necessarily as the socializing agent and the Rest as the socialized or socializing. Still, a residual or soft diffusionism persists in their representations. Cooper falls into it because he fails to properly historicize post-1950 labor disputes in French colonial Africa to reflect their temporality and spatiality. We are left with the impression of inevitable outcome when, after the 1950s, the labor question succumbed to a regional struggle of statehood. This was reflected by the emergent African for political autonomy as means to equality and justice.

While anticolonialism had been about self-governance all along, the staging, meanings, and means to entitlements varied according to temporal and regional understandings of the nature of the envisaged polity and government and their teleologies. When, prior to 1950, France entertained the possibility of citizenship and justice beyond territoriality, state, and nation, African elites and labor operated within different conceptions of modernity and attendant forms of universalism and universality.[95] Then, a substantial number of elected African officials did not (and could not) conceive or accept the notion that the global economy could be parceled out as national economies and that justice could be implemented according to local, cultural, and regional standards. Forced labor and the free access of Europe to raw materials in the colonies were only two indicators that imperial economies straddled territorial boundaries. So did the war efforts.

It was not until after the Marshall Plan envisaged to reconstruct a regional economy in Europe that humanist concepts of the human condition, human solidarity, and social justice gave way to modernist notions of human nature, interdependence, and interest. The new concepts not only displaced the operative idioms and standards of politics in Greater France, but they also institutionalized new forms of politics suited to the emergent international structures of power, economy, and culture.[96] After the Marshall Plan and European reconstruction, Africans were compelled to adjust or retrofit their own visions of economy, justice, and community to fit the emergent liberal order. It remains that related notions of political autonomy, state, sovereignty, and national economies merely reintroduced political tropes that had previously been the means by which "Europe" could dispossess land and property as well as usurp values and their symbols without much worry about historical justice and/or the rights of the dispossessed. In short, time signified by the evolving the dynamics of Franco–African relationships, determined politics in space and not the other way round.

Schaffer's call for translation of concepts in light of "cultural traditions, social organizations, and political practices" is also attractive but deceptive.[97] But the approach is not dialectically comparative in that the "standards that American English speakers use for judging the presence or absence of democracy" still is the prism through which Schaffer judges political forms elsewhere as democratic or not. We have "roughly equivalent words," but the standards are not determined comparatively, they are predetermined.[98] Politically, this is a way of granting agency to Africans while denying them subjectivity in manner akin to past colonial moves that granted African cultural specificity as justification for lesser forms of sovereignty, legal rights, and political immunities and capacities.

While significant, linguistic methods do not always adequately elucidate the cultural and historical differences in comparatively analogous Western and African concepts, thoughts, and discourses. The movement from political thought (ideas, concepts, and their applications) to political discourse (the formulations of thoughts and intentions through the available idioms and language games) is mediated by external factors. In the colonial context, the adoption of certain forms of democracy was a necessary sign of civic or political preparedness to self-rule, but not a matter of choice. Colonial practice too has had very little to do with the inherent relevancy of particular forms to the everyday of populations. Postcolonial practice improved upon colonial ones with varying degrees of experimentation and internalization among others, but also within the constraints of the global order. Africans did not voluntarily settle on liberal democracy as the only possible form of the concept. This event is the culmination of global processes that impose liberal democracy as the only allowable form as well as the only permissible idiom of political competence and thus readiness for self-governance. In determining whether Senegal or any other African country is a functioning (and not merely a functional) democracy, one must entertain the possibility that the discourse of democracy anywhere remains at some distance from the collective aspirations and imaginaries of society and values (or thoughts). While agency originates in the rituals of democracy (voting for instance), subjectivity emanates from the movement that continually seeks to reconcile democratic forms with the values and interests of the collective.

Demokaraasi must not be understood merely as the Wolof approximation of the Greek word for self-government.[99] Any translation must also investigate the connections between practice and the will and historical aspirations, ambitions, and orientations of vast majority for whom self-government extends beyond procedural democracy. The gap between the form and boundaries of the enacted democracy, on the one hand, and the will to self-government, on the other, may in fact serve to explain why government itself appears unstable in Africa generally forty years after decolonization.[100] African communities, it would seem, are still looking unsuccessfully to reconcile their historical aspirations with, on the one hand, the liberal political forms by which they are judged by the West and, on the other, the structures of values, subjects, and rationality underlying global processes of justice, normativity, and utility.

Union Française: Une Grande Famille

In late 1940, the emergent French resistance coined the term Greater France to respond to the imminent entanglement of colonizers and colonized, following defeat, but also to preempt a feared Anglo-Saxon plot to dismantle the French empire.[101] This fear was prompted by widespread proclamations by the United States and British official circles of the end of France as a great power.[102] In the words of one official, "defeat, submission to the reality of defeat, and the consequences of these two events" dictated a French policy of "generosity, trust, and an open mind" toward the colonized, one "decidedly liberal and egalitarian policy" as the sole means to restore French authority over its colonial populations and the world beyond.[103] Still the idea of idea of Greater France had potent political symbolism. It was viewed as the fruit of a "spiritual revolution,"[104] a recognition of the actions of the colonized, and a resignation to their inevitable demands for moral recognition, social equality, individual and cultural freedom, and political representation. Accordingly, France had to reform the empire under a new sense of community reflecting the sacrifice of all.

The revolution was to take form after the war through constitutional deliberations and forms. It effectively started in January 1944 in Brazzaville, the capital of French Equatorial Africa, with a French-initiated "African Conference." The revolution, however, was stillborn. Although convened in Brazzaville to honor Félix Eboué, the "African Conference" betrayed Eboué's humanist ideas and his desire for universal "brotherhood" and citizenship. The empire was to remain "accessory and dependent upon" the Métropole,[105] with no direct African participation in the determination of their own status.[106] Charles de Gaulle was keen to reassure the world of French commitment to colonial reform and goodwill toward Africans, but he was unwilling to meet African demands for, alternatively, total assimilation with equal rights, a federalism of equals, or a cooperation of interest based on enforceable rules.[107]

De Gaulle (and the conference) proposed a constitutional framework for a French Union (as distinct from a Franco-African Union) to be submitted to French nationals in a future referendum. There followed debates, lasting from 1944 to 1946, that led a metropolitan consensus that France, the colonies, and the French Union be endowed with distinct legislative and executive bodies. Under the final constitution endorsed by the socialists and the Mouvement Républicain Populaire (MRP), the French National Assembly would legislate for the Union upon formal advise from the Senate, or Council of the Republic. While the colonies were represented in both bodies, their numbers were greatly limited to preserve their metropolitan character.

The French Union was fitted with one overarching bureaucracy headed by the French president, who cumulated the function of president of the French Union. He appointed the chief of the territorial units dependent upon France. He was assisted in this regard by consultative bodies including formerly colonial subjects: the High Council of the French Union (executive body) and the Assembly of the French Union (legislative). Representations on these two bodies were equally divided between métropolitan France, on the one hand, and the overseas departments and territories, on the other.

The constitutional framework reflected de Gaulle's and the MRP's determination to bring about government stability and an end to political fragmentation (or *morcellement*) and squabbles among political parties in what de Gaulle scornfully termed the *régime of parties*. Yet, political debates converged on positions held by the Communist Party, Socialist Party, and Christian democrat and liberal-led MRP. Given the nonrepresentativity of the extreme right, Christian democrats and liberals of MRP leaned strategically toward the views of de Gaulle, often in opposition to the communists at the other end of the political spectrum. Unable or unwilling to distance themselves from the communists, the socialists emerged from this political landscape as power brokers, with a significant leverage.

The 1946 reforms therefore reflected the growing influence of the socialists. Their candidates (André Philip and then Guy Mollet) were chosen to preside over the drafting of the new constitution while the other two factions were left to select permanent secretaries (rapporteurs): François de Menthon (MRP) and Pierre Cot (radical-socialist) backed by the Communist Party.[108] So too did Vincent Auriol, a socialist, lead the Constituent Assembly. This honor elevated him to the presidency. His advisor on colonial questions was also another socialist: Marius Moutet. Again, the secretariat of the Constituent Assembly went to the MRP in the person of Paul Costé-Floret.

As a result, the socialists prevailed in forwarding their views of the dilemmas facing France. It is now commonsense that they understood, for instance, that the "reality of the defeat" had revealed the fragility of the republican order, and the possibility of collapse of empire. Yet, despite repeated references to the shared and conjoined destiny of metropolitan and colonial populations, the socialists invested the notion of democracy, human solidarity, and political authority with political forms that maximized French access to material and symbolic powers at the expense of the colonized. They tinkered with the principles of decision making such that colonial populations had little involvement in matters concerning the Métropole. Thus, for instance, the constitutional assembly elevated the National Assembly, where representation favored the Métropole, over the Assembly of the French Union, where representation was evenly split between French and colonial representatives. French socialists also opted for a strong centralized government that would secure the necessary "military, diplomatic, and financial means" to ensure "the necessary cohesion" of the French Union.[109] They agreed too to preserve the role of France in the colonies in all circumstances.[110]

The constitution of October 27, 1946, granted France the responsibility to determine the interest of the "France-Africa couple," to
determine the role and place of Africa and Africans in its attainment,
and to secure it from those who would seek to destroy it.[111] The
French National Assembly made laws for its African colonies in matters regarding crimes, civil liberties, political and administrative organizations.[112] The Assembly of the Union was to formally express
opinion on foreign policy, financial and other technical matters, but it
had no power of review or advice, even as one African deputy noted
when the implicated policy presented grave consequences for the
territories and little impact on the Métropole.[113]

By 1946, the idea of a union between and amongst free and
consenting autonomous entities had considerably disappeared from
political discourses. The actualized "big family" was founded upon
the colonial ontology of state, nation, and empire in new guises. With
its virility restored, the once and eternal, "indivisible, laic, democratic, and social" French republic was to endow itself with the proper
state, one capable of dispensing values and institutions to its overseas
departments and territories, on the one hand, and the associated
territories and states, on the other. In sum, the French establishment
arrived at the idea of colonial reform armed with conviction, imagination, and ideological views of values, institutions, and human
endowment and faculties.

Identity, Ideology and Democracy

African reactions to French constitutional debates converged in
many ways. From public and personal records, it emerges that the
majority noted the absence of new approaches to government, entitlements, and privileges. As I show later, representatives of the
colonies noted that while the French establishment had relinquished
any hope of restoring old colonial forms, it lacked the political will
and ideological inclination to effect radical reform. They also pointed
out that France did not appear to be ready to commit sufficient financial resources to the reconstruction of the colonies. The aspects of
the new constitution that troubled most colonial representatives
were the new mechanisms of government, processes of decision making, and the rules of legislation. These were at variance with African
aspirations that, beyond formal democratic elections and rituals, the
new institutions would be informed by yet-to-be-formalized emergent forms of community, solidarity, fairness, and justice. Africans

were generally incensed, therefore, by the instrumentalization of the instruments of democracy, the rules of decision making, and the techniques of government.

Above all, African representatives were astounded by their total exclusion from the Brazzaville Conference and the ensuing constitutional debates. In West Africa, individuals and political entities objected to the language, structures, and institutions of the new constitution. They also contested the role and place assigned to Africa in the French Union and in the world. These "agitators" were former graduates of public and parochial schools who belonged to cultural and recreational associations and trade groups before their enlistment in supportive roles during the resistance.[114] Now mobilized around their objections to the new constitutions and related political discourses, these African intellectuals hoped to reorient politics toward new objectives and within new modalities as well as restore African dignity—*personnalité Africaine*.

The Rassemblement Démocratique Africain (RDA) quickly emerged as a crucial player. Founded in 1946, the RDA appealed to diverse constituencies. It also embodied multiple aspirations, ranging from assimilation and integration to Africanism, *négritude*, nativism, secular progressivism, and radical reformism. Its members originated from the elites, public figures, and intellectuals of the fourteen colonies of French Africa. Its primary mission was to contest elections in the colonies for the three legislative bodies of the French Union viz., the National Assembly, the Assembly of the French Union, and the Council of the Republic.

Between its foundation in 1946–1950, the RDA affiliated itself with the French Communist Party, the radical noncommunist Union Socialiste Radicale et Démocratique, and other metropolitan organizations that professed to support a transformative postcolonial agenda. These groups not only gave political cover to the RDA in metropolitan legislative bodies, they also helped to amplify its criticisms of colonialism and its claims for and on reform. In the latter regard, the RDA was fortified in its positions by the ability of its leaders to articulate plausible visions of the moral order. It was also emboldened by the eroding French consensus about postimperial and postcolonial values, institutions, and modes of knowing. Indeed, the RDA grew in self-confidence in direct proportion with the erosion of the intellectual and ideological capital of the Métropole both at home and overseas.

During these first four years of its existence, the most recognizable face of the RDA before the French public was its general secretary,

Gabriel d'Arboussier. D'Arboussier was the natural child of a French colonial administrator and an African (Malian) woman. At a time when colonial administrators routinely surrendered their mulatto offsprings to public orphanages, the older d'Arboussier bucked the trend. He not only recognized his son and daughter, he also took them to France.[115] For transgressing colonial etiquette, he lost his position in the colonial administration. Gabriel took pride in his father's action and made it a personal challenge to vindicate him by challenging racial prejudice.[116] Gabriel d'Arboussier's mother too had a mixed and impressive lineage. Although a Djavando griot, d'Arboussier's mother's ancestors had been friends and allies of the great Sufi Imam and statesman, El-Hadj Omar Tall: founder of one of the most prosperous theocratic states in nineteenth-century West Africa. The grandchild of Omar Tall, Saidou Nourou Tall, was also married to d'Arboussier's maternal cousin. These maternal associations were also a great point of pride for d'Arboussier.[117] He thus "hoped through his activities to bring about a union between the people of France and the peoples of Africa against the imperialists who caused only war and misery."[118]

D'Arboussier grew up in France where he attended public schools with the likes of François Mitterand, who became president of France. A trained lawyer, d'Arboussier attended the École Coloniale and joined the ranks of idealist humanists who flocked the ranks of colonial administrators in order to effect a progressive colonial policy. To prepare for this task, d'Arboussier cultivated and was fully conversant in French universalist traditions. Indeed, he took striking positions in postwar philosophical debates alongside Marxists, existentialists, phenomenologists, and postmodernists.

Upon completing his training, d'Arboussier first served in his mother's birthplace, then French Sudan. From there, his hope of witnessing a rebirth and transformation of French humanism and republican traditions began to fade due to French hesitations on implementing real reform. It was then that d'Arboussier left the colonial administrator to join the ranks of the RDA and anticolonialists. He was elected its secretary general in recognition of his oratory skills, intellect, and unsurpassable memory—to which he committed French classics alongside Hegel, Marx, Engels, and Lenin.[119] He was also an authority on France and the French political landscape.

Upon entering the Assembly of the French Union, d'Arboussier quickly rose to prominence to assume the vice-presidency. A cursory review of parliamentary debates reveal that d'Arboussier earned begrudging respect from even his staunchest political adversaries. By all accounts, he was among the most articulate, prolific, and influential politicians of that body. (He was also said to be conceited and arrogant.)[120] In the year 1947 alone, d'Arboussier introduced or sponsored over 200 bills or amendments on 48 different subjects.[121] The themes of his interventions ranged from local and metropolitan representations, land tenure and colonial expropriation, to France's relations with its Western allies and their repercussions for Africans. D'Arboussier's representations necessarily reflected the RDA's political agenda of equality among free citizens, fair representation of the territorial units of the French Union, and just exercise of sovereignty. As d'Arboussier articulated them, these themes pertained directly to government of the people (as free and equal citizens), by the people (of all of territorial units), and for the people (whose wills necessarily legitimized law and its execution).

D'Arboussier frequently wondered aloud about the identity of the body politic in light of the orientation of the constitution and the gap between it and the notion of government by the people—plural, diverse, and in need of mutual recognition and respect. He also queried the methods of decision making and the relationships between and among the many layers of territorial spheres created by the consitution. Here, his focus fell on the meaning of government of the people, the need to include them in decision making, and to recognize their techniques for achieving an ethical life. Finally, d'Arboussier kept a watchful eye on the rituals of legitimation, including the techniques of sovereignty, their teleologies, and other demonstrative politics. He gave particular thought to the meaning of shared destiny and interest so centrally assumed in any notion of government for the people.

Staging Democracy: Government by the People

D'Arboussier had hoped for a different kind of union. Central to the constitutional order was a hermeneutic of communal competence that formalized the notion that some questions were too important to be assigned to the colonized.[122] This hermeneutic was "one of race and of racial discrimination" and must be disallowed. D'Arboussier insisted on unanimous applause. The present order is "founded upon a dogma that once served as ideological pillar of the defunct colonial system. This regime is based upon colonial privileges . . . and practices that we must confront today."[123] While French politicians claimed to detest racial privileges, d'Arboussier could detect them in refined constitutional rules and decision-making procedures: "I agree with the irrefutable juridical demonstrations of my colleagues about the fine points of the constitutional texts," he once opined, but "what I reproach to this government is that it takes our opinion as a matter of formality. They will let us debate for as long as we want, for days, even if we exceeded our allotted times and budgets, as long as we do not touch any topics of consequence."[124]

D'Arboussier's counterproposals were transformative. They centered on the principles, rules, and procedures and mechanisms of government. Even as he criticized French officials for their betrayals of democratic principles and their negative orientation toward politics, d'Arboussier elaborated on the meanings of republicanism, democracy, and citizenship after empire and colonialism. He would change the mechanisms of selection of deputies and their numbers, along with the rules of decision making of local assemblies, regional assemblies, and the legislative and consultative bodies in the Métropole. They were all contrary to the ideals of universal suffrage, equal suffrage, and equal representation. Finally, d'Arboussier and others sought to dispense with constitutional duplicity, especially the existence of two voter rolls—one each for black and whites separately—and separate rules for determining the size of their constituencies.[125]

In 1950, posing as educator and master of prose, d'Arboussier opened one of his speeches by arguing that the importance of any electoral law in a colonial context had implication for "the political sovereignty of the peoples of overseas territories, the problem of democracy within the French Union, the problem of participation in the management of public affairs."[126] The proclamation of the French Union was itself a recognition of that will to sovereignty, "the result of gains made by the colonized on the battlefields" which was also heard in the corridors of San Francisco at the inception of the UN Charter.[127] The French could not negate these truths in a vain attempt to deceive Africans in the guise of political pragmatism. He advised that they follow, once again, Africans who elected trust and political goodwill as motivation in considering new political models and experimentations. "We had historical models before us," he declared, "but we chose to take a path that reflects our present and circumstances."[128]

The following is a paraphrase of his arguments: I am not saying that there is no representation in the assemblies for the peoples of the overseas territories. But a true representation is one that effects "sovereignty." This is what is lacking with local assemblies as well as territorial assemblies, municipalities, and others.[129] None of the local assemblies can effectively check the power of the administration, none has the power to effect social and economic policy.[130] Likewise, "there is representation for the colonized at the National Assembly, the Assembly of the French Union, and the Council of the Republic," but I challenge you to take a poll of the elected representatives of the territories, you will find that there is "a unanimous sentiment" that it amounts to very little in regard to sovereignty.[131]

The solution proposed by d'Arboussier was *"une démocratisation générale."* At this point, French liberals and socialists encouraged d'Arboussier to press on because his view on the matter of democracy put his traditional communist allies ill at ease.[132] D'Arboussier obliged them. "All present here today know that democracy is the solution" and that "we know what to do." But France is afraid to "democratize public life in Africa," so deputies here today would like to believe that "the everyday of the Africa does not accommodate such a democratization." But it is really so that they can maintain the colonial system.[133] The crucial feature of democracy, d'Arboussier concluded, was "popular representation" and its essence must be the "attainment of justice based on political reality and efficacy."[134] In the event, electoral justice depended upon the modality of suffrage, the composition of voter rolls, and the nature of the ballot.[135] This is "democratic justice," and "We have the technical knowledge to effect such a democratic justice, to bring about true debates and good policy, whether through proportional representation or not."[136]

To wit, African demand for democratic justice was linked to electoral justice. The latter arose from resentment of the so-called double voter rolls (*collège electoral*). Under the constitution and the law, the natives of each territories were entitled to the same number of representatives as settlers. In Niger, for instance, this meant 150 Europeans sent a representative to the National Assembly for every 1 elected by 70,000 native inhabitants.[137] In the most populous territories the ratio was 1 deputy per 1,000 settlers against 1 per 1 million natives.[138] Ouezzin Coulibaly, also an RDA deputy, opined that his French colleagues "supported the double voter rolls on specious grounds that abused Montesquieu's views while ignoring actual events and the fundamental principles of democracy."[139] For his part, Etienne Djaument argued that it was a parody of reason to insist that settlers and natives be granted equal numbers of seats in separate voter rolls.[140]

Like many African deputies, Djaument recognized the European voter roll occasionally produced progressive and fair-minded settlers who defended the cause of Africans. But the very idea of a separate voter roll for Europeans was "illogic," it negated the principle of a single citizenship for an indivisible republic, the juridical regime upon which the Union was founded.[141] Or, "you will forgive me Mr. Durand-Reville," Djaument rejoined a contesting French deputy, "If by crossing the ocean one is entitled to one's own electoral college then let the two hundred thousands colonial emigres here in Paris an equal number of representatives to the Assembly as their Parisian counterparts."[142] (The applause came only from Africans and a few communists.) So, "we cannot in a single republic grant privileges to some while denying others the same; in a republic everyone must be bound by the same law . . . What we have here is that the alteration of the word republic."[143] Amadou Doucouré added that the French deluded themselves in thinking that the dual electoral college system provided them with security.[144] On the contrary, said Doucouré, it only created new sets of problems among henceforth unequal citizens.[145] If you consecrate this double college, another Omar Ba added, all antagonisms due to interests and values that must be settled through deliberations, would be conflated with "racial antagonism" because "the two voter rolls would be 99 to 100 per cent racially homogenous."[146]

It is understandable then that Africans were most upset about metropolitan attempts to reduce their representation in the sovereign legislative organs—viz., the National Assembly and the Council of the Republic—in favor of greater representation in the consultative body of the Assembly of the Union: "There are now talks of progressively reducing the number of slots reserved to the representatives of the territories in the Council of the Republic in favor of a Federal Assembly whose competency will preclude all essential questions of the Union, notably financial issues, economic issues, and even the right to discuss the extent of the right of deliberation."[147] But sirs, d'Arboussier logically asked, "if you deny Malagasies or Africans the right to decide the fate of the people of France, how do you justify that the French decide the fate of the people of Madagascar and Africa."[148] This time around the applause came mostly from Africans, French communists, and a few socialists.

Taking Folks Into Account: Government of the People

Official France contemplated postwar dilemmas in universal (if not scientific) terms, based on historical views of the human condition (if not nature), the political and cultural foundations of order, and the causes of conflict and anarchy. French elites thus envisaged postcolonial reform in light of their perceived telos of the world order (particularly of international morality and its economy of rights and privileges); the direction of the political economy (indeed, the future of colonial capitalism!); the cultural dislocations of empire (caused by the threshold of rationality and political autocracy); and the question of the other (representations and their contents). But the envisaged institutions and their rituals of legitimation and teleologies often belied philosophical ideals and principles.

D'Arboussier understood it all as he sought to reconcile French anxiety and attempt at self-preservation with the will of anticolonialists to political self-determination. His solution was a republican union of consenting sovereign peoples. The model was based on three separate but complementary principles: (1) *preservation and integrity*; (2) *equal competency based on interest*; and (3) *sovereign reciprocity of rights and duties*. This first principle was consistent with metropolitan norms of communal identity combining territorial identity (*jus soli*) with a "natural" one (*jus sanguini*).[149] Political identity would combine both sources of identity in a nonexclusionary fashion. The reason, and this justified the second principle, was that the "Franco-African" union was a community of interests of indistinguishable entities, already tied together genetically, culturally, economically, and socially by centuries-old interactions. In this context, D'Arboussier envisaged multiple sovereignties according to territory, space, and identity such that deliberations were always universal but sovereign decisions were taken by those most affected related laws. This meant that political competence would be linked directly to a material and/or symbolic base—loss, suffering, gain, contribution, and the like. Sovereignty would not be arbitrarily assigned to those with power, resources, and the hubris to usurp the authority of others.[150]

The union thus imagined would be *democratic* and truly *federal*, one inspired by postwar sensibilities. D'Arboussier contrasted his vision with the existing "*autocratic federalism*" in which Africans were placed in "*magnificently adorned assemblies*" with no responsibility or "right to deliberate and act upon anything consequential to the *raison d'être* of their presence in such bodies."[151] This autocratic system harkened back to the past and its function was to enable France to pursue its colonial policies unobstructed.[152] To d'Arboussier what it did was not sensitive to the fact that anticolonialists no longer conceded "their sacred right born of wartime sacrifice.[153] Having defended the republic, freedom, and democracy, d'Arboussier insisted, Africans were entitled to "venture their views with maximum candor and honesty."[154]

Boubou Hama comforted d'Arboussier's position that Africans had the right to deliberate on all matters concerning the French Union and to do so by speaking candidly and frankly.[155] To paraphrase Hama: "how are we going to obtain truth if we cannot look at reality objectively . . . I understand that reality is relative, but there is one that you do not want to face and this is the point of view of the Assembly of the French Union. We would do well to listen and to draw a synthesis of various and competing truths in order to better serve our common interest."[156] In truth, Hama continued, "you do not want to hear about the horrors of your actions; you cannot endure daily denunciations of such actions; you hope to hide the truth of such acts from the people of France."[157] Freedom of speech was not only a right but, as Hama ventured, it guaranteed "an energetic Assembly of the French Union as well as the future of France . . . its international presence . . . its independence and place in the world."[158]

At the time, Africans noted that honesty and candor would save France from humiliation and defeat in Vietnam. Dien Bien Phu proved them correct. Speaking at hearing on Vietnam, Hama warned against the secrecy that shrouded government actions: "we need to hear from the representatives of the French government," if only to alert us to the implications of the events in Vietnam.[159] Perhaps, he intoned, the government does not want to hear from "the largest and most important group of this Assembly . . . [which] takes its duties to heart." The RDA "simply wanted . . . the government . . . to deal with Ho Chi Minh."[160] The "government must end this war in Indochina, its police actions in Madagascar, and its colonial repression, oppression, and the exploitation of the masses in the territories."[161]

Hama understood early on that the government was not asking the right questions on Vietnam and, thus, was not serving the interest of France and the French Union.[162] "We think that the government is asking the wrong question . . . we believe that the all or nothing approach is ill-suited to this circumstance and that it is dangerous to start from the proposition of Bao Dai or nothing."[163] Hama was also distressed that the government had forgotten that the Vietnamese people had supported the French struggle for liberation; that Vietnam sided with the anti-Fascist coalition; and that it endorsed the Atlantic Charter and the Declaration by the United Nations. During that time, "others [on the French right] comfortably accommodated Nazi enslavement and the plot against freedom fomented by Hitler and Mussolini." The Vietnamese people, he proclaimed, "were not fighting the people of France" and "French soldiers in Vietnam were not defending the Patrie but the [French] Bank of Indochina."[164]

For these and other views Hama was accused of communist sympathies. He responded to this charge with indignity: "I will tell you . . . that we intend to combat the politics of colonialism because it destroys human brotherhood." That is not communism, it is inscribed in the constitution of the French Union and the UN Charter. "I am Marxist but not communist. But I will [be communist] if you push me in that direction, if you convince me that the communists are the ones interested in peace and liberty in the world."[165] In short, both Hama and d'Arboussier fought off political blackmail for advocating *tenable principles* of justice, rights, duties, along with *modalities for their enforcement*.[166]

The cold war, the creeping American influence in French politics, and the ideological transposition of all contests onto the East–West lines of confrontations were tragic events for anticolonialists.[167] Related events effectively shattered meaningful dialogue about global institutions, with effects for political debates in France.[168] Where once he was cheered by liberals for his defense of democratic pluralism,[169] d'Arboussier was roundly rebuked by the same liberals when he turned his attention to global political pluralism, communal integrity, and cultural identity.[170] One liberal deputy suggested that "the communist party and the RDA had become cousins such that it was hard to tell them apart."[171] "The RDA is not the communist party," d'Arboussier angrily replied. "Cousins do not always agree." "We are not cousins of the communists but we get along just fine." Unsatisfied, another metropolitan deputy enjoined, "You must be siamese twins then."[172]

Social Meaning of Democracy: Government for the People

D'Arboussier's vision of the moral order necessitated a new imaginary of community, society, economy, and law. This vision had bearing on the social meaning of all postwar institutions—the French Union, the Council of Europe, the United Nations, and NATO. D'Arboussier argued that any "government of the people," a republic or otherwise, was compelled for its own legitimacy to institute political and legal regimes that reflected the wills of the citizenry. In the context of impending decolonization, European models of politics and their notions and rituals did not meet these requirements.[173] Building globally on the experiences of the Concert of Europe and the League of Nations went along toward postwar reconstruction. But the emerging order was even less credible than its antecedents. The new one was founded upon two distinct and antagonistic blocs: one, Soviet, based on authoritarian materialism and, the other, American, based on liberal materialism.[174] Both kinds of materialism required exclusive alliances of ideology, power, and material interest. They were both hostile to democratic pluralism and political experimentation and in fact mandated uniform approaches to economy, culture, and social life.[175] Neither materialism assuaged the fear of the formerly colonized nor met their needs.[176] It was thus incumbent upon anticolonialists to envision a different moral order for the different emergent "publics," operating within contemporaneously defined public spaces.[177]

A Republic of Publics

D'Arboussier first envisioned a global order of multiple publics, beginning with localities and extending outward to the world.[178] Again, the model was thought through the French experiment. Beginning with local assemblies, d'Arboussier argued that these institutions were the "first element of autonomy through which overseas peoples would assume responsibility over their affairs." Such assemblies confirmed the specificity of local interest, but by not acceding to separation,[179] they put an end to the excessive centralization as well as allowed Africans to "affect the character of government" itself.[180] The means and competencies devolved to them would put to test so-called revolutionary French liberalism, which did not seek to assimilate or subordinate others. This liberalism established a middle ground between total subordination and total autonomy, that is, free association.[181]

Local assemblies also afforded Africans the space from which to flesh out their theory of "revolutionary humanism," a sort to be opposed to colonial humanism.[182] Anticolonial humanism was informed by particular circumstances (for instance, *the right to life of local populations and their particular interests*) without negating the law of development."[183] D'Arboussier wanted to get away from "the colonial pact and its imperial modes of preferences" through philosophical conceptions, legislative enactments, and executive implementations of public utility.[184] These, according to d'Arboussier, were not a neutral or mere technical act. They fostered a false sense of public utility where there were distinctions to be made "between the public utility of France and that of the each territory."[185]

The question of property and expropriation of land for public utility weighed heavily in this debate. D'Arboussier would not agree that the sites of the proprieties to be expropriated had no bearing on the formulation, implementation, and relevancy of public utility. Here too the idea of a uniform notion of public utility of land was worrisome to d'Arboussier who argued that the laws and teleologies of land use, spoliation, and exchange did not lend themselves to easy translation and conversion into colonial contexts and local conceptions of property, commodity, and their modes of operations.[186] "The land issue has extra-juridical dimensions" that require extra-juridical reflections.[187]

Not only were the histories of "land-as-property in France different from the trajectory of property and property rights in the colonies," the inhabitants of the Métropole and the territories had different dispositions toward land and property. In metropolitan France, for instance, no property was beyond spoliation, speculation, and privatization—that is, appropriation by public or private agents for public or private purposes. This was not the case in the colonies. There, the question of proprietorship and the juridical status of land had to be augmented inevitably with consideration of local "principles of conservation," their conceptions of nature, connections of land to ancestors, and "the right of the occupants to dignified life."[188] "This is," as d'Arboussier argued, if the goal was "to secure the future," and to "acknowledge that the humanity of overseas representatives has great value that cannot be ignored by this assembly."[189] It follows that the principle of expropriation for public utility of overseas lands must take into account other proprietary principles that are of utmost interest to local populations.[190]

Without explicitly stating so, d'Arboussier hinted at the existence of multiple and different publics, corresponding to different imaginaries, needs, and interests. It is in this light that he thought it consistent with democratic rights that local assemblies be given "real powers" "to determine the manners in which to dispose of their lands and to do it as they see it fit." It was time, d'Arboussier said, to "relinquish the idea that issues related to lands can be resolved through simple juridical techniques."[191] The government was to enter into negotiations with the inhabitants of the territories to discuss the terms and modes of preference and operation of property, particularly land. Before such time d'Arboussier argued that the problem of land, proprietorship of it, and authority over it remained "the foundations upon which the French Union would be built or destroyed."[192]

The entry of France into transnational associations, alliances, organizations, and partnerships with other states also had bearing on the role and place of its African colonies and their populations in world affairs. This was particularly the case with the United Nations, the emergent European Council, the Bretton Woods institutions, the Marshall Plan, and NATO. Specifically, French leaders insisted that related agreements would involve only the Métropole, its executive branches, and the National Assembly and not, as African deputies had hoped, the organs of the French Union with consultation of the representatives of the colonies.[193] Having failed to move French elites in these regards, d'Arboussier contemplated tweaking the modalities of implementation of the related agreements in order to allow for greater participation of the representatives of the overseas territories. Until 1950, he was still confident that the heavy burden and sacrifice of Africans during the war warranted concessions from France and its allies.[194]

Other black deputies too had high hopes that France's humanist traditions would cause it to reverse course and consider their own positions. Gabriel Lisette of Chad advised that France could not ignore the great political questions of the day, which he likened to the momentous events of 1789 and 1848.[195] Barring a general commitment to democratic principles, Lisette warned, "Africans would resist to be drawn into international associations and/or organizations as appendages of France." A retreat from global democracy would be too high a price for Africans to pay for loyalty to France. Referring to darker times, Lisette recalled the days when France and its allies would trade black, white, and brown Africans as slaves.[196] If France could not adhere to the spirit of its own traditions, Lisette continued, it should at least heed the lessons of the war and the Atlantic Charter that every country was entitled to enter into consensual unions founded upon true cooperation of peoples.[197] In short, France should not expect overseas populations to agree to political programs, particularly those involved in the Marshall Plan and the North Atlantic Treaty, that evidently reinforced colonial exploitation for a foreign imperial power.[198]

A Republic of Economies

D'Arboussier esteemed too that the future of the imperial economy was not a technical matter to be left to French bureaucrats and businessmen alone. The economy, after all, was founded upon ethical proposition about exchanges, rewards, relations, and their teleologies. The nature and context of the economy were also of consequence. The idea of national economies was all but fictional at the time of the war. (France had not established a *comptabilité nationale*, or national accounting system, until the mid-1930s.) Imperial economies stretched across vast expanses uniting European capital and industry to native labor in the application of technology to the exploitation of "local" natural resources.[199] Ostensibly, this "interdependence" ensured mutual benefits for all, as promised by the *solidarists* of Third Republic France. In fact, while the system ensured the good life in the Métropoles for a public of consumers of colonial goods, it is more accurate to view that colonialism was a "daughter" of industrial production and mass consumption in Europe than a modernizing force for the empire.[200] Thus, the "French" economy was properly speaking an amalgamate of multiple centers and peripheries, allowing for differentiated modes of production, distribution, and consumption together with equally differentiated social relations among unequal political subjects, rights-bearing individuals, and value-bearing persons. Also, the identities, faculties, and capacities of these entities depended upon overlapping structures emanating from the economy and the political systems.

This situation allowed colonial reformists to envisage a Franco-African economic bloc of more than 200 million producers and consumers with enough financial resources, raw materials, and industrial and agricultural output to sustain economic activities, including consumption, necessary for economic recovery. The speculation was that, if Europe were to be included in such an entity, a postimperial Euro-Asian-African economy would rival the United States and the Soviet Union. Africa alone, it is surmised, was a "reservoir of enough raw materials for all the former métropoles."[201] The French acted on this belief in April 1946 when they created the Investment Fund for Economic and Social Development, or Fonds d'investissement pour le Développement Économique et Social des territoires d'outre-mer (also FIDES). This "fonds" was destined mostly for infrastructure and bureaucratic development to make way for the kind of development envisioned by France—and, as it turned out, not the inhabitants of the territories.[202]

Bretton Woods and the Marshall Plan limited the effectivity of the FIDES, adding to its conceptual and structural flaws. By focusing principally on European recovery, U.S. policy injected new dynamics into existing semi-global imperial economies by repositioning them as national economies according to new geopolitical rationales. Africans were divided on whether the American policy, particularly aid to France, could be tailored to meet African needs. Mamadou Dia, not the RDA, offered the most coherent arguments from the standpoint of the French government on the transition of global capitalism from colonial exploitation to one with a new human face.[203] Addressing his African colleagues and the French left, he warned that the "grandiose programs coming out of Washington," should not be resisted merely on ideological grounds or fear that America would undermine France in the colonies.[204] "The Truman plan may be a discovery to the opinion and government of the United States," he declared, "but the paternity of the idea of assistance to European territories goes to France." The latter, in Dia's mind, "had already in place institutions and organizations specifically designed to accomplish what Truman has proposed on a larger scale": to equip and modernize the colonies.[205] "It seems," Dia concluded that France "should go along with the Truman Plan" while keeping in mind that necessary rectifications would be needed in the colonies "at the expiration of Marshall Plan credits" due to its "ill orientation."[206]

RDA spokesmen at the time were not convinced that Western imperialism and capitalism were undergoing a process of "humanization." For one, the structures of global flows had not been reversed as the benefits of the new order accrued mostly to the former colonial powers. No longer métropoles in the imperial sense, Britain, France, and other colonial powers stood to introduce new ethical precepts of justice and solidarity according to which they would disentangle themselves from their old colonies while retaining most of the benefits, rights, and privileges created by the old economies.[207] The transformation began at the Bretton Woods conference when the United States refused to allocate credits to support local economies in colonial territories.[208] On the contrary, in order to conform to the new exigencies, France unilaterally and without consultation with local authorities introduced measures that devaluated its colonial currency as well as limited credit allocations to territorial projects.[209]

Second, the Marshall Plan reinforced Western positions in other regions by creating the condition for the differentiated expansion of capitalism such that it unevenly benefitted communities around the world. It also significantly altered existing relationships between France and its territories. This plan was presented as a generous gift to Europe and in many ways it was. But the plan did not come without conditions. One, contained in Article II of the bilateral implementation agreement, required that France consult with the United States concerning their plans for industrial developments. This was a point of consternation for both French and the leaders of the territories. For France, it was another blow to Gallic pride that a foreign country, not the least the United States, would dictate the terms of French conceptions of solidarity and assistance.[210] A socialist member of parliament noted thoughtfully that the Franco-American accord would startle the partners of the French Union. He wondered aloud what France would make of the consultative role of the democratic organs of the Union and how it could guarantee to respect the rights of non-metropolitan entities and states. But Alduy concluded that the Marshall Plan remained a necessary evil.[211] Besides, added the French foreign minister, "we are facing a unilateral offer from the government of the United States. It is absolutely impossible for us to intervene in the laws of the United States when the government of the United States predicates a bilateral agreement on American law."[212]

D'Arboussier and his colleagues saw the evil in the American-initiated European reconstruction plan, but not the necessity. To be sure, France laid financially anemic and its industry ruined at the end of the war. But the Marshall Plan was not a disinterested gift. America too needed the plan to boost markets to relieve its excess capacity. In addition, it was not clear whether the United States applied the same economic logic to others as it did to itself. Specifically, it was not clear that the United States understood that France needed to create viable economies in Africa to ensure its own future. This was demonstrated by the fact that the United States could not provide assurance that Marshall Plan credits would flow in the territories. The most distressing (and disingenuous) dimension of the American plan was its resuscitation of the colonial logic of modernization. Whereas before the plan France had staked colonial reform on new understandings of human solidarity and assistance, the Marshall Plan now enjoined France and other colonial powers to turn to their colonies for raw materials in the reconstruction efforts.

It seems to the colonized that America had revived a nearly defunct notion of trusteeship according to which civilized nations had free access to the resources of their territories provided the end be the mutual benefit of the guardian and the trustee.[213] This policy was enforced by the demand that aid and infrastructure development in the territories be undertaken by the colonial power in conjunction with the United States and U.S. capital. In the event, France was only to serve as intermediary for aid to its former colonies.[214] In the meantime, France awarded exclusive and semi-exclusive access to vast natural resources in Africa to American corporations through government-sponsored contracts.[215] The new arrangement was the justification of colonialism that Africans had managed to jettison before the arrival of the Marshall Plan. Significantly, it put into play a new African sovereignty and rights to land and natural resources.[216]

D'Arboussier also worried that the geopolitical rationales of the Bretton Woods institutions and the Marshall Plan foreshadowed an old-new ontology as material and symbolic foundations of the global economy and the international system. Whereas the U.S.-mandated European Reconstruction Plan aimed to bring prosperity to former enemies (e.g., Germany, Italy, Portugal, Greece, and Turkey), it assigned a subordinate place and role in the global order to African entities, "once allied to it and its Allies in the fight against German Nazism, Italian Fascism, and Japanese militarism." The point was not that the United States or Europe should not have offered assistance to Germany or Italy. Nor was it that the former enemies were unworthy of reconstruction. It was to highlight a contrast according to which, after Bretton Woods and the Marshall Plan, it became less and less natural to empathize with Africans or to think of "Africa" as deserving of solidarity and reconstruction as others. From 1948 onward, the base-presumptions of Africa-related discussions shifted drastically away from common dignity and interest to the specificity of African existence, which required less than the empathy owed to others, say Germans and Italians.

Second, d'Arboussier complained that France did not practice a politics of conviction by adhering to the essential principles of the French Union. Coming on the heels of the European Reconstruction Plan, the belated change of heart betrayed the sacrifice and burden born by Africans during the war. The shift in priority also signified a lack of imagination. The Union was indeed endowed with enough material wealth, natural and cultural resources, and base populations to sustain an economic experiment on the scale of the somewhat successful political experiment. Prior to the American aid package, Africans had not imagined aid. Rather, they had hoped for viable industrial and agricultural policies and open free trade; mutually agreed economic exchanges, not economic trusteeship; fair financial and commercial instruments, not ones exclusively designed to benefit one part of the world. The goal of the resulting economies would be free and fair competition, but not rivalry, among admittedly unequally endowed states and political entities.[217]

Conclusion: Democracy's Heartless Home

D'Arboussier had precise ideas of the requirements of a postcolonial order that included concrete spatial enactment of sovereignty (will), interest (desire), and value (affect and sensibility). Specifically, he aspired to establish regimes of common laws uniting all political entities, organized across multiform regional and global associations and organizations with multiple modes of legitimacy and sovereignty. For instance, he suggested as acceptable principle of a Franco-African Union that France consult Africans whenever it entered into agreements that implicated Africans' collective and/or individual interests—whether political, cultural, financial, and/or economic. In return, Africans would restrain from intervening in French domestic politics and policies. Decisions would implicate parties according to their interests and dispositions, which defined zones of sovereignty.

Initially, these ideas seemed attractive and plausible to French authorities. However, as the Trans-Atlantic Alliance grew—specifically upon Bretton Woods, the Marshall Plan, and the North Atlantic Treaty Organization—French authorities began giving precedence to their newfound strategic interests. France was swayed in the American direction by political weakness and moral debt to the United States. As a result, successive French presidents of the Council of Government assented to the wishes of the Truman and Eisenhower administrations to not only "liquidate" the empire but to do so within the frameworks of both the American plan for European reconstruction and the emergent East–West antagonism. The majority of French elites and politicians initially resented American dictates and interference in French colonial affairs. But, resentment quickly gave way to acquiescence in return for increased French role in world affairs. The new associations had afforded France permanent membership at the UNSC (United Nations Security Council), the hosting of UNESCO, a seat in NATO command structure (until the 1960 de Gaulle-initiated exit), and most importantly access to new financial and economic structures. These "assets" made the former colonial power less dependent on the territories and therefore less attentive to them. As it happened, France and the United States split responsibility for the collapsing French empire. The United States inherited France's troubles in Indochina, while France sank deeper into the Algerian quagmire.

It would be unwarranted, however, to attribute the change in French attitude and orientation toward the empire to U.S. pressure. France gained from European reconstruction. It offered an opportunity for restoration, if not of French grandeur, then of French claims to symbolic, cultural, and civilizational specificity and indispensability. Restoration brought back memories and confidence in metropolitan values, institutions, and moral science. It also rekindled a language of command as primary modality of engagement of the colonized. The primary instigator of this movement of return toward a language of command was the French political right and center. Progressively, the French political left too lost its inhibitions and humility to embrace Bretton Woods, the Marshall Plan, and NATO. Specifically after 1948, the French left earnestly began to retreat from wartime associations and positions that it had steadfastly maintained in relations to "universal republicanism" guided by humanism. By 1950, the socialists had aligned themselves with the political right in reserving for France the authority and exclusive privilege to lay out the norms, rules, and standards of France's relations with the former colonial entities.

The new situation had implications for Africans: French reconstruction required African raw material and political goodwill;[218] NATO plans required the "full use" of French territories in Africa;[219] and the Bretton Woods institutions imposed policy "burdens" on the French Union, which included African entities.[220] Yet, American policy makers insisted on the sovereign character of the related policies thus compelling France to exclude Africans from deliberations and decision making.[221] This created tensions between the Métropole and anticolonial elites who rejected French request for "understanding" of its new "pragmatism." The general sentiment was summarized by Alioune M'Bengue in the moderate, semiofficial, and pro-French Senegalese newspaper *Condition Humaine*: that the difficulties encountered by France were due to the fact that it "was too used to reigning" to accommodate postcolonial demands for democracy and equal sovereignty.[222] Others bemoaned the betrayal of ideals by the French left which had thus far supported the African goal of emancipation and dignity. Léopold Sédar Senghor, for instance, resigned from the socialist Section Française de l'Internationale Ouvrière because, while still imbued in leftwing "verbiage," the organization had effectively betrayed its humanist and socialist goals: "it had voted against equality . . . , it had voted against single voter rolls, it had voted against proportional representation, it had voted against democracy in Africa."²²³ Once again, d'Arboussier was impatient: "We cannot be held indirectly to be incompetent," he objected. "Either we are competent or we are not" to exercise our rights and to be included in decisions regarding the Union.²²⁴

By 1950, it was evident that French authorities had failed to win their arguments with anticolonialists on the new pragmatism. Anticolonial obstinacy was particularly sensitive when France faced open conflicts in Algeria, Syria, Vietnam, and Madagascar among others. The French government thus resolved to directly confront the key recalcitrants, among them RDA members. At first, the government directed a campaign of denunciation and ostracism against the body. This strategy did not last because the RDA remained the largest organization of the empire with a solid regional base. Then the government shifted to political coercion, economic bribery, and personal incentives for the "moderate wing" of the party. In a crucial 1950 meeting between Vincent Auriol (president of the Republic), Rene Pleven (president of the Council), François Mitterand (minister of Overseas France), and Felix Houphouet-Boigny (president of the RDA), the latter undertook the task of severing working relationships between the RDA and the Communist Party and other noninstitutional organizations. In exchange, the French government promised greater RDA inclusion in decision-making processes.²²⁵

The government also asked Houphouet-Boigny to expel "radicals" from the ranks of the RDA.²²⁶ The principal target was d'Arboussier. With the assent of government, Houphouet-Boigny began to give resonance to a whisper campaign that d'Arboussier was not African and that, as an anti-French communist, he was a careerist unconcerned by the plight and needs of Africans. The government had already enlisted the Indépendants d'Outre-Mer in this campaign. Among them, Mamadou Dia had warned Africans against confusing the sentiment of pride that necessarily guides the struggle for dignity and the cult of pride, a charge leveled at RDA elites who Dia claimed desired to be constantly loved and honored by the masses.²²⁷ This cult of pride, or vanity, was presumably nursed by those who took their "gifted with oratory skills as predestination . . . and not merely a gift of creative talent."²²⁸ Dia also warned Africans to learn "to not be so impressed as to confuse political courage with demagoguery." Political courage, Dia argued, "is founded upon honest analyses of particular and general interests, a global vision of problems to be solved, and a lucidity of mind before complex and grave problems." By contrast, demagoguery is based on linguistic "artifices and political calculus based on private interests that have little bearing on larger concerns."²²⁹ Dia's comments were directly at "radicals at large" but they echoed the more specific one of Houphouet-Boigny against d'Arboussier: "he brings everything down to himself whereas we should be concerned with the future of our Movement by practicing the politics of the possible, nothing but a politics of the possible."²³⁰

Upon his conversion to French pragmatism, Houphouet-Boigny set to prove that d'Arboussier was diverting the "African" struggle for emancipation toward a self-interested communist crusade that ill-served African populations.²³¹ Where once the RDA's ambition was to transform Franco–African relations on anticolonial lines, Houphouet-Boigny now argued that the mission of the RDA was "no longer to occupy itself with the distant future . . . or faraway issues."²³² What interested the RDA was "the immediate future . . . and the realization of the French Union in mutual understanding."²³³ Houphouet-Boigny was now "convinced that it is possible . . . to construct a larger union toward social justice, order, and peace" through accommodation.²³⁴ Houphouet-Boigny also asked for a revision of RDA's PanAfricanist vision because "it was a geographic reality" that French Africa was an "island at the heart of the Western world." The RDA could no longer stand for d'Arboussier's vision of "an Africa of 100 million people . . . an independent Africa from Dakar to Zanzibar, from Chad to the Cape of Good Hope!"²³⁵

Houphouet-Boigny complemented these rebukes with a campaign to exclude d'Arboussier from the leadership of the RDA on account of the latter's identity. Just as "the most disinterested of untouchables cannot hope to lead in India," Houphouet-Boigny intoned, d'Arboussier cannot be one of our leaders. "His mother is 'djavando [*sic*] . . . a sub-caste of griots." This irritates "our friends from Sudan who had warned me of endorsing d'Arboussier" because "they say there that one should always beware of the head of a djavando."²³⁶ We cannot ignore these considerations of ancestry: "A griot is a griot and must remain so." "I am sorry to speak the truth." "D'Arboussier is Mulatto." "I have lots of Mulatto friends throughout Africa and in France: Jean Delafosse, Guillabert, Boissier-Palun, to name only a few." But it is the case that no matter their personal qualities, our Mulatto brothers have seldom been capable of leadership in our communities, nor have they been judged by their communities of possessing sufficient leadership qualities. "Can we then trust Gabriel d'Arboussier who is both djavando and mulatto? Is he honest and disinterested? Does he really know African realities?" "These are the facts," proclaimed Houphouet-Boigny: "the decision to exclude d'Arboussier manifested itself clearly . . ."[237]

Houphouet-Boigny's comments were gratuitous, ungenerous, unkind, and untrue on the whole. But they were politically effective. The highest officers of the French state with responsibility for the colonies—the president of the Republic (Auriol), the president of the Council (Pleven), and the minister of Overseas France (Mitterand)—collectively signed on to Houphouet-Boigny's campaign.[238] It should also be noted that, due to recovery of grandeur and European and transatlantic alliances, French officials had by then lost interest in the creation of a larger republic uniting France and Africa. As French officials desired, Houphouet-Boigny and others now asked for nation-states founded upon narrow notions of Africanism and autonomy. It did not matter that the new states would be resourceless because they would not be dependent (or closely aligned) on France for their domestic survival and international presence.

CHAPTER 5

DANIEL OUEZZIN COULIBALY: DESCARTES WASN'T ALWAYS RIGHT, DIDEROT MAYBE

The defenders of the double voter rolls abuse and exploit Montesquieu by going so far as to deny that the law of numbers is a fundamental element of democracy.

— *Ouezzin Coulibaly, Journal Officiel, April 1951*

These words of Diderot come to mind: There is something more odious than slavery: it is having slaves and calling them citizens. (Loud applause on the extreme left. Strong protestations at the center and the right. Prolonged noise).

— *Ouezzin Coulibaly, Journal Officiel, June 1949*

Descartes was not always right.

— *Alfred Bour, Annales de L'Assemblée de L'Union Française, July 1948*

Rumor has it that Henry Morton Stanley perplexed over a quandary facing colonialists: "we cannot justify our presence among "natives" if we do not educate them; but I suspect that we are not prepared for what they will say about us when and if we do teach them to write."[1] Stanley correctly predicted that "natives" would have different understandings of the colonial act and that what appeared to the colonizers as virtues and necessities may well appear to the former as weaknesses and acts of barbarism. Stanley's ruminations also show that the colonial act was accompanied by anxieties over the eventual *prise de parole* by natives, that is their self-conscious expressions of thought on colonialism. The core of these anxieties has been whether postcolonial discourses can be aligned on the rationalizations of the colonial act by its agents.

These concerns extend today to all dimensions of postcolonial relations, including the dynamics of politics and knowledge production. For instance, before he went to Britain in 1990, Nelson Mandela told reporters in Dublin that the British government should talk to the Irish Republican Army (IRA). Neil Kinnock, then leader of Labour, called the suggestion "extremely ill-advised."[2] MP Teddy Taylor said the comments made it "difficult for anyone with sympathy for the ANC and Mandela to take him seriously."[3] Mandela "made similar waves in the US when he refused to condemn Yasser Arafat, Colonel Gadafy and Fidel Castro."[4] He recently earned the scorn of American and British policy makers for suggesting on the eve of the 2003 Anglo-American war on Iraq that "America was a threat to world peace."

To cite Gary Younge, few expected "The kindly old statesman who forgave his jailers" to use "that sort of language" or to so boldly stake out moral visions of the political order that contrasted with their own.[5] They conveniently forgot that the kindly old African was also a political strategist with deep moral commitments. At home, Mandela instigated national reconciliation amongst South Africa's blacks and whites; anti-apartheid activists and backers of apartheid, liberals and communists; Xhosas and Zulus, among others. Mandela earned a Nobel Peace Prize for the ensuing peaceful transition. On the international stage, Mandela defied centuries-old Western political wisdom—presumably extending from Thucydides to Machiavelli to Hobbes—by voluntarily and unconditionally dismantling South Africa's nuclear weapons program. In addition, Mandela sought to orient South African society and science away from militarism and militarization.[6] Above all, Mandela correctly presaged the inevitable. Great Britain did talk to the IRA. The United States embraced Gadafy. And the official justifications of the Iraq War have all but dissipated.

It is symptomatic of Western postcolonial anxieties that Mandela and other third world leaders are seldom viewed as deep thinkers with legitimate perspectives on international relations. They are conveniently if not condescendingly viewed as either "kindly old gents" or "sinners"; "moderate" or "radical"; "authentic" or "alienated"; but seldom considered to hold legitimate political interests or rationalities. Nor are they deemed to hold legitimate political imaginaries, discernable ethical positions, and/or dependable moral orientations. Few have considered it fruitful therefore to index the imaginaries, political idioms, moral discourses, and concepts and referents of the likes of Mandela as coherent models of politics. Instead, analysts often settle on the latter's "reflexes" and "intuitions" as basis for determining their legitimacy as moral agents.

This orientation to postcolonial agency and thoughts is prevalent in theory. Take Mandela again. Although the list of his deeds is as long as his judgment impressive, he does not appear in IR as a symbol of particular orientation to politics, with determinate ethical moves, discernable referents, and observed outcomes. This honor goes to the likes of U.S. President Woodrow Wilson who, for instance, appears in IR as a great internationalist and idealist who dreamed peace for Europe and the world. It does not matter that the gentleman from the American South returned black veterans of World War I to a segregated society or that his pragmatism on colonialism led to untold miseries for colonial populations. Other more meritorious Western politicians have been ridiculed for their naivety. These include Aristide Briand and Frank Kellog, authors of the 1928 Briand-Kellog Pact, that sought to renounce war as instrument of national policy. Those who are inducted in professional indexes and guidebooks as "Wise Men" are ones who charted the course of events like the cold war: for instance, "Dean Acheson, Charles Bohlen, Clark Clifford, George Kennan, W. Averell Harriman, Robert Lovett, and John McCloy."[7]

Unlike them, Mandela did actualized "Bryant-Kellog" by peacefully returning Walvis Bay to Namibia and charting a new course in South Africa's relations with its neighbors that stressed peaceful co-existence. Mandela also lived up to the letter of what was only a dream of the American financier Bernard Baruch by giving a nod to F. W. de Klerk's decision to dismantle a nuclear arsenal under international supervision. While de Klerk was motivated by fear and political uncertainty, Mandela and other black leaders insisted that nuclear weapons were "not part of South Africa's future" on moral grounds.[8] It would seem, therefore, that Mandela's thoughts and deeds would constitute truths and wisdom that can be attained through science to serve as bases for a new political pragmatism and disciplinary aesthetic. But the *Longman Guide to World Affairs* that list Acheson among modern-day Wise Men only identified Mandela as "South African nationalist . . . spokesman for black civil rights . . . [who] negotiated the end of Apartheid . . . and became South Africa's first truly democratically elected President . . . [and] was awarded the Nobel Prize for Peace . . ."[9]

This present chapter appeals to the postcolonial gaze as basis for challenging the existing commonsense and archives of "world affairs" away from Euro-referentiality and its self-reassuring teleology.[10] It is divided into two sections. The first section deals with the sovereign proclamation by postcolonial intellectuals of authorial autonomy, or the "right" to independently engage in inquiry, analyses, and criticisms based on their own perceptions and modes of thought. It focuses on questions on the validity of a postcolonial epistemic proposition (viz., *reverse ethnography*[11]) and a related mode of engagement (sarcasm and irony). So-called reverse ethnography stands for the position that the outward gaze of the formerly colonized may shed new lights on modern politics, its political ethos, cultural roots, and intellectual rituals. This proposition has been rejected by Western analyses on both methodological and ontological grounds involving the value of the postcolonial gaze at the West and the neutrality and credibility of postcolonial representations of Western practices, political programs, and thoughts, particularly those implicated in the colonial act. The principle of the postcolonial gaze has been advanced with a principled determination by postcolonial entities to not seek prior institutional authorization and to not abide disciplinary referentiality on the object and form of inquiry. These positions have raised alarm because they lead to nonnormativity (of speech acts) and nonconformity to method (in the sphere of theory production) in contexts supposedly better suited for dialogue and communication.

The second section of the present chapter contrast two teleologies related to the sovereign postcolonial *prise de parole*. The one forwarded by reverse ethnography and its forms is to legitimize new identities — based on more inclusive definitions of the place, role, and function of the agents, actors and subjects of global politics — and to validate their perceptions and responses to existing practices, rituals, and ethos of global politics. In the inverse, the aim of the bulk of objections to the postcolonial gaze and its modes of engagements is to impugn the credibility and legitimacy of any knowledge produced outside of existing Western canons, its analytical methods, and discursive traditions. The reasons are political and ideological, as the objections are often accompanied by extra-discursive means intended to silence postcolonial criticisms.

I use for illustrations French reactions to readings by Daniel Ouezzin Coulibaly, political director of RDA from 1947 to 1950. The context is

Coulibaly's reading of the aims of postwar French political programs. As I show, the postwar context, particularly upon the Trans-Atlantic Alliance, is devoid of moral respect for anticolonialists. Nor are French deputies interested in engaging their anticolonial critics on the substance of arguments alone. Their ill-will toward anticolonialists are only thinly disguised by cynicism and the desire to either assimilate, co-opt, or silence critics of the emergent policy rationalities. The resulting marginalization of Coulibaly and other RDA radicals illustrates both the power of institutional affectations and a longstanding ambivalence and opposition to the gaze of the colonized and its expressions.

Sufficient Truths, Inappropriate Questions

Although coming from different disciplinary and regional perspectives, Tzvetan Todorov[12] and Anthony G. Hopkins[13] proclaim commitment to intellectual, cultural, and political exchanges between Western intellectuals and others. They propose humanism (for Todorov) and British cultural history (for Hopkins) as the proper if not exclusive contexts of global values, norms, and institutions—the bases of global exchanges and communications. They are miffed by the insistence of postcolonial critics that there exist links between humanism, colonialism, and modernity, on the one hand, and global material inequities and social malaises, on the other. Against related postcolonial criticism, Todorov and Hopkins have recently felt the need to defend European ideas, cultures, and empires against the "sort of science" practiced by postcolonial scholars[14] and the "new direction" taken by postcolonial scholars in regard to "imperial" history.[15] Together they charge that the methods of postcolonial theorists are nonnormative, eclectic, and nonsensical and that postcolonial critics are not interested in good-faith communication and the free exchange of ideas. Second, they reject as misguided postcolonial views of Western scientific and cultural practices, particularly in regard to their connections to the "colonial project." Indeed, they admonish postcolonial critics to abandon their "wayward ways" and modes of inquiry in order to necessarily embrace the epistemological and ontological fields charted by Western canons and intellectuals.

Textual "Warfare": Normativity and Cultural Reductionism

Todorov's views of postcolonial utterances are indirect, that is only through associations of the former with anti-humanism and relativism.

Todorov demurs their faulty science, specifically their failure to appreciate the value of post-Enlightenment humanism as an instrument of progress. He detects a lack of subjective affinity on their part with the objects of their criticisms: authors and texts. Todorov associates postcolonial scholarship with these forms of relativism and anti-humanism because the former needlessly maintains "that the experience of the other—individual or collective—is essentially incommunicable . . . forever impossible." Like naturalists and anti-humanists, therefore, postcolonial theorists oppose the idea of elaborating a universal language in which human experiences can be made intelligible to all.[16] Todorov reserves his scorn for the idea that postcolonial critics may productively engage in *reverse ethnography*— by which he means an ethnography of the West by those who formerly assumed the role of object of colonial anthropology: "the former indigenous people may of course 'ethnographize' the Europeans, but the result will not be different from the result that the Europeans themselves could achieve, after *detaching* themselves from their own society."[17]

Todorov's aim is to ascertain the truth-value of humanism against the errors of anti-humanism and relativism reflected by arguments on nationalism, racism, and exoticism.[18] To defend the merits of humanism and its relevance to ethical life today, Todorov reappraises the influences of the likes of Rousseau, Montesquieu, Montaigne, La Bruyère, and Diderot on modern French thought and moral discourses broadly construed. Todorov weaves a history of thought together with political moral philosophy in order to clarify humanist ideas of race that are central to postcolonial criticisms of the Enlightenment.[19] He is not interested in the doctrines of race that justified conquest, but he wishes to raise questions about the meanings of texts and their political, ethical, and philosophical implications.[20]

In this latter regard, Todorov likens the attitudes of anti-humanists and relativists toward the Enlightenment and humanist texts to "textual warfare."[21] He confesses to have practiced it himself: "I have not always avoided it." Still, he reproaches anti-humanists and relativists of feeling "only hostility" toward certain ideas and texts in a way that makes "dialogue impossible." This is particularly the case when critics rely on "satire and irony."[22] Postcolonial critics too use irony and satire to drive home their messages. Given Todorov's associations of postcolonial critique with anti-humanism and relativism, he must assume that the formerly colonized are also uninterested in dialogue.[23]

A cultural historian of the British empire, Hopkins too is alarmed by the methods of postcolonial scholarship that, he maintains, undermine productive exchanges in the academy and the emergence of universal norms.[24] Yet, he has different concerns than Todorov. While Todorov imputes anti-universalist thought to nineteenth-century nationalism and racism, Hopkins seeks to defend the virtues of empire against denigrations by postcolonial criticisms based on eclectic views, drawn on the findings of multiple disciplines: particularly historical revisionism, deconstruction, and postmodernism.[25] He insists that the empire produced an elite and culture that laid "the foundation of a global, fully integrated, universal order for the benefit of all humanity"[26] — in short, today's international morality.[27]

Against this background, he regrets that postcolonial cultural criticism has not helped to develop "a novel type of comparative history, one that spans colonial borders and joins Africa to Australia."[28] Such a history might "demonstrate the complementarity of colonial history and indigenous history and the ways in which cultural and material forces have interacted . . . for good or for ill."[29] Instead, according to Hopkins, postcolonial criticisms provide only emotional, subjective, and irrational responses to cross-cultural relations and global politics.[30] They tend to postulate a "stereotype of the European master narrative" and to project a totalizing enterprise "on to an identikit picture of subject peoples, referred to as the Other, in order to demonstrate that many Europeans held racist views."[31] He then echoes the widely shared view among critics of postcolonial scholarship that the latter perspectives are ill-motivated, incompetent, and not conducive to truth-seeking and political pragmatism[32] These critics also argue that postcolonial perspectives are hindrances rather than contributions to cross-cultural and cross-regional engagements.

Neither Todorov nor Hopkins directly comment on the substance of postcolonial thoughts or ideas. They conclude that postcolonial theorists are uninterested in communication across cultural, intellectual, and territorial boundaries on the sole basis of their "observations" of postcolonial modes of expression or forms of analyses.[33] Hopkins is put off by the fact that, under the inspiration of Edward Said, postcolonial theorists reduce science (philosophy or history) and its objects, "realities," to "representations" and thus prefer "texts" to "contexts."[34] This is to say that postcolonial critics of imperialism and its cultures favor speech acts with great rhetorical effects over the scientific validity of their claims. If Hopkins is to be taken seriously that postcolonial speech acts have no truth-value, then their primary signification would be that "the empire strike back" rather than "write back"—in English.[35] Hopkins's arguments point to Todorov's view of textual warfare, a situation that obtains "when one has nothing in common with the author one is confronting, when one feels hostility for his ideas, [when] dialogue becomes impossible."[36]

Whereas Hopkins berates postcolonial scholarship for its "lack of humor" and "eloquent capacity for self-parody," Todorov complains that postcolonial speech acts (writings) are gratuitously ironic, sarcastic, satirical, and worse. Irony, according to the *Oxford English Dictionary*, is a figure of speech in which the intended meaning is the opposite of that expressed by the words used.[37] Satire, in this logic, is a rhetorical form, prose, or speech act in which the author holds up prevailing follies or vices to ridicule.[38] Finally, a parody is a composition in prose or verse in which the characteristic turns of thought, phrase, or action are imitated in such a manner as to prove them ridiculous or ludicrous.[39] On the other hand, sarcasm is said to be a "sharp, bitter, and cutting expression or remark; a bitter gibe or taunt" intended to make false pretenses conspicuous. In this sense, sarcasm has much in common with irony.[40] Sarcasm is believed to be unsuited to sustained composition, although it figures prominently in debates as retort. It affects as well as reflects the general context of the exchange and the dynamics and formulations of language.[41] Satire, on the other hand, is believed to be a higher rhetorical form. It is a prose or speech-act in which the author holds up prevailing follies or vices to ridicule.[42]

There are significant differences between these modes of expressions that underscore their validity in different contexts. The first differences are between satire, irony, and parody, on the one hand, and sarcasm, on the other. One is that satire, irony, and parody lend themselves to sustained and formal arguments and, as such, are easily susceptible to systematic prohibition. Sarcasm, in contrast, depends more on the contexts of utterances than their composition. It retains a degree of ambiguity toward its objects, which can only be clarified by the context of the exchange. This is to say that the effectivity of sarcasm depends equally upon the author's intentions and the listener's sensibilities. In other words, sarcasm is most effective when the target (its object) succumbs to the author's intended effects or impressions.

Based on these distinctions, it is ironic that, although they complain about postcolonial "textual warfare," Todorov and Hopkins refuse to substantively engage postcolonial scholarship. This rule of no-engagement rule depreciates the truth dimensions and/or scientific validity of the latter in that it is based on a caricature, or set of comic imitations, that depreciates its objects. One omitted dimension of postcolonial analyses is that they are at once discourses of self and criticisms of colonial projects and programs. But these are not monological theoretical models. Rather, than describe a singular colonial experience and a singular colonial act, postcolonial analyses emerge from multiple colonial legacies and trajectories and as such reflect diverse colonial histories, distinct linguistic and scientific reasoning, and loci of enunciations.[43]

This kind of parody was the cachet of colonial anthropology and ethnography of natives unrecognizable to themselves. The elements of this parody are not only inaccurate, its motivation is principally the kind of intellectual or political cynicism against which the colonized frequently opposed sarcasm—a short corrective retort pretended as a complement but is actually a devastating rejoinder. In the colonial context, sarcasm often served as a *rappel á l'ordre*, or a call to order, that countered colonial self-centeredness and its twin oblivion to the other. A rhetorical taunt, sarcasm is used to signal disagreement with texts and/or their authors. The utility of sarcasm lies in the fact that it is more difficult to root out, as the author can easily feign innocence when confronted by his/her "victims." For these reasons, colonial authorities frequently sought to identify those most likely to resort to sarcastic remarks for the purpose of preemptive actions, including censure, imprisonment, and worse.[44] Nor has the academy's reaction to sarcasm been charitable. For instance, in a telling moment, Hopkins offers "passing sympathy for Herman Goering's otherwise wholly deplorable reaction in drawing his revolver on hearing the word culture."[45] By this remark, Hopkins sought to signify the abuses of "the word and world of culture" in postcolonial theories.

The use of sarcasm is not without paradoxes. The audience—authority or listener—may dismiss a sincere rejoinder on the grounds of nonnormativity. The authority that feels "victimized" by sarcasm may repress its authors. In this latter context, public authorities (including the colonial state) frequently take sarcasm to imply the absence of good faith and goodwill depending on their inclination, interest, and power. Under these circumstances, the charge of sarcasm necessarily shifts attention away from the substance of the parties' competing positions or claims in the interest of power disguised as norms. Otherwise, sarcasm does not in itself obscure the truth dimensions or meanings of the critiqued "texts" or authors.[46] Nor is sarcasm unconnected to truth claims.

The temptation of critics of postcolonial sarcasm is often to disallow or ignore something called criticisms on account of their forms—and not substance. This temptation is at once misguided and dangerous. It is misguided because postcolonial analyses and discourses necessarily reflect the legacies of different colonial trajectories, their modes of administration, and the extent of participation of subject populations in the political economic and the production of knowledge. The degree and sphere of this participation continue to affect contemporary memories of empire and related topics and themes of inquiry. The call to censure ignores this context and unduly privileges the locutionary effects of speech acts over both the condition of possibility of utterances and the context of their reception. Second, the temptation to censure is dangerous because of its totalitarian and repressive impulse. As I show later in the context of French legislative debates, censorship seeks to disallow speech acts and utterances that are routinely practiced across space and time, including in liberal and humanist traditions, as legitimate forms of retort and counterpoint as well as effective instruments of communication.

Whither Reverse Ethnography

Reverse ethnography is neither a science nor a method. It is a name given by critics of postcolonial approaches to an analytical proposition that commands postcolonial entities to set their gaze outward on Europe and the West as means to understanding modern society, law, and morality. Lately this proposition has led to a number of "offensive" analyses and formulations. One is that geographical Europe is but a province of both the moral and physical universe. This view is adjoined by the view that the mythical or symbolic Europe of Occidentalist fantasy and Western theory has no superior attributes over other moral entities. Finally, it is premise of reverse ethnography that Europe and the West are not above reproach and their behavior and policies are the proper object of analyses. To provincialize Europe, in this context, is to position oneself against the political, cultural, and economic structures upon which the West had built its claims to political hegemony, moral authority, and economic exploitation of the Rest. Reverse ethnography thus construed brings back Europe into moral discourses as interlocutor of others, themselves once objectified by Western sciences, particularly anthropology, as less than equal being.

Todorov rejects the viability of *reverse ethnography*. He is particularly contemptuous of the notion that there exist semiotic structures, idioms, and discourses of universalism and rationalism outside of Enlightenment ideologies and its their successor intellectual movements.[47] He is also unconvinced that the formerly colonized have shown independent endogenous capacity as analysts and readers to separate themselves from their potential objects: Western societies and texts. To bolster his arguments, Todorov denounces the influence of cultural relativism and anti-humanism on postcolonial criticism which, he assumes, are a function of the rise of structural Marxism, phenomenology, existentialism, and associated theories and perspectives in the aftermath of World War II. Todorov argues that related approaches negated not only the legitimacy of Western values, institutions, and science but also their relevancy to global salvation. By relying on them, reverse ethnography devolves in revisionism and reductionism and, thus, contributes to the breakdown of cross-regional exchange and the quest for universal values.

Based on Todorov's accounts, reverse ethnography amounts to a futile but dangerous exercise. First, reverse ethnography lacks scientific rationale in that it rests principally on parochial preoccupations whereas "ethnological knowledge itself is inconceivable without reference to universality, of the sort practiced by modern science."[48] Second, reverse ethnography rests on parochial preoccupations whereas modern science depends upon the faculty of reflexivity. This is the capacity of the properly instructed scientists to symbolically and emotively detach or distance themselves from their own societies. Reflexivity leads to self-criticism, skepticism, realism, and transparency.[49] The observer thus detached or distanced from the self is able, in a second movement, to approach the other empathically as point of comparison or construct.[50] According to Todorov, this second movement is indispensable to the necessary comparative approach to self-understanding.[51]

These two principles are the bases of *ethnographic distancing*, an epistemic move already perfected by Western humanists and liberals. According to Todorov, ethnographic distancing is predicated upon the motivation of the self due to reason to consider the other or to adjust to the needs of the external observer. It also assumes that the self is capable of transcending the biases and limitations of its methods and modes of thought in order to meet the requirements of any external observers. The teleology of ethnographic distancing is the attainment of more useful information or knowledge, one likely to lead to mutual understanding and impartial (better) judgment of the behaviors of the self and others. On these counts, Todorov claims, Western theorists possess sufficient methodological designs to reach objectivity by metaphysically removing themselves from the ontological grounds upon which their societies have imposed coherence on social knowledge and its representations.

I do not question the merit of ethnographic distancing. Michael J. Shapiro, for instance, has eloquently demonstrated the value of ethnographic distancing in comparative analyses that involve one's own society and/or culture.[52] Unlike Todorov, Shapiro does not claim the sufficiency of ethnographic distancing. For, while ethnographic distancing comes from self-awareness and thus provides a standpoint for reflexive thought, it does not necessarily alter the gaze or its direction. Nor does ethnographic distancing necessarily or inherently dispense with the Eurocentrist or Occidentalist filters through which the Western gaze takes effect.

Reflexive or not, the pathos of ethnographic distancing (an instance of the Western gaze) and reverse ethnography (an instance of the postcolonial gaze) are similar. They necessarily reflect subjective biases. For this reason, ethnographic distancing and reverse ethnography seldom converge in function and teleology. Thus, one cannot expect ethnographic distancing to be sufficiently and reassuringly empathetic to its other. I suspect that Todorov's (and Hopkins's) anxiety around the postcolonial gaze suggest a discomfort at being misunderstood once postcolonial scholars set aside Western rationalism, its modes of inquiry, and self-referentiality.[53] In short, ethnographic distancing and reverse ethnography perform two distinct functions. Specifically, reverse ethnography affords the postcolonial analyst the freedom to gaze and to autonomously analyze. It is an empirical question whether the analysis is reflexive or not. But, from an ethical point of view, there are no grounds to authorize ethnographic distancing while proscribing reverse ethnography, or vice versa. A better solution might be to declare both reverse ethnography and ethnographic distancing valid because they collectively foster cross-cultural and cross-regional comparison of the respective understandings of self and others.

The opposite solution is rife with problems. Thus, in order to abide ethnographic distancing and to dispense with reverse ethnography, Todorov must return to two pillars of Occidentalist ethnographic thought. The first is that, while all persons are endowed with subjective faculties, only rationalists (i.e., Western subjects) have both the capacity to discern and the motivation to judge in an objective manner. Self-judgment is given only to persons and entities with adequate customs, artistic and scientific expressions as well as familiarity with government and the laws of property and exchanges.[54] The few thus endowed are capable of reliable judgment, that is one with redeemable truth value.[55] Because these persons and moral entities are reliable judges of themselves and their actions, they are not fallible in the same manners as others. They can redeem themselves.[56]

In contrast, others are largely presumed to be less curious, less motivated, and less influenced by the passage of time. They are thus less able to detach in order to attain the requisite objectively necessary for scientific observations. They are not qualified therefore to legislate for themselves and the self. Consistently, Todorov does not think that, at the moment of reverse ethnographic gaze, postcolonial theorists are capable of distancing themselves for purposes of reflexivity.[57] Unlike himself, a stand-in for rational humanists, postcolonial critics are presumably incapable of reflexivity, detachment, and translation or comparative analysis. Whereas the self may legitimately proclaim detachment while conducting an ethnography of the other, Todorov preemptively holds the others' critical gazes to be suspect by attributing to them priori motives of revisionism and disinterest in "observable realities" and "knowable facts".

Again, Todorov is not alone in his contempt of the idea that postcolonial critics may productively engage in reverse ethnography. For Hopkins, the mind's eyes of the British cultural historian and "his" methods remain the incontrovertible means to understanding the imperial project and its cultural legacy.[58] While Todorov is not as attached to imperial history and culture as Hopkins, he is insistent that Western theorists, philosophers, and publicists possess the appropriate methods for attaining objectivity. Ethnography, combining the findings of yesteryear's anthropology and today's ethnographic distancing, allow the rational theorists to metaphysically remove themselves from the ontological grounds upon which their societies imagined themselves as coherent entities. Having proclaimed the sufficiency of these two movements to the social scientific enterprise, Todorov does not seem to value reverse ethnography. Besides, reverse ethnography might yet be beholden to the prediscursive motivations, incompetence, and deviancy of the formerly colonized.

Methods, Exocriticism, and Disciplinary Exchanges

Todorov's insistence on dialogue among cultures and regions is not new. Yet, he underestimates the degree to which the worlds of the other influenced, through socalled exocriticism, Enlightenment-era constructions of both modern "reality" and the "empirical evidence" for it. Exocriticism allowed humanists and anti-humanists alike to internalize native voices in fashioning their criticisms of their own social environments. These natives voices were also the means by which they demonstrated the truth dimensions of humanism and liberal sensibilities. The likes of François-Marie Arouet (Voltaire)[59] and Dénis Diderot[60] espoused *exoticism and exocriticism* as points of departure of reflexive philosophy. Voltaire envisaged exocriticism as possible commentaries by the native, or "man-in-nature," on the perversities of European life. Diderot, on the other hand, took the presumed standpoint of the native as point of departure of comparative analysis intended to map out cultural possibilities for liberal(izing) forces in Europe. In many ways exocriticism assembled elements of ethnographic distance and reverse ethnography. It also combined analytical methods favored by reverse ethnography, including the use of nonnormative speech acts as means to highlighting the inadequacies of existing orthodoxies and the everyday. Indeed, in their scorn of conservative French orthodoxies and prejudices, both Voltaire and Diderot combined conventional political writings with irony and satire. These writings and speech acts were intended to sow doubts in the minds of those converted to French orthodoxies by exposing the fallacies and spaciousness of conservative arguments.[61]

Voltaire used the figure of the other to bolster his case against political and religious conventions and customs. The terms of comparison were straightforward: to expose the rigidities of French customs (particularly social mores) and the datedness of its authoritarian political traditions, Voltaire imagined what the simple-minded native would think of them. The imaginary looking eye of the native added perspective and potency to his arguments, given that French political and cultural pretensions were bound up in imperial conquests among others. Accordingly, the imaginary commentaries of the native necessarily captivated the attention of conservatives and their opponents for the purpose of debating the rigidities of French social environment.

In *L'Ingénu*, Voltaire depicts a simple-minded Huron who comes to France only to find a less than ideal country. He is disappointed to discover that French existence did not coincide with the dictates of religion and humanism.[62] Despite his critical observations, the Huron must still defer to French rationalism. Not only does the ingénu continuously remind us of the absurdity of his past way of life, Voltaire insist upon pointing endlessly to the simplistic methods of inquiry by which the Huron exposes the conjuncture of oppression in French society. Once the ingénu concedes that his wayward manners do not compare with rational sensibilities, and thus should be abandoned as a matter of wisdom, he is spared from persecution. In the end, Voltaire implores his readers to tolerance for even the unwise—"those who expose themselves to persecution in their pursuit of esoteric disputes." The tormentors of the unwise, he opines, "seem to me to be monsters."[63]

As with Voltaire, Diderot's native is an affable character who invites tolerance and empathy from "those for whom the love of liberty is the deepest of all feelings." Indeed, Diderot begins his *Supplement to the Voyage of Bougainville* with denunciations of the manner in which the native Tahitian, "a brother," is illegitimately "ensnared like an animal."[64] This brother offered "his fruits, his wife, his daughter [and] his hut," only to be "killed ... for a handful of beads which he took without asking."[65] For these sorts of behavior, "The Tahitian either fails entirely to understand [French] customs and laws, or he sees them as nothing but fetters ... which can only inspire indignation and scorn."[66] Then, Diderot exhorts his countrymen to "Witness in your mind's eye" the spectacle of Tahitian hospitality and "to tell me what you think of the human race."[67] Diderot imagines the resulting narrative about humanity to dispense with "holy orders" and to "show gratitude," to accept the ways of Tahiti.[68]

The ways of Tahiti are exemplified and narrated by Orou, "your host and friend." It is Orou who conclusively shows Diderot the limits of imperial reason and colonial rationality: "You can't condemn the ways of Europe in the light of those of Tahiti, nor consequently the ways of Tahiti in the light of those of your country."[69] It is also at Orou's behest that Diderot must find "a more reliable standard" of judgment, one that defies the dialectic of rationalism, neither severe nor lax, one that maximizes the "general welfare and individual utility."[70] Orou himself is not without judgment of French ways, for one who is severe is a "beast fighting against nature" and one who is the opposite is a useless imbecile.[71] These teachings are as significant for bourgeois and decadent France as Orou's views of "justice and property," the institutions that allow modern men to "be arbitrary," that is to "attribute or deny good or evil to actions on no other grounds than whim." For it is property that brings individuals to "suspect one another . . . to trample upon others . . . to become envious, jealous, deceitful, distressed, secretive, covert, spying upon another to take him or her by surprise." It is the quest of property and the desire to acquire it at the expense of the other that "misery" to colonies and, conversely, brings dishonor to the idea of legislation. Here, as in the realm of private morality, "a law is published, a dishonorable world invented, a punishment determined."[72]

Diderot is nonetheless clear that while one must "wear the country you visit," one must also "keep your own clothes for the journey home."[73] The journey home was the site of translation, when the writer determines the value of other cultures and their relevance to their own social context. This is where imperial reason must prevail. In Diderot's "mind's eyes," Orou must be allowed to satirize and parody French conservative ways and authoritarian orthodoxies, but only insofar as he affirms his liberal (hedonist?) sensibilities.[74] In the final analysis, however, Orou must defer to French wisdom and sovereign authority. The teleology of contact for Diderot remains the conversion of the native to French civilization, albeit cleansed of superstition and conceit.

Exocriticism proved successful in the context of early Enlightenment. The illustration of the "obvious" through the "standpoint of man-in-nature" was a marked improvement upon earlier self-adulating forms of reflexive philosophy. It allowed individuals like Voltaire and Diderot to present their criticisms of French society and institutions comparatively as possible commentaries by the other. Yet, the methods had limitations. Exocriticism lacked the hermeneutic and linguistic tools for an empathetic comparative approach of the Métropole and so-called native societies. It depended principally on fictionalized accounts of native perspectives on the Métropole on terms defined alternatively by European (here French) humanists and naturalists. In the hand of humanists like Voltaire, the imagined native visitor was made to make observations and appreciations that only served to reinforce the universality of the human condition and the equally universal human responses to it. For their part, French anti-humanists such as Diderot represented native cultures as self-sustaining systems or models with the explicit purpose of highlighting alternative modes of being and the need for Europe to change "outdated" traditions. In both instances, exocriticism was founded upon furtive and self-serving analogies, resemblances, and differences such that its internalized native voices necessarily supported the relevant metropolitan sensibilities. In both, the "encountered," Europe was presumptively the object of the gaze, but the terms of observations were seldom those of the "encounterer"— dare I say discoverer!

Exocriticism was inevitably inattentive to the diversity and complexities of "native" traditions, it was assimilationist in character. It reflexively internalized native voices, perspectives, and commentaries on the Métropole. As a result, the colonized native could not offer unauthorized critiques and commentaries—certainly not ones founded upon their own experiences of alienation, the desire for autonomy and emancipation, and the will to freedom. Second, whether intended or not, exocriticism paradoxically endorsed the legitimacy of the collective French will to hegemony and the colonial enterprise. While it effectively drew attention to the rigidities of French social environment, exocriticism comparatively upheld one central tenet of colonialism: the asserted superiority of French civilization over native cultures and traditions.

Reflexive Thoughts: Ethnographies and Criticisms

Exocriticism may serve as a good metaphor for ethnographic distance in that both depend upon the revelations of the "mind's eyes." But exocriticism provided something that is lacking in ethnographic distancing. In exocriticism, the "mind's eyes" is presumptively that of the other. It placed stock in the others' perspectives, even if those perspectives were imaginary and translated and narrated entirely by the self for itself. In contrast, ethnographic distancing effects reflexivity through self-conscious but endogenous movements away from the sources of affective attachments to self and toward objective self-discovery. To this end, adepts hope to develop scientific or discursive methods or rationalism that favor objectivity in research and reflection. Thus imbued with confidence, adepts of ethnographic distancing dismiss comparative approaches, whether real or fictive, to culture, politics, and ethics.

Whatever the intentions of their authors, exocriticism and ethnographic distancing have been more than intrusive and usurpatory in practice. They both have erased and/or silenced the other in significant way. Voltaire and Diderot, for instance, canvassed native culture for attractive cultural traits; but they were not interested in comparative appreciation of the other(s)' cultures. The worthy or interpellated native recognizes the inherent superiority of Western civilization. Hence, the little Huron necessarily held France in esteem and was only disappointed that the monarchy and the religious hierarchy did not live up to the ideals of French grandeur. Orou too was a worthy native because of the correspondence of his views with those of the enlightened and emergent French liberals. In both instances, the natives necessarily admired French society and progressive traditions and, as a result, were deferential to their French translators and interlocutors. In return, their role and attitude cast the *ingénu* and Orou as mature, reasonable, and worthy of consideration. These characters have since defined the types of natives who are worthy of solicitation. Others, especially those who are hostile to the colonial-ascribed role and function, are to be ignored, repressed, and/or silenced outright.

Prior to decolonization, sociology, cultural history, and reflective philosophy generally mirrored Western self-consciousness. This self-consciousness was the basis of social science. Whether inspired by rationalism or naturalism, social theory reflected this consciousness by giving into corporeality through academic disciplines or symbolic fields of signification. These modern disciplines and fields gave meanings to diverse social realities while organizing them hierarchically to reflect the primacy or superiority of Europe, the West, and their values, institutions, and methods. Self-consciousness was also the basis of understanding the other. Again throughout the modern era, French humanists and naturalists recognized the value of cross-cultural exchanges and dialogues. But they invariably spoke for the other: the simple-minded, unambitious Huron (Voltaire's ingénu) and the kindly old gent Orou (Diderot's interlocutor).

Corresponding to such fields of signification, Orientalism and Africanism for instance translated native knowledges, rationalities, and aspirations for the self. Orientalism and Africanism thus complemented Occidentalism by both fostering analyses that questioned the legitimacy of the "non-West" to enact international morality and casting doubts on the capacity of the non-West to forward their own modes of inquiry and thought, including political analyses, programmatic narratives, and ethical discourses. Like Occidentalism, Orientalism and Africanism emerged from a European act of sovereignty that claimed for the West the right and authority to not only speak for itself, but to legitimately assume the role of proctor, trustee, and translator for the other. These functions allowed the

West to confidently determine the bases upon which non-Western constituencies would be interpellated.

This Enlightenment-initiated Occidentalist conceit lasted until the end of colonial rule. As a result, rationalists and naturalists alike preached cultural and social transformations through dialogue and exchanges while failing to anticipate the moment of transformation when Europe could not longer internalize the other's views and contain their passions and desires. The conditions of this moment were twofold. One was the predicted familiarization of the colonized with Western religious, intellectual, and ideological canons. The other condition of change, less predictable in its effects, was the colonized's experiences of Europe and thus observations of European actions particularly regarding rights, liberty, and subjectivity.

Upon decolonization, the colonial figure of a kindly old native undergoes transformation. The postcolonial Orou may no longer be content to simply demand that Europe and the West adhere to their own moral codes or that they respect their own laws as an act of generosity. The new "native" now judges the act of conquest to be profoundly oppressive. He understands that the genealogy of this oppression does not rest simply in aberrant behaviors, resulting merely from a discrepancy or contradiction between humanism and rationalism, on the one hand, and the quotidian lives of Europeans, on the other. The seasoned Orou experienced colonialism as a life disrupting event, the result of pernicious political programs rooted in authoritative and, from the standpoint of the West, legitimate traditions. Orou reached this conclusion from observation of events that cast doubts on the premises of humanism and rationalism as well as their claim to dispense liberty and equal justice for all. In short, the new Orou rejects colonial interpretations of the past. So too does the emancipated autonomous Huron now attach distinct meanings to colonial relation, particularly to its political and cultural rationalities as well as its idioms.

It is therefore clear that Todorov's and Hopkins's discussions of postcolonial thoughts and modes of expressions illustrate broader questions in politics, social science, and the humanities about the value, nature, function, and utility of the views, ideas, and thoughts of others. These questions are particularly pertinent to cross-cultural and cross-regional exchanges when the views of the others might reflect on the self, its ideas, and actions. Upon decolonization, rationalism and naturalism no longer retain the monopoly of imagination, narrative, and political discourses pertaining to the encounter of the self and the other. The postcolonial other must assume its own subjectivity as a matter of sovereignty and, as a matter of authorial privilege, determine new ethical standards of judgment, some of which may exceed the normative boundaries envisaged by the colonizers.

In the section that follows, I intend to show that arguments against postcolonial criticisms and modes of expressions are often a red herring. They emanate from the fact that rationalists and naturalists have not accommodated themselves to the new setup. Few visit with ease the sites and narratives of the colonial encounter through postcolonial imageries and sentiments. Specifically, Todorov and Hopkins imagine the postcolonial setup to be inherently hostile or antagonistic to the self. They would rather that postcolonial dialogue reproduce the relationships between European authors and the mythical Orou or the *ingénu* or contemplate censure. At any rate, the scenarios and conditions of scientific and cultural exchanges proposed by Todorov and Hopkins would preserve the integrity of colonial canons and institutions against challenges by the colonized. Unsurprisingly, anti- and postcolonialists reject Occidentalist scenarios and conditions. Postcolonialists too entered the world as knowing subjects and with the intention of validating and/or justifying their views of the colonial event and the postcolonial order.

Specifically, reverse ethnography must not be viewed as a substitute for reflexivity, including "ethnographic distance," and vice versa. To its defenders, *reverse ethnography* is a fitting reply to Western self-understanding, particularly as it relates to its own *anthropological and ethnographic ambition and knowledge* of the other. The telos of sarcasm is getting attention rather than the jibe itself. This means that sarcasm does not inherently dispense wisdom; it merely demands modification of arguments or behavior of an opponent during an exchange. Nor is reverse ethnography a substitute for reflexivity. The former is analogous to a window through which the formerly colonized cast its gaze through available methodologies upon colonialism and its ontology, beyond self-professed intentions. This window allows the formerly colonized to shed light on certain moral questions bearing on the universal human condition that may fall outside of the expressed concerned of the former colonial powers. Indeed, it allows the formerly colonized to capture the West in its most unsuspecting and unauthorized moments and, through its modes of inquiry to reexamine the claims made by the cultural historian and the reflexive philosopher.

The point here is *not* to ascertain that reverse ethnography produces the "better results." Each standpoint allows for the examination of questions that are peculiar to their subjects' understandings of self and international existence. Thus, in contrast to reverse ethnography, ethnographic distance is the metaphorical mirror that imperial reason holds to itself in order to show to others that which it wishes them to see. Like Enlightenment-era exocriticism, the implied reflexivity of ethnographic distance does not unto itself guarantee transcendentalism, or transcultural communication and moral exchange. Nor are its methods and discourses uniquely redemptory, that is that they guarantee ethical outcomes in human interactions. In short, neither reverse ethnography nor ethnographic distancing leads inherently to goodwill in regard to trans-boundary (transcultural) communications. They merely enrich our moral dispositions—including empathy, identification, detachment, distance, assimilation, syncretism—and enrich the quality of our judgment.

The Other Side Of Time: No Longer Kindly Old Gents

Something akin to reverse ethnography played a significant role in anticolonial commentaries on French and Western policies. The similarities begin with the setup. First, wartime events and postwar French political experiments offered an opportune moment to the colonized to offer their views on the international order and international reality. Second, the reversal of roles between the colonizer and the colonized as subject and object of the analytical gaze. This shift in the direction and function of the scientific gaze was not without consequences. In particular, it created a high level of anxiety and discomfort within the French public and political establishment. Third, both reverse ethnography and anticolonial commentaries invest the anthropological gaze with a moral and political ambition. In the following section, I focus on tensions in the French Senate and political scene arising from comments by Daniel Ouezzin Coulibaly. As senator, Coulibaly aspired to, first, debunk the mendacious notion that imperial reason may provide a credible critique of colonialism and, two, to make a case against the postwar French political fantasies, or pathologies.

Imperial Anxieties, Political Languages

Like any country, France is ultimately an amalgamation of individuals and communities, and cultures and institutions. These entities exist naturally within complementary (inclusive) as well as conflicting (exclusive) relations. Consistently, postwar French politicians asked complementary as well as conflicting questions about the causes and consequences of defeat and "submission to the reality of defeat." This was especially true of the political left. However reluctantly, they generally contemplated postwar dilemmas in universal (if not scientific) terms based on like claims about human nature and/or condition, the political and cultural foundations of order, the causes of conflict and anarchy. They entertained in equally universal terms questions about the telos of the world order (particularly of international morality and its economy of rights and privileges); the direction of the political economy (indeed, the future of colonial capitalism!); the cultural dislocations of empire (caused by the threshold of rationality and political autocracy); and the question of the other (representations and their contents).

French elites also had to contend with a new reality. Political tragedy had revealed the fragility of the imperial order and undermined one of its pillars: that France was inherently slated to produce the public good and to lay the institutional and constitutional foundations of politics, political deliberations, and governance. France, at least the dissidence, also had contracted a 'blood debt' (*dette de sang*) from colonial subjects (and their Western allies too). These subjective factors of weakness, debt, and vulnerability propelled postwar French politics toward a deliberative and voluntary thrust. These events also influenced the direction of politics, the paths of French anticolonialists, and the languages of politics.

The outcome was mixed. As illustrated in chapters 3 and 4, the rethinking of politics was infused with sympathy for and gratitude toward the colonized for their role in the war. This sentiment was augmented by longstanding traditions of anticolonialism among the French left—and to a limited degree on the political right. Untold numbers of intellectuals and politicians active in the resistance had also established political ties with anticolonialists on the African continent and, as such, could boast personal knowledge or acquaintance with the circumstances of the colonized. Indeed, a number of left-leaning French citizens represented African constituencies in French legislative bodies. Significantly, they engaged the colonized in post-Enlightenment idioms thus making these idioms the principal media of communication in postwar France and in the colonies.

On the other hand, French elites did not pose new questions on public morality, political economy, and rationalism. Instead, they rephrased old questions regarding the origin, nature, and trajectory of sovereignty, capitalism, and the rule of law. They placed their observations in the context of their perceived limitations, if not failure, of post-Enlightenment philosophical and political reason as well as related values and institutions. The goal was to explore the relationships between ways of knowing individual and collective experiences and the imagination of the proper means of survival. They also sought to channel the postwar mood toward an examination of time and the temporal dimensions of politics. Related debates fostered philosophical skepticism and the relativism of cultures and traditions.

The return to the Enlightenment-era themes of the human condition and solidarity testified to the rebirth of consciousness about the uniformity of life and its exigencies everywhere. It also signified a real willingness of a significant part of the French left to engage the colonized.[75] Still, state actions both fostered and hampered transimperial solidarity and political action. For instance, Vichy's collaboration with the Nazi regime, its deportation of Jews, and the reaffirmation of French colonial ambitions created sympathies and, in some instances, unity of purpose among factions of the colonized and metropolitan minorities such as Jews. These entities were not only unified by the betrayal by "official France" of the humanist ideals of solidarity by surrendering Jews to Vichy, but also by reneging on the wartime promise to break with colonial traditions, and thus prolonging the experience of racism and discrimination for colonial populations. Indeed, on such occasions, despite the unevenness of their material endowments and institutional capacities, the concerned subjects drew on comparable moral resources and faculties to aspire to a different moral order.

Nor could the state singly orient all cultural and intellectual flows that traversed the colonial settings of state and empire. French political organizations and cultural associations often brought together disparate constituencies into political and ideological alliances to explore political rationality in the context of the respective experiences of their members with modernity, empire, and the international system. They helped to channel and orient political sentiments and actions. Related processes of exchange, teaching, and learning did not result in a single dynamic as colonizers and colonized participated on equal terms in the determination of the appropriate political and moral course. Held against the background of Vichy, wartime and postwar reflections centered on the state, society, and the law, or public morality, on the one hand, and humanism, its institutions, and moral sciences, on the other. Such reflections encompassed skepticism if not suspicion of the sufficiency of reason (rationalism), structuralism, and Marxist dialectics, and their manifestations in politics: sovereign violence, militarism, authoritarianism, totalitarianism, and Nazism.

It remains that the experiences and memories of the various entities of the empire with modernity and violence, the trauma of war, historical rootlessness, imperialism, and political subjectivity varied greatly. The relationships of subjects to state and empire accounted for some of the variations. In turn, these variations resulted in different moral and political orientations. This to say that political and ethical concerns were mediated thus by identity, the experiences with violence and traumas, and degrees of alienation from the state. They were also shaped by ideological perceptions of the causes of subjective privation—identity, religion, culture, language, territory—and their expressions in law, politics, and moral discourses. In short, political and moral discourses were invariably attentive to questions of state, empire, society, and law, but these questions were suffused in consciousness, memory, and intentionality, resulting from differentiated experiences.

It is to be expected, therefore, that not all metropolitan reflections resonated with the colonized. The ones that did were inspired by Marxism, existentialism, and phenomenology, all implicated in fundamental critiques of modernity. Their adepts were influenced by the likes of F. G. W. Hegel, Friedrich Nietzsche, Sigmund Freud, Edmund Husserl, Martin Heidegger, and other proponents and critics of modernity who had diagnosed the crises of modern European society, science, and culture. Among them, French existentialists—including Maurice Merleau-Ponty,[76] Jean Paul Sartre,[77] and Albert Camus[78]—established connections between modernity (as manifested by Western rationalism), war (as manifestation of violence), and technology (particularly the bourgeoning industry of violence). Whether communist or not, they reflected on the meanings of modernity and the implications for it of the increasing role of violence, driven particularly by the ideology of sovereignty and the imperial act of conquest, slavery, and colonialism. These reflections also provided insights to the place of historical consciousness and intentionality in imagining the future. They were also among the first groups to openly accept the notion that the war might have been experienced differently across time and space. They highlighted the particularity of capitalism and colonialism in a bid to rescue universalism from a compromised colonial pragmatism. They denounced capitalist exploitation and colonial autocracy and authoritarianism; yet, warned against the dangers of anticolonial alienation and violence. They also postulated the possibility of disentangling the rationalist project of human emancipation from the history and trajectory of the colonial project and its cartography (if not economy) of power and rights.[79]

A great many Marxists and existentialists, for instance, rethought the relationships between France and the empire. Consistently, they sought to rid themselves of colonial prejudices and their structure of ideologies and social relations. Existentialists in particular struggled with their personal ambivalence and the ambiguities of their positions vis-à-vis the world of politics. Merleau-Pointy put their dilemmas in starker term as a choice between "living the unreflective life through engagement and experience, but then being unable to reflect; or withdrawing from the everyday in order to reflect, but then losing the ability to apprehend the real structures of the everyday."[80] Likewise, Marx(ists)' "vision of emancipation entailed a journey beyond the notion of juridical equality that liberalism holds so sacred."[81] In short, the new theories and views augured "radical" beginnings on the role of subjectivity, the nature of science and rationalism, and their derivative values and institutions.

Whether in the political or theoretical spheres, French gestures and overtures toward the colonized occurred within the parameters of centuries-old intellectual and political traditions and related cultural practices. They suffered from colonial and historicist views of the others, their cultures, traditions, and habits. The colonial order placed an emphasis on the identity and subjectivity of participants such that one side, the colonizer, was identified duly as sovereign, autonomous, and knowledgeable and, thus, legislator and teacher with will, desire, and interest, all deducible from intentionality. In this colonial ontology, the identity and subjectivity of the colonized depended upon their subordinate status, their inability to will, their lack of intentionality, and thus their capacities for moral learning and sociability.

These political discourses rendered the colonized and the empire visible to the French public. African anticolonialists appreciated these French perspectives as much as they did the political support of some segments of the French left. This appreciation accounted for the choice of language of colonial representatives as well as the general direction anticolonial analyses and political and moral discourses. Yet, there still remained significant differences between the French left and African anticolonialists. French intellectuals and politicians who successfully resisted the state-sanctioned colonial agenda and its anthropological views were nonetheless seduced by their central propositions and thematic about self and others. Thus, although they recognized the "ontological ambiguity" of human reality and the human condition, postwar French philosophy and theory pertaining to the other did not undergo significant readjustments and/or transformations from the reigning orthodoxies. Still swayed by the endemic historicism of Hegel, Kant, Husserl, and Marx, their followers frequently succumbed to Orientalist views of so-called natives, their traditions, cultures, and habits.[82]

The relevant perspectives and their adepts could not countenance the demands of the colonized for both accountability and redirection of postwar domestic and international relations. Specifically, their visions of decolonization failed to provide guarantees of a halt in the colonial project. They left in place the structures of violence and repression that protected subjective privileges. The envisaged postcolonial subjects lacked real power domestically or internationally and, therefore, no hope for recognition or justice through legislation, negotiation, or otherwise. Spatially speaking, postcolonial subjects were to inhabit a resource-diminished state; restrained within them by the superior military might of the former colonial powers; disenfranchised by subordinated local or national governors; stripped of rights and entitlements under imposed constitutional arrangements. That future looked too domesticated and too compromised to be satisfactory.

Reverse Ethnography and Colonial Anxieties

Prior to 1948, few Africans quarreled with the notions and principles of underlying the Union: a Franco-African community (*communauté*) of goodwill (*bonnes intentions*), mutuality (*volontés mutuelles*), and human solidarity (also brotherhood). RDA members were among those who had hoped at first to free the international order itself of colonial traditions and morality in order to implement a different kind of modernity based on new forms of identity, sovereignty. The direction of French policy—particularly after Bretton Woods agreements, the United Nations, Marshall Plan, and NATO— compelled the colonized to imagine separate futures. Upon these events, French authorities began to revalorize a hierarchical order of regions, cultures, institutions as bases or structures of interdependence and collective security. The corresponding policy options undermined anticolonial objectives: for mutual recognition, equality, and justice. These objectives were not easily accommodated by the emergent ideological binaries of liberalism versus communism, humanism versus naturalism, and progressivism versus colonial racism.

Now, the Franco-African debates highlighted differences of view about the need and meanings, and therefore political and institutional implications, of particular forms of recognition, equality, and justice. Related positions invariably conformed to the material and symbolic resources available to contestants and their expectations of the future. It is thus that anticolonialists began to object to authoritative French inflections of the terms that goodwill and cooperation, for instance, signified African acceptance of French (or Western) leadership as necessarily indispensable to progress and international peace. The anticolonialist objections centered on new conditions imposed by France on Africans in response to changes in the international scene.

The political question for French authorities was whether they could moderate or modulate the degrees and manners in which former colonial subjects would exercise their new roles. This question was both temporal and ethnographic. In the first instance, French authorities were convinced that decades of colonial education regarding French traditions, spirits, and achievement in arts, sciences, and morality would impel deference and thus temper the autonomist ambition of the new citizens. Relatedly, the Authority assumed the sufficiency of its legal idioms, particularly in regard to the protection of persons; the acquisition and exchange of goods; and the weight given to culture within politico-symbolic space of the French Union.

The response of the colonized to postwar reconstruction and postcolonial reform focused less on ideology and more on the truth and symbolic dimensions of politics. Indeed, the status of politics and truth emerged in imperial legislative and consultative bodies as the focal point of contestations about budget allocations, voting procedures, political alliances, educations, and national security among others. Once again, RDA members and their sympathizers were most adamant about truth-telling in politics. The politics of truth was always a delicate one and African deputies took pains to remark on its teleology in order to soften its effects. First, RDA members took care to admonish French officials, "who were unaccustomed to negotiating with the colonized," to "repudiate this bad habit" of resorting to "brutal force" and to return to the "other traditions of justice and liberty. (Applause on the extreme left)"[83] Second, Africans insisted that legislative debates be constructive without avoiding "painful events," for the latter had to be recalled "for the purpose of establishing truth."[84] Third, the guarantees of the 1946 constitution of liberty and equality could not be reversed for, while the authorities could not countenance equality, Africans knew to exercise their liberty.[85] Finally, it had to be established that "Africans who had enthusiastically taken up arms against the Nazis found it repugnant that they should be asked to arm themselves against their [colonial] brothers. (Applause on the extreme left)"[86]

The question of French repression in Vietnam, Madagascar, and Algeria, and of French entry into NATO proved most controversial for African deputies. They were also the issues over which French authorities were most uncompromising. To begin, Africans were "distressed that French authorities would expel elected French representatives from the assembly in order to prevent them from speaking the truth about [these matters]."[87] Second, militarism was a cause for worry: you tell us that "These police planes will be equipped with two machine guns and four 50kgs bombs," Mohamadou Djibrilla Maiga intoned, and you think that we do not suspect where they will be used.[88] "We would be very happy that you tell us, Minister, the destination that the Government envisages for them . . . We remember that in a separate debate it was said that airlifted troops could be sent all over Indochina . . . Are these airplanes the response to that request?"[89] The "weight and performance of these crafts tell us they are not really capable of defending the French Union."[90]

Repression and censure proved costly and counterproductive. French officials had applied political blackmail, ostracism, and isolation to d'Arboussier to no avail. They had also tried outright physical elimination on the persons of Senator Victor Biaka Boda[91] and many others. The alternative response to growing African radicalism was therefore political and economic bribery aimed at enlisting allies among Africans who could help counter growing criticisms of French policies among their own ranks. The authorities would allow freedom of speech and so-called truth-telling, but African deputies had to agree to modify their modes of expression and discursive methods, on the one hand, and apply pragmatism to their exigencies, on the other. The relevant steps augured an era of French intervention in intra-colonial relations for the purpose of pitting "authentic" and thus "legitimate" "native voices" against non-authentic and thus less than legitimate ones. Again as previously discussed, this presumptive support for "authentic" and "legitimate" representatives of the colonized only served as pretext to rid anticolonialist movements of so-called radical elements. Except for the case involving Gabriel d'Arboussier, this French policy too would prove difficult to implement until the 1950 disaffiliation of the RDA from the French communist party.

Ouezzin Coulibaly: Neither Gent Nor Kind

Daniel Ouezzin Coulibaly was perhaps the most eloquent critic of "imperial reason" and its cultural and intellectual underpinnings. Coulibaly was born in Upper Volta (now Burkina Faso), where he spent his formative years. The young Coulibaly's trajectory was not unlike that of many évolués. He was chosen to go to school by his family, from among many other siblings, who helped to support him. He was expected to play an important yet subordinate role in the colonial administration. Having distinguished himself at school in his native territory, he was awarded a fellowship to the trade school of William Ponty, in Dakar, Senegal. There, he trained as *médecin africain*—a category of nurses and physician assistants trained to attend to local health needs. In this capacity, Coulibaly lived in the ambiguous sphere inhabited by all évolués, halfway between full emancipation and colonial subjectivity: a medical professional expected to be a mere subordinate and instrument of colonial management of health. Coulibaly would soon discover another paradox: that even as an accomplished intellectual he would be reduced to a cultural agent of colonial rule.

While attending Ponty, and afterward, Coulibaly took interest in politics and, for this reason, cultivated great interest in French literature, philosophy, and politics. His first elected position was as president of the alumni association of the graduates of Ponty. This position led to a career change from medicine to politics. In 1946, he was a founding member of the RDA in Bamako. He was subsequently elected deputy to the French National Assembly in 1947 from the Côte d'Ivoire, the territory encompassing his native Upper Volta. Coulibaly served in the National Assembly between 1947 and 1953, when he was elected to the French Senate, or Council of the

Republic. In these capacities, he followed other Africans in seeking affiliation with metropolitan individuals and organizations, mostly from the ranks of progressives.[92]

As an intellectual and the political director of the RDA, Coulibaly professed helped to establish *Le Démocrate*, a mimeographed daily that he cowrote and edited for the RDA branch of the Côte d'Ivoire. The themes, events, and places covered by *Le Démocrate* reflected Coulibaly's self-professed crusade on behalf of truth, liberty, justice, and equality. From September 1948 to July 1950, for instance, Coulibaly wrote editorials on the politics of symbolism (September 27, 1948); the treatment of African veterans (June 13, 1949); the victims of modern barbarism (September 5, 1949); the simulacrum of elections and democracy (December 12, 1949); the passage of history (January 2, 1950); and a letter to Joliot-Curie (July 3, 1950). These articles were notable for their intellectual depths and attention to international events. The majority of his essays rivaled in tone and seriousness of his August 1948 editorial entitled *J'accuse*, with deliberate reference to Emile Zola's essay in the Dreyfus affair.[93] Subtitled "Resistance to Oppression is a Consequence of Human Rights," this essay scolded France for its betrayal of the colonized, for its willingness "to sacrifice human beings to the altar of national interest" and its "desire to rule over others without their consent."[94]

Coulibaly's political reflections covered worldwide thematic, philosophical, regional, and topical debates. He became an avid reader of philosophy and literature as well as daily newspapers from around the world. While preparing for his political career, he developed fondness for Dénis Diderot, Emile Zola, Molière, and Voltaire among other French intellectuals who had demonstrated political courage based on moral principles. Coulibaly's own *J'accuse* was modeled after Zola's famed letter denouncing the absence of moral courage in France during the Dreyfus affair. Coulibaly had also cited Voltaire's stand "in the Hugo Calas Affair," Courbet's interventions before the Paris Commune, and declaration by "honest French citizens" who have historically honored France by taking the side of truth over convenience.[95] Coulibaly was reputed to be among the few parliamentarians who could fit in one speech moral teachings from Diderot and Montesquieu, the sentiments of Paul Robeson and John Colliers alongside editorials and commentaries from the *New York Herald Tribune*, *La Gazette de Lausanne* as they pertained to events in the Philippines, Cuba, Hawaii, Santo Domingo, and colonial French Africa.[96]

In contrast, Coulibaly was distrustful of those who espoused philosophical universalism but benefitted from political actions oriented toward parochial gains. He understood such positions to amount to a pernicious kind of cynicism: to know the truth, but to abstain from revealing it either for lack of courage or for reasons of convenience regardless of the consequences of such actions for others.[97] This kind of cynicism bothered Coulibaly. He resented it even more when French intellectuals and politicians alike attributed their cynical positions to something called pragmatism. Looking past France, Coulibaly was bothered by the pervasiveness of similar cynicism in U.S. political culture, particularly with respect to their attitudes toward native Americans and blacks. What he saw in France and America, two countries for which he otherwise had grudging admiration, was the political and philosophical betrayal of the colonized, native Americans, and blacks. He could not therefore countenance the persistent and self-motivated identification of the West as exclusively and conclusively democratic, tolerant, and plural even as, he often pointed out, the lynching of black Americans and the confinement of native Americans and Australian Aborigines to unproductive political and economic life continued unabated.[98]

Even those who disagreed with Coulibaly could not easily dismiss him. He was recognized for his extraordinary intellectual and oratory talents, his extensive readings of history, and his devotion to truth.[99] In her never-completed biography of Coulibaly, Claude Gerard fondly remembers that Coulibaly "expressed himself and wrote with remarkable ease. He possessed a singular style: a soft and gentile combination of irreverence, humor, and sarcasm.[100] The vehemence of his indignation [at postwar Western designs] and the power of his arguments were paralleled by a distinct style in evidence in his articles, his speeches, and parliamentary interventions."[101] Coulibaly oriented these talents and his energy to demonstrating that a "number of factors of political, economic, and social orders, originating domestically and internationally," negatively influenced postwar thinking about postcolonial relations, particularly between the Métropole and the colonies.[102] They necessarily subordinated the colonies and their status to the Métropole and its parochial interests.

The global economic factor threatening the Franco-African union was the pending economic crisis and the Marshall Plan which aimed to correct it.[103] Here, following Gabriel d'Arboussier, Coulibaly noted that the Marshall Plan introduced a radical shift in the immediate postwar culture and practice of consultation within the empire: "from the report of the director general of economic affairs of the High Commission on Africa," we can now deduce that "from concessions to concessions, your economic policy now consists of obedience to American command."[104] "Because of you, our countries are about to become American subsidiaries and our economies placed in a strict dependence upon the fluctuations of the dollar."[105] This would be so because "our economies are based on goods from the land and we are now dangerously threatened by the falling prices of agricultural products in the US" while due to your "concessions to Americans nothing ensures that the protection currently in place will hold."[106] "Our fate, which is the fate of all dependencies, is to be subject to a form of mercantile exploitation," with French merchants now as middlemen, to trade African goods with maximum profit to them.[107] "Let it be, at least, that commercial accords that introduce new policies implicating our countries do not exclude us."[108] Such accords must not exclude a priori the principals while granting concessions over them to "foreign countries."[109]

The economy was not Coulibaly's primary interest, however. It was the emergent international order, particularly the ascendency of militarism and militarization driven by the cold war. "History contain lessons that must guide all our activities and ethos" Coulibaly began in his memorialized speech of July 26, 1949.[110] These lessons of history, he continued, "apply to questions embedded in the Atlantic Pact." In the aftermath of World War II, all allied nations gathered in San Francisco signed a document from which I can extrapolate the following: "if some peoples have recovered national sovereignty, which they lost four years ago, we are forgetting that other equally oppressed nations heard the promises made there and that they may now seek the freedom that has been so touted for months."[111] Coulibaly favorably compared the San Francisco (UN) Charter to the Atlantic Pact, whose Article 2 "says that its aims is to preserve Western civilization and the democratic institutions that Western nations consider their common heritage." Pointing to the apparent philosophical dissonance injected by the latter in the emergent global sensibilities, Coulibaly noted that the implicit dangers of superpower rivalry: "we are now told that civilization is threatened again by war and there is need to preserve it by placing a security dispositif around the geographic space where this so-called Western civilization would blossom."[112] "Do we understand that Black Africa and Madagascar would not be dragged into a war resulting from this pact and its consequences?"

"There is no confusion as to the answer when one reads the constitution of the French Union." Citing its preambles, Coulibaly noted that "The French Union is composed of nations and peoples that put together, in an equilibrium, their resources and efforts in order to ensure their common security."[113] "Article 62 adds to this declaration that members of the French Union put all their resources together for the defense of the Union. The French government assumes coordination of the appropriate means and policy to this end." Finally, Article 60 encompasses our territories in its understanding of France and its geographical sphere.[114] Evidently, "this means that the Atlantic pact, whether an instrument of security or war, binds us and engages us without explicit reference to us while simultaneously excluding us."[115] "It is an impressive somersault but one that does not fool us." "To convince doubters that the Atlantic pact engages Africa, let me quote from around the world articles from newspapers that neither communist or communist sympathizing (*communisant*)."[116] One, the *New York Herald Tribune*, stated that "French Africa, from the southern coast of the Mediterranean to Belgian Congo, is for the first time in the line of defense of NATO. The new organization will facilitate the realization and extension of the Atlantic Pact. The US already has in place agreements with France, allowing American airplanes the use of Nord African bases."[117]

Coulibaly anticipated the rebuttal that the United States meant well because it is an "anti-colonial power."[118] "I advise them to read the study by the American John Colliers who has established the dossier of American colonialism in a remarkable study by the Fabian Society in London."[119] In fact, "Liberia gives us a good example in Africa of the kinds of republic that America has established . . . in the Philippines, Cuba, Hawaii, Santo Domingo. Or think of lynching in continental America. (Applause on the extreme left)."[120] But, such actions as lynching are "prohibited by the Constitution of the French Union which also denounces racism and colonialism." "And now you want us in an alliance with the US for which we might sacrifice our lives in campaigns of pacification of other natives in for their raw materials."[121]

Coulibaly was comforted in this idea by the views of Paul Robeson on the link between the Marshall Plan and NATO: For us in Africa, warnings about the American record on colonialism and racial exploitation come also from "the other side of the Atlantic from the people of color themselves." "The democrat Robeson" is in agreement with me that there is a link between the Atlantic Pact and the

Marshall Plan. Robeson says that "the real impact of the Marshall Plan will be total slavery for the colonies."[122] Coulibaly surmised that the Marshall Plan would create economic entanglements and bankruptcy for European bankers and their governments might offer African resources to American business in exchange for European debts: "How are the English, the French, and other bankers of Western Europe going to pay back Wall Street? Solely by turning over the natural resources [of the colonized] such as gold, copper, zinc, groundnuts, cocoa, oil, sugar, bananas from where? Well! from South Africa, Nigeria, East Africa, French Africa, Guatemala, Vietnam, Malaysia."[123] Under the circumstances, "The Atlantic Pact would offer legal sanction for sending troops in the colonies in order to implement slavery. They will shoot at the African [and Vietnamese] people as they lynch in Mississippi. This is the other side of the coin. (Loud protestations in the center, on the right, and some benches on the left)."[124]

The protestations grew louder as Coulibaly developed his theses. But it is when he seemingly enlisted Diderot to his side that Coulibaly brought chaos to the house. "These words of Diderot come to mind," he poignantly noted, "there is nothing more odious than having slaves and calling them freemen." The comment drew sustained applause from some corners on the left. The majority was not amused. Besides interruptions from the center and the right, one Pierre Montel called on the presiding legislator to censure Coulibaly: "Do you tolerate such speech acts, Madame President? This is scandalous!"[125] To Montel's call for censure, Gabriel Lisette, a legislator from Chad rejoined: "Are you now renouncing Diderot?, Mr. Montel"[126] The president of the session interrupted in turn to declare ceremoniously: "I cannot censure Diderot, Mr. Montel." The left bursted out into loud applause.[127]

Cynicism, Censure, and the Postcolonial Order

While the rules prevented the presiding legislator from censuring either Diderot or Coulibaly, the latter paid a price for quoting his irreverence—that is from quoting Diderot in a manner deemed inappropriate by the French political establishment. As Claude Gerard notes, there was resentment that Coulibaly's speeches and writings were invariably "peppered with *specks of humor and sarcasm as well as poetic notes and unpredictable but moving images . . .*"[128] On this occasion, Coulibaly had just delivered his "most memorable intervention on the tribune of the National Assembly." Unfortunately for Coulibaly it was about the Atlantic Treaty, one that even conservative French elites would just as soon signed without fanfare. According to Gerard, the speech was met with enthusiastic reception among Africans and some on the political left, but the "exuberance" of the delivery "provoked indignation among colonialists." It also created discomfort within a good fraction of the left, particularly among those of the establishment. At any rate, "All present forever remembered that speech."[129]

Coulibaly was known "to mock everything and everybody but always with extreme genteelness."[130] He always laughed even when attacked, or "when asked if he was Christian, Muslim, or animist." In fact, he was baptized Christian and attended Catholic Church. But he also attended Muslim prayers as well as visited local healers. This attitude and his inability to conform to expectation and parliamentary decorum were all points of annoyance to many of Coulibaly's French colleagues. But, if Gerard is to be believed, Coulibaly understood his colleagues' "problem" to be constitutive of a larger struggle over identity and subjectivity as well as the will to power, that is to authoritatively determine the rules and methods to truth and to adjudicate value.

In this light, Coulibaly's sins were threefold, both linked to postcolonial and global restructuring. One was his refusal to pass off French cynicism for pragmatism. Second was his opposition to the idea of an unconditional African support, commitment, and contribution to the reconstruction and defense of the Métropole and "Western civilization." The third was his insistence on the inclusion of Africans in decision making and the benefits of the economic prosperity under both the Atlantic Charter and the Marshall Plan. By these actions, Coulibaly clearly ventured beyond the boundaries of the symbolic order set by the French with respect to the role of the colonized within the emergent French Union. He refused to abide the notion of inherent French leadership and sovereignty, which constitutionally reserved "foreign policy," "security," "economy," and "education" to the Métropole. Nor would Coulibaly defer to French legislators and in these regards.[131]

If Coulibaly was politically and ideologically motivated, French reactions to him were neutral and merely normative. The content and substance of his speeches, not the forms of their delivery, were at stake. So too were the principles of free speech, truth-telling, and public morality. Indeed, the reviled behaviors were integral to French parliamentary customs and widespread among anticolonialists.[132] Certainly, verbal taunts and jibes, including sarcasms, were legitimate discursive techniques in French legislative and consultative bodies. Metropolitan legislators legitimately embraced brazen interruptions and walkouts as effective communicative practices without regard to the fact that such actions transgressed, say, West African cultural sensibilities. Second, French authorities accommodated anticolonial critics, including *négritudistes*, who were equally critical of colonial rule and French policies[133] and, as such, satirized and parodied official French invocations of humanist universalism for cynical reasons.[134] The legitimacy of the actions of the concerned individuals was never in doubt so long as they conformed to parliamentary traditions, if not norms.

Africans also accepted as legitimate French parliamentary rituals, such as brazen interruptions or walkouts that were otherwise unacceptable in their own cultural milieus. RDA deputies who were disproportionately from West Africa would have found French rules of deliberation, specific body languages, and mannerisms to be offensive. Specifically, under the rules protecting political speech, French parliamentarians freely accused their African interlocutors of ill-will, subversive intentions, and maliciousness without the burden of proof or explanation. Further, in certain West African cultural milieus, it is not acceptable for a wrongdoer to interrupt person(s) that s/he recognizes to have aggrieved in discussions concerning the offense. Consistently, it was poor form on the part of colonial powers to incessantly interrupt Africans with the aim of refuting the latter's recount of the colonial experience. By analogy, it is poor form to counterpose colonialist texts and interpretations of colonial expansion as ground for dismissal of an anthropology of Europe that focuses on European actions and their effects.

From the previous paragraphs, it appears that Coulibaly merely engaged in ordinary parliamentary rituals. While it is indisputable that Coulibaly had a great sense of humor and sarcasm, he did not intend political theater. French responses to him proved that point. Coulibaly staked his arguments on the illegitimacy (as opposed to the constitutionality) of the prerogatives sought by France as well as the sanctity of the democratic principles of equality, reciprocity, and justice for all in a postcolonial order. Related positions and demands frustrated French elites no longer interested in firming up the postcolonial agenda initiated in 1940. Aided by transatlantic their recovery of French grandeur, after 1949, French elites now resented the "indignity" of having to justify themselves to a skeptical African audience. The French administration too was piqued that Africans were no longer sanguine about political assimilation and conversion to the central tenets of post-Enlightenment rationalism, liberalism, and their derivative ideologies. A shift in debates away from the nature of the emerging global order, postcolonial reforms, and related French policies only obscured these tenets.

In this context, the focus on his personal demeanor and discursive style was but diversion from a much larger political contest over constitutional prerogatives. It effectively shifted attention away from French policies and their underlying imaginaries of political community, economy, and international morality. Censoring the speaker on account of nonnormativity, therefore, was a convenient way of censuring the content of the "offensive speech" without appearing to object to the speaker's freedom of speech. It was properly a way of countering Coulibaly's declared "sovereign right" to gaze— to look, observe, and comment—without prior imperial authorization as to methods or grounds. This right claim was the real danger to the French drive to reestablish the authority of France over the colonies. In this case, Coulibaly's detractors wished to silence the speaker or to discount the truth of his arguments, along with the ethical impulses behind his concerns. To this end, they cynically pointed to mode of delivery and determined that it was simply too sarcastic. In the end, Coulibaly toned down his opposition to the emergent order. Even so, he was constantly denounced by colleagues.

Coulibaly was still senator when he died on September 7, 1958. To date, there are speculations about the origin of the disease. The commonsense is that he succumbed to a poison that he ingested unsuspectingly after his January 1958 victory over the local ally of the French colonial administration, in the biggest political crisis of the colony. As fate would have it, Coulibaly died only days before the empire-wide referendum that was to determine whether the French Union survives the collapse of the Fourth Republic.

Even in death, Coulibaly was vindicated in his predictions that international developments would be to the detriment of the interest of "Africa" and "Africans." The Atlantic Alliance, including France, ultimately succeeded in restoring global politics along lines associated by the discipline with realpolitik. Indeed, with the formalization of the Bretton Woods agreements, the institution of the veto power at the United Nations, and the advent of the Marshall Plan and NATO, France and its Western allies successfully secured for themselves the essential executive roles within such universal organizations as the United Nations as well as specialized agencies such as the International Monetary Fund and the Bank for International Reconstruction and Development, or World Bank.[135] These crucial steps ensured a political ethos of unilateralism that capitalized on the material advantages of the West over others.[136]

These successes have had a darker side. The Marshall Plan aided in the reconstruction of Europe but the prior Lend-Lease accords and Marshall Plan-related agreements set the colonies up merely as sources of raw material. The terms of these agreements and French policies evolved later, but there is no denying that the Marshall Plan singularly excluded the colonies from its investment plans while encouraging the former colonial empires to prey on the colonies for raw materials. NATO too helped defend Western Europe from the threat of communism. But in Africa, from Algeria to the Congo to South Africa as from East Africa to West Africa, the Atlantic Pact helped to defend colonialism and to prop up moribund colonial powers such as Portugal—and for a while France. NATO also entered into partnership with dictators and minority regimes, notably in Congo/Zaire and the apartheid regime in South Africa. From the 1960s onward, the United States led the way in opposing genuine colonial reform as well as rejecting "unfavorable" democratic outcomes. The result has been disastrous for Africa as U.S. allies laid countries to waste. Mobutu Sese Seko's Congo entered a long period of civil war at the end of his reign. So too did Angola suffer from U.S. and NATO support for Jonas Savimbi and his political movement: the National Union for the Total Independence of Angola, known by its Portuguese acronym as UNITA. Apartheid South Africa's support for the Mozambican National Resistance (RENAMO) has the same effect. In both Angola and Mozambique, the rebels and Apartheid South Africa had American blessing. The numbers of the dead and amputees resulting from the resulting conflicts as well as the magnitude of ruin to the ecology testifies to the effects of the transplantation of the cold war ethos of permissiveness to Africa.

It is not merely antipathy that led colonial officials and deputies to routinely reject anticolonial arguments. In politics as in the academy, there remains a tendency to censure or repress inconvenient and disagreeable thoughts on account of their modes of expressions or methods. Similar positions are found Todorov's and Hopkins's comments on postcolonial criticisms and reverse ethnography. Again, as in the colonial context, the objectors to nonnormativity have the power to exclude or to cause chains of events leading to the exclusion of undesirable authors from academic debates. Ironically, such exclusionary tactics do not conform to the apparent norms of academic engagements. At any rate, just as in the political arena, the exclusion of individuals has never been as significant as the eradication of objectionable ideas, concepts, and their applications from academic discourses and their idioms. Consistently, all attempts to give voice to anticolonialism and postcoloniality, on the one hand, and to provide sustained accounts of the connections between Western modernity, Occidentalism, and certain forms of violence, on the other, have met with skepticism and/or contempt. Again the grounds of dismissal are often related to their nonconformity with disciplinary methods and conventions.

Conclusion: Analyses, Criticisms, and Discourses

Europe and the West were not alone in reflecting upon the consequences of the war specifically the chaos, horrors, and disintegration of social order it engendered. The colonized too confronted the near-uniform existential questions about modern times, political rationality, and the moral foundations of the international system. Consistent with its own temporality and political spatiality, the French empire boasted communities whose complex identities and subject positions shaped political discourses. Like colonial elites everywhere, the political class in Africa approached related issues from their subject position as colonized. They spoke from various positions in the colonies and the Métropole with diverse intellectual, cultural, and political sensibilities. In this regard, the tendency among them was to ally themselves with French progressives and skeptics in asking whether Western values (culture), science (reason and technology), and institutions (social organization) were adequate or uniquely suited to meet the requirements of the imminent world.[137] But the colonized ask different questions. They also invested the postwar ideals of human solidarity, international friendship, and global goodwill with new meaning and thus new standards, rules, and norms—more open to interrogation, reflection, and improvement in regards to their pertinence to justice, equality, and peace.

Although anticolonial thoughts embraced the politically salient ideas and concepts of the postwar era, their discourses produced effects that often diverged from metropolitan ones. To stress a belabored point, anticolonialists did engage Western authors, texts, and policies; but they did so on the basis of a new political imaginary and for the purpose of expanding on the latter's ethical and ontological boundaries. This is why one should expect Africans to envisage new allegories and metaphors of solidarity—and, by extension, freedom, justice, equality, and the like. Thus, it emerges from anticolonial thought, for instance, that goodwill meant that no party to postwar contests could claim advantages or privileges based on history alone; no party devalued the contribution of another during the war; that the legal bases of existing inequities be overturned; and full and equal citizenship and not national or civilization origin be the basis of political participation and decision making.[138] It also appears that many colonial entities conditionally accepted Western leadership in laying the foundation of the new order but not in justifying imperialism and structures of domination and exploitation. Further, justice was to allow for equal access to resources and the ennobling of human dignity. To ensure this outcome, anticolonialists envisaged means other than the implementation of "individual rights," especially when such rights could be traced to colonial origins.[139] Finally, anticolonial views of peace meant not only a stable world order, but one that ensures justice and mutual solicitation as well as prohibits militarism and the militarization of society and economies.

Anticolonialists also produced legitimate lines of inquiry that in turn, led to different interpretations of international events. For instance, anticolonialists agreed with nearly all at the beginning of World War II that the "sclerosis" of the international system principally comprised Nazism, Fascism, and other forms of totalitarianism. But the larger crises of empire, state, and governance were not far behind. Those crises concerned the core institutions and structures of value and interest upon which Western humanists and universalists had built their ideas of freedom, political autonomy, sovereignty, and self-determination. These observations gave form and substance to African deliberations. The political lexicons and languages of analyses of such groups as the RDA may be judged today to be antiquated or mistaken. I am not sure. But not their "grammar" or ethics of engagements (or ethics) proved to be salutary to France and the international system in crisis time. By obscuring them, IR impoverishes its own narratives and, ultimately, international theory. Again, this is not to say that the methods of postcolonial criticism, including reverse ethnography, better serve truth and wisdom (and ultimately justice). Nor am I suggesting that humanists and rationalists cannot, through ethnographic distancing, arrive at ethical position that may serve justice. I am suggesting, however, that international theory will remain incomplete if it does not assimilate anticolonial and postcolonial thoughts with respect to ontology and the productive exchanges that must foster international security, peace, and justice—if indeed these objectives are still central to the teleology of IR and international theory.

Conclusion

The key determinants of the legitimacy and credibility of the process of discovery and knowledge have undermined the universalist ambition of IR. These are Eurocentrism and statecentrism. Eurocentrism has generated archives, lines of inquiry, and modes of signification that posit Europe as morally coherent and ontologically superior and therefore the source and inspiration of international morality and norms. For its part, statecentrism takes the modern state to be necessarily and empirically the primary agent of international order and morality and thus conflates its absence with lawlessness or anarchy. Related assumptions are inadequate at best. Indeed, rather than provide inspiration to other international systems, modern "Europe" instituted practices and norms that undermined the autonomy and viability of other regional systems and their units as condition of its own ascent to hegemony. Nor did the Westphalian system of sovereignty chart the course for other regional orders that sought to attain emancipation and justice through equality and autonomy.

The European encounters with others were far more complex than allowed by Eurocentric and state-centric commonsense. These encounters generated at once sympathy and antipathy, gift and barter, commercial exchanges and usurpation, hospitality and ethnic cleansing among the participants. But none of these outcomes was inevitable or necessary. Nor was the related violence happenstance. While responding to individual dynamics, the turns taken by these encounters were greatly influenced by Western modernity, rationalism, and instrumentalism. The latter set the context for the ethos, practices, and violence that later prevailed everywhere, including Europe. Modern European thinkers and policy makers not only imagined the "national" and "international" as two separate spheres subject to separate moralities, they reduced "international morality" to the mere will to dominate (as suggested by realists) or to survive (as implicit in liberalism) of competitive rival entities. Related views are often simplistic and self-serving.

Contrary to disciplinary commonsense, international existence has occurred mostly within *overlapping structures* of spaces encompassing empires, states, colonies, and regions. The constitutive rules of the relevant orders were mediated by both the internal constitution of the units—that is, whether the state was imperial, republican, democratic, pluralist—and the morality that they promoted through conventionalized norms. The latter obtained from specific cultural, diplomatic, theological, and commercial contexts. In the case of Europe, resident governments—elected officials, dictators, and/or potentates alike—adhered to an international morality that set the contexts for such values as freedom and justice within "international orders" that incorporated others under European or Western tutelage.

The illustrations provided by this book, particularly the actions and interventions of évolués, suggest that the will to dominate has not been the primary motivation of global relations and that anarchy is relative to given orders. That story shows that, even upon the disappearance of the imperial colonial state, the colonized generated a distinct political rationality, based on historical conceptions of solidarity and humanism that allowed for actions on behalf of the collective, including the colonizer. Indeed, the évolués experimented with new political ethos, practices, and rituals. These were inspired by their own self-understandings as well as interpretations of African values and traditions.

While drawing on Western canons, the évolués also took exception to the colonial act and related political practices. I selected the speeches, analyses, and actions that informed the views and politics of a few African publicists because they illustrate the postcolonial moment: the ushering in of a worldwide consciousness of the common fate of humanity, accompanied by the irreparable puncturing of the myth of Western moral superiority and institutional exceptionalism together with the delegitimization of colonialism. Indeed, World War II sensitized communities worldwide to the dangers of racial ideologies and totalitarianism, both represented by Nazism and Fascism. It also gave led to the proclamation by the formerly colonized of their "sovereign right" to gaze: that is, to look, observe, and comment on the world beyond without prior imperial authorization as to methods or grounds. This right to gaze is rooted in the rejection of the mendacious notion that imperial reason stands alone as the exclusive means and context of self-criticism. It adheres to a basic subjective but profoundly ethical principle to an entitlement to inquire, discover, and speculate about the practices, cultures, and institutions and values of entities that, for centuries, claimed superior access to science and morality and the necessity to looked at others unfavorably in self-justification.

Operationally, the postcolonial gaze denounced the kind of intellectual utilitarianism and instrumentalization of difference that accompanied the colonial act. Related criticisms focused on the Western gaze and its historical, anthropological, and aesthetic apparatuses of the Western gaze: historicism, comparativism, and hermeneutics. Historicism has been primarily implicated in rationalist and institutionalist conceptions of nature and reason that both distorted the spatial and temporal operations of global politics and condoned the underlying violence. It led to a comparative views of "Man" and society and morality and law that erroneously posited Europe, particularly the European experience and trajectory, as universal and transcendental models of development and moral existence. In turn, this comparativism was sustained by an "ethnography" that mapped distinct notions of "place," "religion," and "culture" onto self-serving cartographies of "Europe," "Africa," "Near East," and "Middle East" as distinct provinces corresponding to parallel operations of morality, recognition, and therefore, engagements. In the theoretical instance, these cartographies established relationships between identity and science and normativity and pragmatism based on allegories and metaphors of progress and stagnation, order and anarchy, property and lawlessness, and the like.[1]

Postcolonial criticisms highlight political subjectivity, archives, and their translation. As discussed throughout the book, some have taken issues with the very idea that Africans and other formerly colonized entities possess equal faculty to contemplate international morality as well as equal capacity to transcend their self-interest for the universal good. This idea has led to "imperial" and/or "proprietary" anxieties about the place of Western intellectual, cultural, and political traditions, on the one hand, and postcolonial methods, lines of inquiry, and modes of signification, on the other. However, postcolonial criticisms generally seek to complement or, according to circumstances, counter the Western gaze with new (re)sources and to orient reflection toward postcolonial futures. Consistently, some postcolonial inquiries and visions do approximate Western liberalism, humanism, universalism, and relativism. Yet, even as they extend recognition and validation to others, including former colonizers, postcolonial analyses often include referents and ontologies that exceed the terms of European and Western conventions.

While postcolonial methods and lines of inquiry do not have higher moral claims on truth, their incorporation into the corpus of disciplinary verities and commonsense may add greater sensibilities to understanding international existence and global politics. At the very least, they might stretch IR conceptions of social life, its intellectual artifices, and ethical conventions. Specifically, postcolonial analyses also provide rich accounts of modernity and its manifestations across space and time; of the ascendency of state sovereignty; and of the nationalization of public identity (subjectivity), thought (or memory), and morality (ethics). They are less reserved about the corrupting effects of Western foreign policy rationalities and the darker, egotistical, and violent processes of Western modernity and the colonial enterprise. Above all, the singularities of postcolonial thoughts rest in their teleologies and relationships to the multiple pasts and presents.

In illuminating global politics and their values and institutions, postcolonial scholars insist on a corresponding social science agenda that envisages methods and lines of inquiry that account for plural temporal and spatial social experiences and their varied conceptions of law and morality. Transposed to IR, this means that inquiries must abide the multiplicity of human resources and the diversity of planetary existence. Scholars would thus catalogue knowledges and moral arguments on the sole basis of their pertinence to inquiry, discovery, and truth. They would also envisage the possibility that modes of thoughts, concepts, and their base-values and institutions mutate upon migration beyond the spaces of their inceptions to suit new necessities and contexts. Finally, they would take it for granted that political languages and idioms may be infused with new referents at the moment of their (re)assembly as instruments for imagining the terms of global coexistence.

Thus conceived, IR must be less "pragmatic" in its lines of inquiry and more responsive to the experiences of the subjects, agents, and actors whose existence the discipline signifies. IR must also consider the possibility of the insufficiency of its methods and rules of inquiry as well as the desirability of translation across cultural and geographical lines of differentiation. As a sign of this humility, it must be open to all methodologically coherent intellectual artifices and modes of signification. As the primary ethical requirement of knowledge, the quest for truth would thus entail meaningful comparison and translation of all actions and their idioms. Again the purpose would be not only to obtain better judgments but also to accommodate mutual beliefs, attitudes, and values as well as institutions, idioms, and political languages that converge toward the intelligibility of international existence.[2]

Notes

Acknowledgments

1. Siba N'Zatioula Grovogui, *Sovereigns, Quasi-Sovereigns, and Africans* (Minneapolis: University of Minnesota Press, 1996).

Introduction   Truth and Method: Identity, Science, and Political Horizons

1. Michel-Rolph Trouillot, *Silencing the Past: Power and the Production of History* (Boston: Beacon Press, 1995), 1–30.
2. Charles W. Kegley, Jr., "The Neoidealist Moment in International Studies? Realist Myths and the New International Realities," *International Studies Quarterly*, no. 37 (1993), 131–146.
3. Ibid.
4. Ibid.
5. The concepts of "Europe," "European," "Occident," "the West," "Western," "Orient," "the Rest," and "Africa" are malleable metaphysical fictions. So are such categories as "colonized," "colonial," and "third world." Their meanings and functions have shifted across time and space according to political contestations. They are nonetheless historical products with great effects in political contexts. My usages reflect the changing temporal and spatial contexts of their deployments by political actors and agents.
6. I later discuss a number of scholars' works pertaining to these points. They include, for instance, Thomas Risse-Kappen, James Mayall, and others on the virtues of transnationalism involving nongovernmental, multinational, and international organizations; Friedrich Kratochwil and Nicholas Onuf on the context of global politics and international norms and society; and Kathryn Sikkink and others on formal and informal transnational networks.
7. See Steve Smith, Ken Booth, and Marysia Zalewski, *International Theory: Positivism and Beyond* (Cambridge: Cambridge University Press, 1996).

8. Gene M. Lyons and Michel Mastanduno, *Beyond Westphalia?* (Baltimore: Johns Hopkins University Press, 1995) and Thom Kuehls, *Beyond Sovereign Territory* (Minneapolis: University of Minnesota Press, 1996).

9. Mervyn Frost, *Ethics in International Relations: A Constitutive Theory* (Cambridge: Cambridge University Press, 1996).

10. For a range, see, for instance, Andrew Linklater, "The Problem of Community in International Relations," *Alternatives*, xv (1990); Chris Brown, *International Relations Theory: New Normative Approaches* (New York: Columbia University Press, 1992); and Martha Finnemore, *National Interests in International Society* (Ithaca: Cornell University Press, 1996).

11. Smith et al., *International Theory*, 5–6.

12. See, for instance, V. Spike Peterson, "Transgressing Boundaries: Theories of Knowledge, Gender and International Relations," *Millennium: Journal of International Studies*, vol. 21, no. 2 (1992), 183–206.

13. Margaret E. Keck and Kathryn Sikkink, *Activists Beyond Borders* (Ithaca: Cornell University Press, 1998).

14. An imaginary is the combination, foundation, and structure of mental images related to an object. A political imaginary encompasses distinct structures of subjectivity or identity and the historically formed objects of social relations. In the practical, the imaginary also guides the conscious and subconscious processes and structures that define the political will and desire.

15. Francis Fukuyama, *The End of History and the Last Man* (New York: Perennial, 2002).

16. Samuel P. Huntington, *The Clash of Civilizations and the Remaking of World Order* (New York: Simon & Schuster, c. 1996).

17. Michael W. Doyle, "Kant, Liberal Legacies, and Foreign Affairs," *Philosophy and Public Affairs*, vol. 12, nos. 3 and 4 (1983), 205–235 and 323–353.

18. As defined by Talal Asad, an authoritative utterance or discourse is neither necessarily true nor strictly wrong. It may combine facts, hearsay, and legends mobilized and organized within institutional contexts to oppose radically different utterances or perspectives. The idea of authoritative discourse has more bearing on the context and justification of discovery than on truthfulness. Talal Asad, "Anthropology and the Analysis of Ideology," *Man*, no. 14 (1979).

19. For illustrations on these points, see, for instance, Robert O. Keohane, ed., *Neorealism and Its Critics* (New York: Columbia University Press, 1986); David A. Baldwin, ed., *Neorealism and Neoliberalism: The Contemporary Debate* (New York: Columbia University Press, 1993); John Fitzpatrick, "The Anglo-American School of International Relations: The Tyranny of A-Historical Culturalism," *Australian*

Outlook, vol. 41 (1987), 45; Ole Wæver, "The Sociology of a Not So International Discipline: American and European Developments in International Relations," *International Organization*, vol. 52, no. 4 (1998), 687–727; Stanley Hoffmann, "An American Social Science: International Relations," *Daedalus*, vol. 3, no. 106 (1977), 41–60; and Ken Booth, "75 Years On: Rewriting The Subject's Past—Reinventing Its Future," in Steve Smith et al., eds., *International Theory: Positivism and Beyond* (Cambridge: Cambridge University Press, 1996), 331, 328–339.

20. Thomas Kuhn, *The Structure of Scientific Revolutions* (Chicago: University of Chicago Press, 1970), 23–34.

21. These include the totality, classification, and content of documents pertaining to history as well as artifices—monuments, arts, museums, and national holidays—that serve as reference for memorialized history.

22. Marianne H. Marchand, "Different Communities/Different Realities/ Different Encounters: A Reply to J. Ann Tickner," *International Studies Quarterly*, vol. 42, no. 1 (March 1998), 199–203.

23. Ibid.

24. Anthony G. Hopkins, *The Future of the Imperial Past* (Cambridge: Cambridge University Press, 1997).

25. See, for instance, Claude Paillat, *Vingt Ans qui Déchirèrent la France* (Paris: Editions Robert Laffont, 1972), vol. II.

26. There are exceptions, notably Michael J. Shapiro, *Violent Cartographies: Mapping Cultures of War* (Minneapolis: University of Minnesota Press, c. 1997) and Chris Brown, "Cultural Diversity and International Political Theory: From the Requirement to Mutual Respect?" *Review of International Studies*, vol. 26, no. 2 (April 2000), 199–213.

27. Brown, "Cultural Diversity and International Political Theory," 200–201.

28. F. H. Hinsley, *Sovereignty* (Cambridge: Cambridge University Press, 1986) and Robert H. Jackson, *Quasi-States: Sovereignty, International Relations and the Third World* (Cambridge: Cambridge University Press, 1993).

29. See Stephen Krasner, "Realism, Imperialism, and Democracy: A Response to Gilbert," *Political Theory*, vol. 20, no. 1 (1992), 48–49 and Jackson, *Quasi-States*, 202.

30. They numbered African chiefs and other black elites, including teachers, nurses, colonial administrators, soldiers, veterans, and other professionals.

31. I borrow the expression and its formulation from Naomi Schor, *Bad Objects: Essays Popular and Unpopular* (Durham: Duke University Press, 1995), 1–17.

32. Vichy officials perceptively contrasted African rebellion against victorious France at the end of World War I with the sympathy shown

to defeated France during World War II. *Centre des Archives d'Outre-Mer,* 1Affpol/928/2.
33. Both this image and arguments are taken from V. Y. Mudimbe, ed., *The Surreptitious Speech: Présence Africaine and the Politics of Otherness, 1947–1987* (Chicago University of Chicago Press, 1992).
34. Ibid., xv.
35. These were recurring points of reference and contestation in the various legislative and consultative bodies set up by France after 1946 in a bid to reform colonialism. Albert Sarraut on Man. République Française, "Ratification de L'Accord Economique avec les Etats-Unis," *Annales de l'Assemblée de l'Union Française* (July 1, 1948), 653.
36. Michel Foucault, *Power/Knowledge: Selected Interviews and Other Writings, 1972–1977,* Colin Gordon, ed. (New York: Pantheon, 1980), 78–133.
37. John Gerard Ruggie, *Constructing the World Polity* (London: Routledge, 1998), 62–84.
38. Jens Bartelson, *A Genealogy of Sovereignty* (Cambridge: Cambridge University Press, 1995), 6.
39. See, for instance, David A. Baldwin, ed., *Neorealism and Neoliberalism: The Contemporary Debate* (New York: Columbia University Press, 1993), 3.
40. Nicholas Onuf, *The Republican Legacy in International Thought* (Cambridge: Cambridge University Press, 1998), 173–190.
41. Dispesh Chakrabarty, *Provincializing Europe: Postcolonial Thought and Historical Difference* (Princeton: Princeton University Press, 2000, 45), 16.

Chapter 1   Encounters: Theory, Difference, and Representations

1. See "Forum on Alexander Wendt," *Review of International Studies,* vol. 26, no. 1 (January 2000), 123–163. The book reviewed by this forum was Alexander Wendt, *Social Theory of International Politics* (Cambridge: Cambridge University Press, 1999).
2. Roxanne Lynn Doty, "Desire All The Way Down," *Review of International Studies,* vol. 26, no. 1 (2000), 137–139.
3. Steve Smith, "Wendt's World," *Review of International Studies,* vol. 26, no. 1 (2000), 151–163.
4. David Campbell, "International Engagements: The Politics of North American International Relations Theory," *Political Theory,* vol. 29, no. 3 (June 2001), 432–448.
5. Campbell, "International Engagements".
6. Friedrich Kratochwil, "Constructing a New Orthodoxy? Wendt's 'Social Theory of International Politics' and the Constructivist Challenge," *Millennium: Journal of International Studies,* vol. 29, no. 1 (2000), 73–101.

7. Richard Rorty, "Habermas and Lyotard on Postmodernity," in Richard J. Bernstein, ed., *Habermas and Modernity* (Cambridge: MIT Press, 1986), 169. Quoted from Dispesh Chakrabarty, *Provincializing Europe: Postcolonial Thought and Historical Difference* (Princeton: Princeton University Press, 2000, 45).

8. Jürgen Habermas, for instance, estimates that Europe, "more than any other culture, faced and overcome structural conflicts, sharp confrontations and lasting tensions, in the social as well as in the temporal dimension." See Jürgen Habermas, "Why Europe Needs a Constitution," *New Left Review*, no. 11 (2001), 20.

9. See Wang Ning, "Orientalism versus Occidentalism?" *New Literary History*, vol. 1, no. 28 (1997), 57–67 and Ian Buruma and Jonathan D. Spence, "Two Cheers for Orientalism: The Chan's Great Continent: China in Western Minds," *The New Republic*, vol. 29 (January 4, 1999).

10. Meltem Ahiska, "Occidentalism: The Historical Fantasy of the West," *The South Atlantic Quarterly*, vol. 102, no. 2/3 (2003), 351–379.

11. Fernando Coronil, "Beyond Occidentalism: Toward Nonimperial Geohistorical Categories," *Cultural Anthropology*, vol. 11, no. 1 (1996), 52, 51–87.

12. See, for instance, Patrick Thaddeus Jackson, "Defending the West: Occidentalism and the Formation of NATO," *The Journal of Political Philosophy*, vol. 11, no. 3 (2003), 223–252.

13. According to Jurgen Habermas, for instance, the justification of the European project after World War II could not have been possible without the explicit appeal of its founding fathers to the Christian West. See Jurgen Habermas, "Why Europe Needs a Constitution," *New Left Review*, vol. 11 (September 2001), 7.

14. For instance, in 1999, German President Roman Herzog gathered together a Conference on European Responsibility (or COEUR, the French word for heart) which among other things ascertained that "Europe has reversed the drift of history in crucial respects." These included the presumed internal "initiative to reverse colonialism," "the initiative for global ecological action," and the invention of international morality through international law. Garret Fitzgerald, "Getting to the Heart of our Common European Identity," *The Irish Times*, March 6, 1999, 16.

15. See, for instance, Richard Falk, *Explorations at the Edge of Time: Prospect for World Order* (Philadelphia: Temple University Press, 1992), 5.

16. R. B. J. Walker, *Inside/Outside: International Relations as Political Theory* (Cambridge: Cambridge University Press, 1995).

17. Falk, *Explorations at the Edge of Time*, 5.

18. Roxanne Lynn Doty, "Desire All The Way Down," *Review of International Studies*, vol. 26, no. 1 (2000), 137–139.

19. Anthony Pagden has argued that "the process by which the 'other' is constructed is not, as has so often been claimed, a rather simple act of

political appropriation." Anthony Pagden, *European Encounters with the New World* (New Haven: Yale University Press, 1993), 184.

20. Tzvetan Todorov, *On Human Diversity: Nationalism, Racism, and Exoticism in French Thought*, trans. Catherine Porter (Cambridge, MA: Harvard University Press, 1993), 68.

21. Ibid.

22. Ibid.

23. See, for instance, Ivan Hannaford, *Race: The history of an Idea in the West* (Baltimore: Johns Hopkins University Press, 1996), 187–396.

24. Ibid., 80.

25. Ibid., 95

26. For a view of the justifying historiography and its generative discourses, see Edward W. Said, *Orientalism* (New York: Vintage Books, 1979).

27. Pagden, *European Encounters*.

28. Ibid.

29. Ibid.

30. Ann Laura Stoler, "Colonial Cultures and their Affective States," Seminar Anthropology Department, Johns Hopkins University (April 26, 1999).

31. Ibid.

32. Janet L. Abu-Lughod, *Before European Hegemony: The World System AD 1250–1350* (New York: Oxford University Press, 1989), 24.

33. Hedley Bull, *The Anarchical Society: A Study of Order in World Politics* (New York: Columbia University Press, 1977), 12.

34. Michel-Rolph Trouillot, *Silencing the Past: Power and the Production of History* (Boston: Beacon Press, 1995), 74.

35. Walter D. Mignolo, *The Darker Side of the Renaissance: Literacy, Territoriality, and Colonization* (Ann Arbor: University of Michigan Press, 1995), 18.

36. Ibid., 187.

37. Ibid., 14.

38. For the literatures on the anomalies or deviations of the postcolonial states, see, for instance, Robert H. Jackson, *Quasi-States: Sovereignty, International Relations and the Third World* (Cambridge: Cambridge University Press, 1993); Jean-François Bayard, *The State in Africa: The Politics of the Belly* (London: Longman, 1989); and Robert H. Jackson and Carl G. Rosberg, *Personal Rule in Black Africa* (Berkeley: University of California Press, 1982).

39. Walt Whitman Rostow, *The Stages of Economic Growth: A Non-Communist Manifesto* (New York: Cambridge University Press, 1990); Crawford Young, *Ideology and Development in Africa* (New Haven: Yale University Press, 1982), 297–324; Jackson, *Quasi-States*; and Jackson and Rosberg, *Personal Rule*, 83–266.

40. L. C. Green and Olive P. Dickason, *The Law of Nations and the New World* (Edmonton: University of Alberta Press, 1989), 1–130.

41. Henry Reynolds, *The Law of the Land* (Victoria, Australia: Penguin Books, 1992), 1–54.

42. Ibid., 9–22.

43. E. W. Bovill, *The Golden Trade of the Moors*, 2nd edition (London: Oxford University Press, 1970), 95–226.

44. James Lorimer, *The Institutes of the Law of Nations; A Treatise of the Jural Relations of Separate Political Communities* (London: W. Blackwood and Sons, 1883–1884) and *The Institutes of Law: A Treatise of the Jurisprudence as Determined by Nature* (London: Blackwood, 1880).

45. Such narrative structures are not a thing of the past. For instance, Naomi Chazan et al. have rejected the main conclusions of *comparative studies on the transatlantic slave trade* by insisting that "It is always impossible to judge how serious this effect was in that there is little evidence on the extent of the disruption, and, of course, we have *no idea of whether similar disruption would have occurred in the absence of the Atlantic slave trade.*" Naomi Chazan et al., eds., *Politics and Society in Contemporary Africa*, 2nd edition (Boulder: Lynne Reinner Publishers, 1992), 231 (My emphasis).

46. Siba N. Grovogui, *Sovereigns, Quasi-Sovereigns, and Africans: Race and Self-Determination in International Law* (Minneapolis: University of Minnesota Press, 1996), 43–76.

47. See, for instance, the debate opposing Seraphin de Freitas and Hugo Grotius in ibid.

48. See, for instance, Jack J. Weatherford, *Indian Givers: How the Indians of the Americas Transformed the World* (New York: Crown Publishers, 1988).

49. See, for instance, Charles Henry Alexandrowicz, *An Introduction to the History of the Law of Nations in the East Indies* (Oxford: Clarendon Press, 1967) and *The European-African Confrontation. A Study in Treaty Making* (Leiden: Sijthoff, 1973).

50. Ibid.

51. Trouillot, *Silencing the Past*, 50–56.

52. Torbjørn L. Knutsen, *A History of International Relations Theory* (Manchester, England: Manchester University Press, 1997), 50–55 and 69–71.

53. See, for instance, Lowell S. Gustafson, ed., *Thucydides' Theory of International Relations: A Lasting Possession* (Baton Rouge: Louisiana State University Press, 2000).

54. See, for instance, James E. Dougherty and Robert L. Pfalzgraff, Jr., *Contending Theories of International Relations: A Comprehensive Survey* (New York: Longman, 2001).

55. Lorimer, *The Institutes of the Law of Nations*.

56. Hannaford, *Race*, 14, 59.

57. Hans J. Morgenthau, *Politics Among Nations* (New York: Alfred A. Knopf, 1964), 4.

58. Hans J. Morgenthau, *Politics Among Nations* (New York: Alfred A. Knopf, 1964), 192 and 197.

59. Ibid., 26–27, 192–197.

60. Ibid.

61. 202–203.

62. E. H. Carr, *The Twenty Years' Crisis: 1919–1939* (New York: Harper and Row, 1964), 38–94.

63. Ibid.

64. Arnold J. Toynbee, *A Study of History* (London: Oxford University Press, 1947), 38–39.

65. Carr, *The Twenty Years' Crisis*.

66. Hans J. Morgenthau, *Scientific Man vs. Power Politics* (Chicago: University of Chicago Press, 1974), 3.

67. Ibid., 198–199.

68. Ibid., 72.

69. Chris Brown, *International Relations Theory* (New York: Columbia University Press, 1992), 24–25.

70. David Campbell and Michael Dillon, "The End of Philosophy and the End of International Relations," in Campbell and Dillon, eds., *The Political Subject of Violence* (Manchester: Manchester University Press, 1993), 1.

71. Ibid., 1–43.

72. Steve Smith, "The Self-Images of a Discipline: A Genealogy of International Relations Theory," in Steve Smith and Ken Booth, eds., *International Relations Theory Today* (University Park: Pennsylvania State University Press, 1995), 1–43.

73. See also, Campbell and Dillon, "The End of Philosophy," 1.

74. Smith, "The Self-Images of a Discipline," 1.

75. As it is with most Occidentalist texts, Carr's skepticism about the faculties and capacities of the other frequently appears in parenthetical notes to other arguments. Carr, *The Twenty Years' Crisis*.

76. Ibid., 224.

77. Ibid.

78. See also Smith, "The Self-Images of a Discipline."

79. For a survey of the ambiguities of the concept and practices of armed humanitarian interventions, see James Mayall, *The New Interventionism, 1991–1994* (Cambridge: Cambridge University Press, 1996); Stanley Hoffmann, *The Ethics and Politics of Humanitarian Intervention* (South Bend: University of Notre Dame Press, 1996); David Campbell, *National Deconstruction: Violence, Identity, and Justice in Bosnia* (Minneapolis: University of Minnesota Press, 1998); and Robert C. DiPrizio, *Armed Humanitarians* (Baltimore: Johns Hopkins University Press, 2002).

80. See, the views of statelessness in Africa, for instance, range from the benign (Bull, *The Anarchical Society*, 59–76) to the monstrous (Robert D. Kaplan, "The Coming Anarchy," *Atlantic Monthly* (February 1994), 44–76.

81. See, for instance, Gerald B. Helman and Steven R. Ratner, "Saving Failed States," *Foreign Policy* (Winter 1992/1993), 3–20; Elizabeth Rubin, "An Army of One's Own," *Harper's Magazine* (February 1997), 44–55.

82. Kaplan, "The Coming Anarchy," op. cit.

83. Ibid. (emphasis in original).

84. See also Carr, *The Twenty Years' Crisis*, 224–239; Bull, *The Anarchical Society*, 101–229; and Adam Watson, *The Evolution of International Society* (London: Routledge, 1992), 265–325.

85. See, for instance, Andrew Linklater, "The Question of the Next Stage in International Relations Theory," *Millennium: Journal of International Studies*, vol. 21, no. 1 (1087), 77–98, "Men and Citizens in International Relations," *Review of International Studies*, vol. 7 (1991), 23–37, and "The Problem of Community in International Relations," *Alternatives*, vol. xv (1990), 135–153. See also M. Hoffman, "Critical Theory and the Inter-Paradigm Debate," *Millennium: Journal of International Studies*, vol. 16, no. 2 (1987), 231–249.

86. Linklater, "Question," 84.

87. Linklater quoting approvingly Robert Keohane, ibid., 77.

88. For postmodern perspectives, see, for instance, Richard K. Ashley and R. B. J. Walker, "Reading Dissidence/Writing the Discipline: Crisis and the Question of Sovereignty in International Studies," *International Studies Quarterly*, vol. 34, no. 3 (1990), 367.

89. This problem is identified by Michel Foucault as "the void left by the disappearance of Man." Quoted in Richard K. Ashley and R. B. W. Walker, "Speaking the Language of Exile: Dissident Thought in International Studies," *International Studies Quarterly*, vol. 34 (1990), 259–268.

90. Ashely and Walker, "Reading Dissidence/Writing the Discipline," 367–416. See also R. B. J. Walker, "*The Prince* and 'The Pauper': Tradition, Modernity, and Practice in the Theory of International Relations," and Richard K. Ashley, "Three Modes of Economism," *International Studies Quarterly*, vol. 27 (1983), 463–496.

91. See, for instance, Richard K. Ashley and R. B. W. Walker, "Speaking the Language of Exile," 259–268.

92. Ibid.

93. Jim George and David Campbell, "Patterns of Dissent and the Celebration of Difference: Critical Social Theory and International Relations," *International Studies Quarterly*, vol. 34 (1990), 269–293.

94. See, for instance, V. Spike Peterson, "Whose Rights? A Critique of the 'Givens' in Human Rights Discourses," *Alternatives*, vol. xv (1990), 303–344.

95. V. Spike Peterson, "Transgressing Boundaries: Theories of Knowledge, Gender and International Relations," *Millennium: Journal of International Studies*, vol. 21, no. 2 (1992), 183.

96. Ibid., 190.

97. Arjun Appadurai, "Disjuncture and Difference in the Global Cultural Economy," *Public Culture*, vol. 2, no. 2 (Spring 1990), 1.

98. See, for instance, Ramashray Roy, R. B. J. Walker, and Richard K. Ashley, "Dialogue: Towards a Critical Social Theory of International Politics," *Alternatives*, vol. XIII (1988), 77–102.

99. Ibid.

100. R. B. J. Walker, "Genealogy, Geopolitics and Political Community: Richard Ashley and the Critical Social Theory of International Relations," in Roy, Walker, and Ashley, "Dialogue," 84.

101. Abu-Lughod, *Before European Hegemony*, 20–21. See also, Jerry H. Bentley, *Old World Encounters: Cross-Cultural Contacts and Exchanges in Pre-Modern Times* (New York: Oxford University Press, 1993).

102. Ramashray Roy, "The Limits of Genealogical Approach to International Politics," in Roy, Walker, and Ashley, "Dialogue," 82.

103. Ibid.

104. See, Mignolo, *The Darker Side of the Renaissance*.

105. Ibid.

106. Eric Wolf, *Europe and the People Without History* (Berkeley: University of California Press, c. 1997), 9.

107. Chakrabarty, *Provincializing Europe*, 3–9.

108. Ibid.

109. Ibid., 4.

110. Aijaz Ahmad, *In Theory: Classes, Nations, Literatures* (London: Verso, 1992).

111. See, Douglas Brinkley and David R. Facey-Crowther, eds., *The Atlantic Charter* (New York: St. Martin's Press, 1994).

112. Michel Foucault, "Introduction," in Georges Canguilhem, *On the Normal and the Pathological*, Carolyn R Fawcett and Robert S. Cohen, eds. (London: D. Reidel Publishing Company, 1978), xi. For analogies in the colonial context, see also Gil Anidjar, *The Jew, The Arab: A History of the Enemy* (Stanford: Stanford University Press, 2003), 42–50.

113. Congressional hearings on postcolonial theory targeting Edward Said and NYU Near Eastern Studies Department; Campus Watch and its connections to the Bush administration Middle Eastern policy advising groups; and so on.

114. In turn, this reception deters others from referring to them as inspiration for their own analyses. See Ahmad, *In Theory*.

115. See, Todorov, *On Human Diversity*; Hopkins, *Future*; and Pagden, *European Encounters*.

Chapter 2   Leclerc's Mosaic: Historicism, Institutionalism, and Memory

1. Edmund Husserl quoted in Dipesh Chakarbarty, *Provincializing Europe: Postcolonial Thought and Historical Difference* (Princeton: Princeton

University Press, 2000), 29; see also Edmund Husserl, *The Crisis of European Sciences and Transcendental Philosophy*, trans. David Carr (Evanston: Northwestern University Press, 1970), 281–285.

2. Chakarbarty, *Provincializing Europe*.

3. Johannes Fabian, *Time and the Other: How Anthropology Constructs Its Object* (New York: Columbia University Press, 2000).

4. Edward W. Said, *Orientalism* (New York: Vintage Books, c. 1994).

5. Felix Gilbert, *History: Politics or Culture* (Princeton: Princeton University Press, 1990), 23.

6. Ibid.

7. Michel-Rolph Trouillot, *Silencing the Past Power and the Production of History* (Boston: Beacon Press, 1995).

8. Despite begrudging acknowledgment of some role to the non-West in the development of international morality, the English School holds steadfastly to the notion that international society and morality are Western (if not English) gifts to international community. See, Hedley Bull and Adam Watson, eds., *The Expansion of International Society* (Oxford: Clarendon Press, 1984), 1 and 2. See also B. A. Roberson, ed., *International Society and the Development of International Theory* (London: Pinter, 1998).

9. Anthony Hopkins, *The Future of the Imperial Past* (Cambridge: Cambridge University Press, 1997).

10. For institutionalist views of the virtues of transnational networks and formal government interventions, see, for instance, Thomas Risse-Kappen, ed., *Bringing Transnational Relations Back In: Non-State Actors, Domestic Structures, and International Institutions* (New York: Cambridge University Press, 1995); James Mayall, ed., *The New Interventionism, 1991–1994: United Nations Experience in Cambodia, former Yugoslavia, and Somalia* (Cambridge: Cambridge University Press, 1996); and Margaret E. Keck and Kathryn Sikkink, *Activists Beyond Borders: Advocacy Networks in International Politics* (Ithaca: Cornell University Press, 1998).

11. Keck and Sikkink, *Activists Beyond Borders*, 39–78.

12. Frederick Cooper, "Networks, Moral Discourse, and History," in Thomas M. Callaghy et al., eds., *Intervention and Transnationalism in Africa* (Cambridge: Cambridge University Press, 2001), 28.

13. See, for instance, Stephen Krasner, "Power Politics and Transnational Relations," in Thomas Risse-Kappen, ed., *Bringing Transnational Relations Back In: Non-State Actors, Domestic Structures, and International Institutions* (New York: Cambridge University Press, 1995), 257–279.

14. Such is particularly the case with Andreas Hasenclever et al., *Theories of International Regimes* (Cambridge: Cambridge University Press, 1997).

15. I will return to this theme in relation to Margaret E. Keck's and Kathryn Sikkink's work on transnational networks. Keck and Sikkink, *Activists Beyond Borders*.

16. Micheline R. Ishay, for instance, has done an impressive rendition "internationalism" by looking at the persistence of Enlightenment-related idioms of reason and solidarity. She holds these to be the most compelling grounds of protest and imagination of political future at a time when these very ideas were contested in vast colonial expanses. See Micheline R. Ishay, *Internationalism and Its Betrayal* (Minneapolis: University of Minnesota Press, 1995).

17. Aihwa Ong, *Flexible Citizenship: The Cultural Logics of Transnationality* (Durham: Duke University Press, 1999), 1–26.

18. This group extends to theorists of transnational networks, international civil society, and social movements. See, Thomas Risse-Kappen, ed., *Bringing Transnationalism Back In: Non-State Actors, Domestic Structures, and International Institutions* (Cambridge: Cambridge University Press, 1995); Peter M. Haas, ed., "Knowledge, Power, and International Policy Coordination," *International Organization*, vol. 46, no. 1 (Winter 1992); and Kathryn Sikkink, "Human rights, Principles Issue-Networks, and Sovereignty in Latin America," *International Organization*, vol. 47, no. 3 (Summer 1993).

19. Sikkink, "Human rights, Principles Issue-Networks, and Sovereignty in Latin America."

20. For an appreciation of the debate see David A. Baldwin, ed., *Neorealism and Neoliberalism: The Contemporary Debate* (New York: Columbia University Press, 1993).

21. See, for instance, Robert L. Phillips and Duane L. Cady, *Humanitarian Intervention: Just War vs. Pacifism* (Lanham: Rowman and Littlefield Publishers, 1996); Gene M. Lyons and Michael Mastanduno, eds., *Beyond Westphalia? Sovereignty and International Intervention* (Baltimore: Johns Hopkins University, 1995) and "International intervention, state sovereignty and the future of international society," *International Social Science Journal*, vol. 45 (1993), 517–532.

22. Krasner, "Power Politics," 257–279.

23. This is particular in the case with transnational networks of epistemic communities. See, particularly, Peter M. Haas, ed., "Knowledge," abstract and 3.

24. Ibid.

25. William E. Connolly, *The Ethos of Pluralization* (Minneapolis: University of Minnesota Press, 1995), 21.

26. See, Eric J. Hobsbawm, *Nations and Nationalism Since 1780: Program, Myth, Reality*, 2nd edition (Cambridge: Cambridge University Press, 1992) and *The Age of Empire, 1875–1914* (New York: Vintage, 1989).

27. Keck and Sikkink, *Activists Beyond Borders*.

28. Ibid., 7.

29. Ibid.

30. Ibid., 35.

31. Ibid., 2.

32. Ibid., 2.
33. Ibid., 35.
34. Ibid., 3.
35. Ibid., 33.
36. Ibid., 30
37. Ibid., 25.
38. Ibid., 30.
39. Ibid., 39–78.
40. Ibid., 5.
41. Ibid.
42. Ibid., 8.
43. Keck and Sikkink acknowledge that such linkages are not without their share of frictions. Ibid., 12–13.
44. Francis Fukuyama, *The End of History and the Last Man* (New York: Perennial, 2002).
45. My own intellectual mentors and sources of inspiration include all prominent Western intellectuals.
46. Cooper, "Networks," 32.
47. Ibid.
48. Ibid.
49. Mustapha Kamal Pasha and David L. Blaney, "Elusive Paradise: The Promise and Peril of Global Civil Society," *Alternatives*, no. 23 (1998), 417–450.
50. Ibid., 418–421.
51. Ibid.
52. Ibid., 420.
53. Ibid., 422.
54. Keck and Sikkink, *Activists Beyond Borders*, 33.
55. Ibid.
56. Ong, *Flexible Citizenship*, 1–26.
57. Ibid.
58. Ibid., 1–28.
59. Ibid.
60. Ibid., 87–136.
61. Ibid., 6.
62. For a sample of opinions, see, for instance, Arundhati Roy, "The Algebra of Infinite Justice," *The Guardian* (September 29, 2001); "Confronting Empire," *Z-Net* (January 28, 2003); "The Day of the Jackals: On War and Occupation," *Counterpunch* (June 2, 2003); and "Mesopotamia. Babylon. The Tigris and Euphrates," *The Guardian* (April 2, 2003).
63. Ariel Dorfman, "The Last September 11th," American University School of International Service, September 24, 2001.
64. Pheng Cheah and Bruce Robbins, eds., *Cosmopolitics: Thinking and Feeling Beyond the Nation* (Minneapolis: University of Minnesota Press, c. 1998).
65. Ibid. See also Ong, *Flexible Citizenship*, 1–28.

66. Ong, *Flexible Citizenship*, 87–136.
67. See, Mayall, *The New Interventionism*, op. cit.
68. R. B. J. Walker, *Inside/Outside: International Relations as Political Theory* (Cambridge: Cambridge University Press, 1992).
69. Jean Bodin, *Les Six Livres de la République*, Christiane Frémont, Marie-Dominique Couzinet, and Henri Rochais, eds. (Paris: Fayard, c. 1986).
70. The proper referent of anarchy in the writings of Thomas Hobbes, Baruch Spinoza, and others is the unmediated chaos that befell Europe from the sixteenth century to the middle of World War II.
71. Siba N. Grovogui, "International Morality and the African Condition," *European Journal of International Relations*, vol. 8, no. 3 (2002), 315–338.
72. Jane Guyer, "The Atlantic as a Region," Johns Hopkins University Lecture, March 26, 2001.
73. Eric Williams, 1944; Walter Rodney, *How Europe Underdeveloped Africa* (Washington, DC: Howard University Press, 1981).
74. Guyer, "The Atlantic."
75. Cooper, "Networks," 28.
76. Ibid., 24–25.
77. Ibid.
78. Ibid.
79. Ibid., 37.
80. Catherine Akpo-Vaché, *L'AOF et la Seconde Guerre Mondiale* (Paris: Karthala, 1996), 13–26 and 95–146.
81. See, Jean-Pierre Bondi and Gilles Morin, *Les Anti-Colonialistes (1881–1962)* (Paris: Editions Robert Laffont, 1992), 207–226 and Serge Wolikow, *Le Front Populaire en France* (Paris: Editions Complexe, 1996), 169–206.
82. Léon Blum's view of governmental reform was spelled out in *La Réforme gouvernementale*; see Wolikow, *Le Front Populaire*, op. cit.
83. Ruth Schachter-Morgenthau, *Le Multipartisme en Afrique de l'Ouest Francophone Jusqu'aux Independances* (Paris: l'Harmattan, 1998), 16.
84. Even after the war, Blum and his partisans continued to solicit participation of some "évolués" into metropolitan political debates. As president of the French Council (head of government) in 1946–1947, Blum appointed the Senegalese Lamine Guèye to be under-secretary of state.
85. For a view of Blum's "programme immédiat" see Jean-Pierre Biondi and Jules Morin, *Les Anticolonialistes*, 207–227.
86. Ibid.
87. An *animateur* of the Rothschilds' banks, Réné Mayer was the former's cousin by marriage. He was also the CEO of an oil exploration company and a member of the liberal party known as Parti Radical,

where he represented Algeria. He was also a onetime president of the French Council. A political opponent of Léon Blum, Mayer also feared that the 1930s crisis might be blamed on Blum by French conservatives who saw in it the handiwork of Jews bent on weakening France. Ibid.

88. Ibid.
89. *Centre des Archives d'Outre-Mer*, 1Affpol/917/1–3.
90. Not only were the foot soldiers of the resistance in Africa disproportionately secular Jews and backers of Léon Blum's Front Populaire, other prominent resistance leaders on the continent had Jewish association. For instance, Edgar de Larminat and Lt. General Paul le Gentilhomme were both married to Jewish women: Suzanne Mahé and Louise le Brun, respectively. Etat Français, Ministère de la Justice, Séquestre des Français Déchus, *Décret du 8 Décembre 1940*.
91. The census of persons of Jewish descent and their property was a turning point. Etat Français, "Loi du 2 Juin 1941 Remplaçant la Loi du 3 Octobre 1940 Sur l'Etat des Juifs et Loi du 2 Juin 1941 Prescrivant le Recensement des Juifs," *Journal Officiel* (June 14, 1941), 2475 and 2476.
92. Akpo-Vaché, *L'AOF*, 220, 211, 226, 248, 249, and 259.
93. For a quick profile of African soldiers and officers of the two World Wars, see Myron Eckenberg, *Colonial Conscripts: The Tirailleurs Sénégalais in French West Africa, 1857–1960* (Portsmouth, NH: Heinemann, 1991), 64–69.
94. Etat Français, *Bulletin d'Information Des Troupes Du Groupe De L'AOF* (July 1942), 4–5.
95. Ibid.
96. Pétain argued that France had been drawn needlessly into a foreign war and that "foreign propaganda had succeeded in dividing French opinion" such that everyone doubted themselves and the leader of France while few thought of themselves anymore as French. Ibid.
97. Ibid.
98. Français, "Loi du 2 Juin 1941." See also Etat Français, Commissariat Aux Affaires Juives, *Décret* (July 28, 1941) and *Loi* (November 29, 1941) Instituant Une Union Générale des Israélites en France. Finally, see Etat Français, Ministère de la Justice, Séquestres des Français Déchus, *Décret* (January 27, 1941).
99. Akpo-Vaché, *L'AOF*, 8, 27–44.
100. Ibid.
101. Ibid.
102. The following are alternate references to French grandeur in official French memoranda: *la place traditionnelle de la France dans le concert des nations; le rôle de la France aux côtés des grandes puissances; l'autorité morale de la France dans le monde; le destin de la France; la France en tant que grande et forte nation.* (The translation is as follows: The traditional place of France within the concert of nations; the role of France

among the great powers; the moral authority of France in the world; the destiny of France; France as great and strong nation). *Centre des Archives d'Outre-Mer*, 1Affpol 879/1–13.

103. Etat Français, Vichy, *Marine A. O. F à Ministère des Colonies*, no. 2.324 à 2.327 (1940).

104. République Française, Colonie du Tchad, *Acte du Gouverneur* (August 28, 1940).

105. Ibid.

106. Etat Français, Vichy, Ministère des Colonies, *Documents*, nos. 1.183 and 2.324 (August 30, 1940).

107. Gabriel Lisette, *Le Combat du Rassemblement Democratique Africain pour la Decolonisation pacifique de l'Afrique Noire* (Paris: Présence Africaine, 1983), 157.

108. See Etat Français, Vichy, *Acte Constitutionnel No. 1*, July 10, 1940.

109. République Française, Ministère des Colonies, *Documents*, no. 1229 (September 5, 1940); Etat Français, Ministère des Colonies, *Documents*, nos. 1.183 and 2.324 à 327 (August 30, 1940).

110. Ruth Schachter-Morgenthau, *Le Multipartisme en Afrique de l'Ouest Francophone Jusqu'aux Indépendances* (Paris: l'Harmattan, 1998), 11–25.

111. République Française, Gouvernement de l'Afrique Equatoriale Française, *Acte Organique No. 1* (August 29, 1940).

112. For chronology and successions of events, see, for instance, *Centre des Archives d'Outre-Mer*, 1Affpol 883/14; 889/1–4; 889bis/1–21.

113. Ibid.

114. Martin Blumenson, "Politics and the Military in the Liberation of France," *Parameters* (Summer 1998), 4–14.

115. Ibid., 4.

116. Ibid.

117. Ibid.

118. See, for instance, Larry Collins and Dominique Lapierre, *Is Paris Burning?* (New York: Simon and Schuster, 1965)

119. Echenberg, *Colonial Conscripts*, 98, see also 64–69.

120. Ibid., 88.

121. See, for instance, Benjamin Stora, *Imaginaires de Guerre* (Paris: Editions La Decouverte, 1997).

122. Ibid.

123. Aijaz Ahmad, *In Theory: Classes, Nations, and Literatures* (London: Verso, 1992), 1–42.

Chapter 3 Félix Adolphe Sylvestre Eboué: Republicanism, Humanism, and their Modulations

1. To underscore this point, see for instance a 2001 letter of Hungarian intellectuals to Lionel Jospin, prime minister of France, regarding French actions on behalf of the Roma of Zámoly. *Élet és Irodalom*,

XLV., 12. 2001. március 23. (http://www.es.hu/0112/publi.htm#kis) (Transl. József Böröcz).

2. Alice L. Conklin, *A Mission to Civilize* (Stanford: Stanford University Press, 1997), 5.

3. Michael Walzer, for instance, considers due consideration of third world thoughts, "thirdwordism," an intellectual indecency. See Michael Walzer, "Can There Be A Decent Left?" *Dissent*, http://www.dissentmagazine.org/menutest/archives/2002/sp02/decent.html.

4. J. G. A. Pocock, *Politics, Language, and Time: Essays on Political Thought and History* (New York: Atheneum Press, 1971), 15–18.

5. Ibid., 3–41.

6. John G. Ruggie, "What Makes the World Hang Together?" *International Organization*, vol. 52, no. 4 (1998).

7. Alexander Wendt, *Social Theory of International Relations* (Cambridge: Cambridge University Press, 2000).

8. Ibid., 3–4.

9. Roxanne Lynn Doty, "Desire All The Way Down," *Review of International Studies*, vol. 26, no. 1 (2000), 137–139; David Campbell, "International Engagements: The Politics of North American International Relations Theory," *Political Theory*, vol. 29, no. 3 (2001), 432–448; Friedrich Kratochwil, "Constructing a New Orthodoxy? Wendt's 'Social Theory of International Politics' and the Constructivist Challenge," *Millennium: Journal of International Studies*, vol. 29, no. 1 (2000), 73–101.

10. Campbell, "International Engagements," 432–433.

11. Ronen Palan, "A World of their Making: An Evaluation of the Constructivist Critique in International Relations," *Review of International Studies*, vol. 26 (2000), 578, 575–598.

12. Ibid., 591.

13. Campbell, "International Engagements."

14. Michael J. Shapiro, *Violent Cartographies: Mapping Cultures of War* (Minneapolis: University of Minnesota Press, c. 1997).

15. Ibid.

16. Wendt, *Social Theory*, 8.

17. See, Antonio Gramsci, "Problems of History and Culture," in Quintin Hoare and Geoffrey Nowell Smith, eds., *Selections From the Prison Notebooks* (New York: International Publishers, 1971), 5–120.

18. See John Gerard Ruggie, *Constructing the World Polity* (London: Routledge, 1998), 62–84, 210.

19. See, for instance, Peter Hulme, *Colonial encounters: Europe and the Native Caribbean, 1492–1797* (London: Routledge, 1986); Peter Mason, *Deconstructing America: Representations of the Other* (London: Routledge, 1990); and Eric Cheyfitz, *The Poetics of Imperialism: Translation and Colonization from the Tempest to Tarzan* (Philadelphia: University of Pennsylvania Press, 1991).

20. Mark Laffey and Jutta Weldes, "Beyond Belief: Ideas and Symbolic Technologies in the Study of International Relations," *European Journal of International Relations*, vol. 3, no. 2 (1997), 193–237.
21. Nicholas Onuf, *World of Our Making* (Columbia, SC: University of South Carolina Press, 1989), 36.
22. Nicholas Onuf, *The Republican Legacy in International Thought* (Cambridge: Cambridge University Press, 1998), 1–27.
23. Palan, "A World of their Making," 586.
24. Ibid.
25. Because "international thought must be subject of its own story," it would seem appropriate to take a new look at republicanism because it "took a world of politics, not states, as its frame of reference." Onuf, *The Republican*, 1–27.
26. Ibid., 12–16.
27. Ibid.
28. Ibid., 46
29. Ibid., 163–190.
30. Ibid., 139–190.
31. Ibid.
32. Ibid., 10.
33. Eduardo Galeano, *Memory of Fire: I. Genesis*, trans. Cedric Belfrage (New York: Quartet Books, 1998), 57–58, 84.
34. See, for instance, Dénis Diderot, *Political Writings*, trans. John Hope Mason and Robert Wokler (Cambridge: Cambridge University Press, 1992) and François-Marie Arouet Voltaire, *L'Ingénu et autres contes* (Paris: Bookking International, F 1993).
35. Siba N. Grovogui, *Sovereigns, Quasi-Sovereigns, and Africans* (Minneapolis: University of Minnesota Press, 1996), 28–30.
36. Ibid.
37. Laffey and Weldes, "Beyond Belief," 193–237.
38. Richard Rorty, "Habermas and Lyotard on Postmodernity," in Richard J. Bernstein, ed., *Habermas and Modernity* (Cambridge: MIT Press, 1986), 169 (Quoted from Chakrabarty, *Provincializing Europe*, 45).
39. See, for instance, Jurgen Habermas, "Why Europe Needs a Constitution," *New Left Review*, vol. 11 (September 2001).
40. In a poignant illustration on the consequences of the institutionaliza-tion of select perspectives, Ken Booth has argued that "Cold War International Relations—ostensibly realist—lost sight of both reality and its roots. The subject had started out to combat human wrongs (in the obvious and important form of war) but it had developed into an activity which taught students to ignore other massive human wrongs." Steve Smith et al., eds., *International Theory: Positivism and Beyond* (Cambridge: Cambridge University Press, 1996), 330.

41. See, for instance, Janet Abu-Lughod, *Before European Hegemony: The World System A.D. 1250–1350* (Oxford: Oxford University Press, 1989).
42. Ibid.
43. Ibid.
44. Michel-Rolph Trouillot, *Silencing the Past: Power and the Production of History* (Boston: Beacon Press, 1995), xi–xix.
45. Michel Foucault, *Power/Knowledge: Selected Interviews and Other Writings, 1972–1977*, Colin Gordon, ed. (New York: Pantheon, 1980), 78–133.
46. Sankaran Krishna, "Race, Amnesia, and the Education of International Relations," *Alternatives*, vol. 26 (2001), 401–424.
47. Ibid.
48. Hedley Bull and others from the English School have tried to modify this assumption by recognizing marginal and unsustained roles to others in the production of international morality. But they ultimately attribute authorship of present international society and morality to the mechanisms of empire and colonization. See Hedley Bull, *The Anarchical Society: A Study of Order in World Politics* (New York: Columbia University Press, 1977), xi–xv, 3–20.
49. See Henry Reynolds, *The Law of the Land* (Victoria, Australia: Penguin Books, 1992), 1–54; Basil Davidson, *Black Mother, Africa: The Years of Trial* (London: Victor Gollancz, 1961), 53. See also Abu-Lughod, *Before European Hegemony*, 20–24.
50. Krishna, "Race," 401–424.
51. Ibid.
52. Pocock, *Politics, Language, and Time*, 15–18 and 233–234.
53. Ibid.
54. See, for instance, J. G. A. Pocock, *The Machiavellian Moment: Florentine Political Thought and the Atlantic Republican Tradition* (Princeton: Princeton University Press, 1975).
55. Onuf citing Pocock, *The Republican*, 38. Pocock, *Politics, Language, and Time*, 15–18.
56. Eric Hobsbawm and Terrence Ranger, eds., *The Invention of Tradition* (Cambridge: Cambridge University Press, 1983).
57. Onuf, *The Republican*, 79.
58. Ibid.
59. F. V. Kratochwil, *Rules, Norms, and Decisions* (Cambridge: Cambridge University Press, 1989), 25–44.
60. Kratochwil, "Constructing," 73–101.
61. Kratochwil, *Rules*, 59.
62. Ibid.
63. Ibid.
64. Ibid., 57–59.
65. Onuf, *The Republican*, 37

66. Voltaire (François Marie Arouet), *An Essay On Universal History, The Manners, And Spirit*, trans. Mr. Nugent (Dublin: Bookfeller in Skinner-Row, 1754).
67. See, for instance, Denis Diderot and Jean le Rond d'Alembert, eds., *Encyclopédie ou Dictionnaire raisonné des Sciences, Arts, et Métiers* (Paris: Chez Briasson, 1755).
68. See, for instance, Lynn Hunt, ed., *The French Revolution and Human Rights* (Boston: St. Martin's Press, 1996).
69. Trouillot, *Silencing the Past*, 78.
70. John Locke, *The Second Treatise of Government*, Thomas Preston Peardon, ed. (New York: Liberal Arts Press, 1952). See also Homi Bhabha, "Of Mimicry and Man: The Ambivalence of the Colonial Discourse," in Frederick Cooper and Ann Laura Stoler, eds., *Tensions of Empire* (Berkeley: University of California Press, 1997), 153.
71. Bhabha, "Of Mimicry and Man," 153
72. Trouillot, *Silencing the Past*.
73. Ibid.
74. Ibid., 81.
75. Ibid., 78.
76. See, for instance, V. Y. Mudimbe, ed., *The Surreptitious Speech: Presence Africaine and the Politics of Otherness* (Chicago: University of Chicago Press, 1992), 95–117.
77. *Centre des Archives d'Outre-Mer*, 1Affpol/1164.
78. Ibid.
79. Frederick Cooper, "Networks, Moral Discourse, and History," in Thomas M Callaghy et al., eds., *Intervention and Transnationalism in Africa* (Cambridge: Cambridge University Press, 2001), 28.
80. David Spurr, *Rhetoric of Empire* (Durham: Duke University Press, 1993), 29.
81. Ibid., 34.
82. Mudimbe, ed., *The Surreptitious Speech*, 95–117.
83. Ferdinand Oyono, " 'Palatable' Negroes," *Centre des Archives d'Outre-Mer*, 1Affpol 2127/1.
84. See, for instance, Cooper, "Networks" and Partha Chatterjee, *Nationalist Thought and the Colonial World* (London: Zed Press, 1986).
85. Here I paraphrase Partha Chatterjee's criticism of both Elie Kedourie and Ernest Gellner's modular view of nationalism, which applies to republicanism as well. See Chatterjee, *Nationalist Thought*, 1–35.
86. Christopher L. Miller, *Theories of Africans* (Chicago: University of Chicago Press, 1990).
87. Mudimbe, *The Surreptitious Speech*.
88. Benedict Anderson, *Imagined Communities* (London: Verso Press, 1983).
89. Craig Calhoun, *Nationalism* (Minneapolis: University of Minnesota Press, 1997), 107.

90. Cooper, "Networks," 39.
91. Ibid.
92. Ibid., 23.
93. Ibid.
94. Ibid., 40.
95. Ibid., 40.
96. Conklin, *A Mission*, 5.
97. Ibid.
98. Ibid.
99. Ibid.
100. Partha Chatterjee, *Texts of Power: Emerging Disciplines in Colonial Bengal* (Minneapolis: University of Minnesota Press), 20.
101. Cooper, "Networks," 40.
102. Youssouf Tata Cissé and Wâ Kamissoko, *Soundjata, La Gloire du Mali*, Tome 2 (Paris: Karthala -Arsan, 1991), 162.
103. Ibid., 208.
104. Chatterjee, *Nationalist Thought*, 13.
105. Ibid., 14.
106. Cissé and Kamissoko, *Soundjata*, 207.
107. Chatterjee, *Texts of Power*, 23.
108. Ibid., 24.
109. Ibid., 20.
110. Alberto Moreiras, "The Conflict of Transculturation," CAC Lecture series, Johns Hopkins University, March 7, 2001.
111. Eric Hobsbawm, *The Age of Empire, 1875–1914* (New York: Vintage Books, 1989); Tzvetan Todorov's seminal book *On Human Diversity: Nationalism, Racism, and Exoticism in French Thought*, trans. Catherine Porter (Cambridge, MA: Harvard University Press, 1993).
112. Ibid.
113. Ibid.
114. Spurr, *Rhetoric of Empire*, 28–73 and 76–121.
115. Conklin, *A Mission*.
116. All these impressions may be found, for instance, in Tzvetan Todorov's seminal book *On Human Diversity*.
117. *Centre des Archives d'Outre-Mer*, 1Affpol 879/1–13.
118. One Vichy concurred that "Few nations can be as proud as France for the consistency of its colonial effort. Thanks to hard work, born of the genius and sacrifice of its children, France was able to put together a harmonious and homogenous colonial empire, the foundation of its grandeur and prosperity." Etat Français á Vichy, "Rapport Politique Haut Commissariat de l'Afrique Française, 1940," *Centre des Archives d'Outre-Mer*, 1Affpol 2178/3.
119. Félix Eboué, "Programme du Gouvernement Général," *Journal Officiel* (December 1, 1941).

120. Pierre-Olivier Lapie, "A Monsieur De Gaulle," *Centre des Archives d'Outre-Mer*, 1Affpol 873/19.
121. See Pierre-Olivier Lapie, *Le Tchad Fait la Guerre* (Paris: Office Français d'Editions, 1943), and *Mes Tournées au Tchad* (Paris, 1945).
122. Lapie, "A Monsieur De Gaulle," 1Affpol 873/19.
123. Ibid.
124 Ibid.
125. M. Parr, "Traduction d'un project de dépêche de Mr. Parr au Ministre de l'Intérieur," *Centre des Archives d'Outre-Mer*, 1Affpol 873/3.
126. Ibid.
127. Ibid.
128. "Accord Clark-Darlan," *Centre des Archives d'Outre-Mer*, 1Affpol 877/1.
129. Winston Churchill, "Extraits du Discours prononcé aux Communes, 10 Juin 1941," *Centre des Archives d'Outre-Mer*, 1Affpol 877/1.
130. Réné Pléven, "Libération de Paris," *Centre des Archives d'Outre-Mer*, 1Affpol 879/1.
131. Ibid.
132. Ibid.
133. Ibid.
134. Ibid.
135. Félix Houphouet-Boigny, "Réponse à D'Arboussier," *Afrique Noire*, no. 27 (July 24, 1952).
136. See, for instance, France Combattante, "Procès-Verbal de la réunion du Groupe Colonial et d'Afrique du Nord," (March 10, 1943).
137. World War II occurred only half a century after the Dreyfus affair, which divided French humanists and republicans. The divisions that it caused climaxed in Emile Zola's famous *J'accuse* pamphlet. The advent of Vichy and the deportation of French Jews to Germany also brought to reality the tenuousness of Jewish positions in French society and institutions.
138. Conklin, *A Mission*, 5.
139. Professeur Robert Laffont, "Texte de discours radiodiffusé," *Centre des Archives d'Outre-Mer*, 1Affpol 873/3.
140. Ibid.
141. Ibid.
142. Ibid.
143. Ibid.
144. Ibid.
145. Ibid.
146. Ibid.
147. Ibid.
148. M. Perret, "Affaire Laffont," *Centre des Archives d'Outre-Mer*, 1Affpol 873/3.

149. Ibid.
150. Jean-Pierre Biondi and Jules Morin, *Les Anti-Colonialistes (1881–1962)* (Paris: Editions Robert Laffont, 1992).
151. Gaston de Monnerville, "Introduction," in Sophie Ulrich, *Le Gouverneur General Félix Eboué* (Paris: La Rose, 1950).
152. Félix Eboué, "A Commissaire National de l'Economie, Londres," *Centre des Archives d'Outre-Mer*, 1Affpol 873/1.
153. Ibid.
154. Ibid.
155. See G. Fortuné, "Circulaire Sur la Politique Indigène au Moyen Congo," *Journal Officiel de la France Libre et de l'AEF* (May 1, 1942), 150.
156. Monnerville, "Introduction."
157. Ibid.
158. Ibid.
159. Ibid.
160. Eboué joined a long list of Antilleans who devoted their lives to restoring humanity and dignity to Africans. Gabriel Lisette, for instance, lived and died in Paris.
161. Monnerville, "Introduction."
162. Félix Eboué, "Circulaire Générale," *Journal Officiel de la France Libre et de l'AEF* (December 1, 1941), 687.
163. Ibid., 688.
164. Ibid.
165. Ibid.
166. Ibid.
167. Ibid., 687–699.
168. Félix Eboué, "Le Programme du Gouverneur Général," *Le Courrier Africain*, Edition AEF, no. 25 (January 25, 1941).
169. Ibid.
170. Eboué, "Circulaire Générale," 687.
171. Eboué, "Le Programme du Gouverneur Général."
172. Ibid.
173. Garret Fitzgerald, "Getting to the Heart of Our Common European Identity," *The Irish Tiimes*, March 6, 1999, 16.

Chapter 4   Gabriel d'Arboussier: Democracy Is Not a Magnificently Adorned Hall

1. Francis Fukuyama, *The End of History and the Last Man* (New York: Perennial, 2002).
2. This optimism suffered a blow on September 11, 2001 upon the terrorist attacks in the United States, which were followed by U.S. wars in Afghanistan and Iraq. In turn, this setback has provided

fodder to those opened to Samuel P. Huntington's view of an impending *clash of civilizations*. See Samuel P. Huntington, *The Clash of Civilizations and the Remaking of World Order* (New York: Simon & Schuster, c. 1996).

3. Jacques Rancière, *Disagreement: Politics and Philosophy*, trans. Julie Rose (Minneapolis: University of Minnesota Press, 1999), vii, viii.

4. Michael W. Doyle was among the first to call for a return of theory to liberal political forms in support of democracy. See, for instance, Michael W. Doyle, "Kant, Liberal Legacies, and Foreign Affairs," *Philosophy and Public Affairs*, vol. 12, nos. 3 and 4 (1983), 205–235 and 323–353.

5. Bruce Fetter, ed., *Colonial Rule in Africa: Readings from Primary Sources* (Madison: University of Wisconsin Press, 1979), 96–98.

6. Thomas Francis Power, *Jules Ferry and the Renaissance of French Imperialism* (New York: King's Crown Press, 1944).

7. David W. Dent, *The Legacy of the Monroe Doctrine: A Reference Guide to U.S. Involvement in Latin America and the Caribbean* (Westport, CT: Greenwood Press, 1999)

8. Jurgen Habermas, "Why Europe Needs a Constitution," *New Left Review*, vol. 11 (2001), 5–6. See also Edmund Husserl, *The Crisis of European Sciences and Transcendental Philosophy*, trans. David Carr (Evanston: Northwestern University Press, 1970), 281–285.

9. See, for instance, Emile Durkheim, *The Rules of Sociological Method*, trans. W. D. Halls (London: Macmillan Press, 1982).

10. See, for instance, Sam Whimster, *The Essential Weber: A Reader* (London: Routledge, 2004).

11. Ronald H. Chilcote, *Theories of Comparative Political Economy* (Boulder, CO: Westview Press, 2000).

12. See, for instance, Clifford Geertz, *Local Knowledge: Further Essays in Interpretive Anthropology* (New York: Basic Books, 1983).

13. Marcel Detienne, "Murderous Identity: Anthropology, History, and the Art of Constructing Comparables," *Common Knowledge*, vol. 8, no. 1 (2002), 178–187.

14. Ibid.

15. Ibid.

16. Walter Benjamin, *Illuminations*, Hannah Arendt, ed. (New York: Schocken Books, 1969), 69–82.

17. Ibid.

18. Detienne, "Murderous Identity," 178–187.

19. Although Western metaphysics has long occluded it, Friedrich Nietzsche, Michel Foucault, and Gilles Deleuze have argued in their differing ways that pluralization and polyvalency are in the nature of things. Consistently, disciplinary analyses impose structures of identities upon this inherent pluralism and thus limit and contain the pluralizing potentialities both within and outside the West.

20. See, for instance, Michael C. Williams, "The Discipline of the Democratic Peace: Kant, Liberalism, and the Social Construction of Security Communities," *European Journal of International Relations*, vol. 7, no. 4 (2001), 525–553.

21. Charles W. Kegley, Jr., "The Neoidealist Moment in International Studies? Realist Myths and the New International Realities," *International Studies Quarterly*, vol. 37, no. 2 (June 1993), 131–146.

22. Stanley Hoffmann, *The Ethics and Politics of Humanitarian Intervention* (Notre Dame: University of Notre Dame Press, 1996).

23. Michael Doyle, "Kant, Liberal Legacies, and Foreign Affairs," *Philosophy and Public Affairs*, vol. 12, no. 4 (Autumn, 1983), 323–353.

24. Jean Bethke Elshtain, "What Morality Got to Do With It? Making the Right Distinctions," *Social Philosophy and Policy*, vol. 21, no. 1 (2004), 1–13 and *Just War Against Terror: The Burden of American Power in a Violent World* (New York: Basic Books, c. 2003).

25. Christopher Layne, "Kant or Cant: The Myth of the Democratic Peace," *International Security*, vol. 19, no. 2 (1994), 5–49.

26. John Owen, "How Liberalism Produces Democratic Peace," *International Security*, vol. 19, no. 2 (1994), 87–125.

27. James Lee Ray, *Democracy and International Conflict: An Evaluation of the Democratic Peace Propositin* (Colombia: University of South Carolina Press, 1995).

28. Owen, "How Liberalism," 149.

29. Ibid.

30. Ibid.

31. Williams, "The Discipline," 536.

32. Thomas Risse-Kappen, ed., *Bringing Transnational Relations Back In: Non-state Actors, Domestic Structures, and International Institutions* (New York: Cambridge University Press, 1995), 492.

33. Williams, "The Discipline," 527.

34. Ibid., 526

35. John Macmillan, "Democracies Don't Fight: A Case of the Wrong Research Agenda," *Review of International Studies* (1996), 22 and 275–299

36. Edward D. Mansfield and Jack Snyder, "Democratization and the Danger of War," *International Security*, vol. 20, no. 1 (1995), 5–38.

37. Ibid.

38. Williams, "The Discipline," 528.

39. James Lorimer, *The Institutes of Law: A Treatise of the Jural Relations of Separate Political Communities* (London: Blackwood, 1883).

40. Ibid.

41. Robert Latham, "Democracy and War-Making: Locating the International Liberal Context," *Millennium: Journal of International Studies*, vol. 22, no. 2 (1993), 139; also 139–164.

42. Ibid., 139.

43. Williams, "The Discipline," 419–423.
44. Tarak Barkawi and Mark Laffey, "The Imperial Peace: Democracy, Force, and Globalization," *European Journal of International Relations*, vol. 5, no. 4 (1999), 403–434.
45. Uday S. Mehta, "Liberal Strategies of Exclusion," in Frederick Cooper and Ann Laura Stoler, eds., *Tensions of Empire* (Berkeley: University of California Press, 1997), 59–86
46. Pheng Cheah and Bruce Robbins, eds., *Cosmopolitics: Thinking and Feeling Beyond the Nation* (Minneapolis: University of Minnesota Press, 1998), 1–41.
47. Joshua Cohen, ed., *For Love of Country: Debating the Limits of Patriotism* (Boston: Beacon Press, 1996).
48. See, for instance, Barry Holden, ed., *Global Democracy: Key Debates* (London: Routledge, 2000).
49. Andrew Linklater, "Men and Citizens in International Relations," *Review of International Studies*, vol. 7 (1981), 23–37
50. Rony Brauman, "L' Humanitaire et le politique: une relation ambigue?" *Le Monde*, October 28, 2003.
51. Cohen, ed., *For Love of Country*.
52. Ibid.
53. Sissela Bok in ibid., 38–44.
54. Ibid.
55. Elaine Scarry, "The Difficulty of Imagining Other People" in ibid., 98–110.
56. Ibid.
57. See, specifically, David Held, ed., *Prospects for Democracy* (Cambridge: Polity Press, 1993); and *Democracy and the Global Order: From the Modern State to Cosmopolitan Governance* (Stanford: Stanford University Press, 1995).
58. Held, *Democracy and the Global Order*, 270–272.
59. Ibid., ix and 1–27.
60. Andrew Linklater, "The Problem of Community in International Relations," *Alternatives*, vol. xv (1990), 141.
61. Held, *Democracy and the Global Order*, IX and 141–218.
62. Ibid., 219–286.
63. Ibid., XI.
64. Ibid.
65. See, for instance, Martha C. Nussbaum, *Women and Human Development: The Capabilities Approach* (Cambridge: Cambridge University Press, 2000) and, with Jonathan Glover, eds., *Women, Culture, and Development: A Study of Human Capabilities* (New York: Oxford University Press, 1995).
66. Chris Brown, "International Political Theory and the Idea of International Community," in Ken Booth and Steve Smith, eds.,

International Relations Theory Today (University Park: Pennsylvania State University Press, 1995), 90–101

67. Linklater, "Men and Citizens," 23–37.

68. Linklater, "The Problem of Community," 141.

69. Linklater, "Men and Citizens," 23–37.

70. Bruce Robbins, "Cosmopolitanism," in Cheah and Robbins, eds., *Cosmopolitics*, 5.

71. Stanley Hoffmann, *The Ethics and Politics of Humanitarian Intervention* (Notre Dame: University of Notre Dame Press, 1996).

72. Robert H. Jackson, *Quasi-States: Sovereignty, International Relations, and the Third World* (Cambridge: Cambridge University Press, 1993), 202.

73. Ibid.

74. Roger D. Hansen, *Beyond the North-South Stalemate* (New York: McGraw-Hill, 1979).

75. Chris Brown, "The Modern Requirement: Reflections on Normative International Theory in a Post-Western World," *Millennium: Journal of International Studies*, vol. 17, no. 2 (1988), 339–348.

76. See, for instance, David Gillies, *Between Principle and Practice: Human Rights in North-South Relations* (Montreal: McGill-Queen's University Press, 1996); Charles A Jones, *The North-South dialogue: A Brief History* (New York: St. Martin's Press, 1983); and Jagdish N. Bhagwati and John Gerard Ruggie, *Power, Passions, and Purpose: Prospects for North-South Negotiations* (Cambridge, MA: MIT Press, 1984).

77. Brown, "The Modern Requirement," 339.

78. Ibid., 339.

79. Ibid., 340.

80. Ibid., 340.

81. Ibid., 339.

82. Boutros Boutros-Ghali, "An Agenda for Democratization at the International Level," in Barry Holden, ed., *Global Democracy: Key Debates* (London: Routledge, 2000), 105–124.

83. Daniele Archibugi, Sveva Balduini, and Marco Donati, "The United Nations as an Agency of Global Democracy," in Barry Holden, ed., *Global Democracy: Key Debates* (London: Routledge, 2000), 125–161.

84. The one exception is Great Britain. Since 1973, by my count the United Kingdom has voted only three times in favor of a SC resolution that the United States had opposed or actually vetoed. This count does not include the number of times that the United Kingdom abstained in face of an American veto. Further, the United Kingdom has only twice proposed a resolution that it knew the United States would veto. This pattern holds whether the ruling party is Conservative or Labor.

85. Frederick Cooper, *Decolonization and African society: The Labor Question in French and British Africa* (Cambridge: Cambridge University Press, 1996).

86. John Darwin, *Britain and Decolonization: The Retreat from Empire in the Post-War World* (New York: St. Martin's Press, 1988).
87. Ibid., 451–453.
88. Ibid.
89. Cooper, *Decolonization and African society*, 465
90. Frederic C. Schaffer, *Democracy in Translation: Understanding Politics in an Unfamiliar Culture* (Ithaca: Cornell University Press, 1998).
91. Schaffer, *Democracy in Translation*, 1–20.
92. Ibid., 2.
93. Ibid., 9.
94. Ibid., 10–11.
95. Cooper also erroneously criticizes Frantz Fanon on the latter's views of the turn taken by African struggles after 1950, when national elites practiced politics of rights and entitlements that undermined African standing in the global moral order as well as led to forms of authoritarianism that were apparent to Fanon and others at the time. Cooper, *Decolonization and African society*, 466–472.
96. Mamadou Dia, "Le Point IV Truman ou le Capitalisme s'Humanisant," *Condition Humaine* (February 11, 1950).
97. Schaffer, *Democracy in Translation*, 14.
98. Ibid., 13.
99. Shaffer's spelling of the Wolof term for democracy.
100. Mahmood Mamdani, *Citizen and Subject: Contemporary Africa and the Legacy of Late Colonialism* (Princeton, NJ: Princeton University Press, 1996).
101. *Centre des Archives d'Outre-Mer*, 1Affpol/409.
102. *Centre des Archives d'Outre-Mer*, 1Afpol/360.
103. *Centre des Archives d'Outre-Mer*, Secret Memorandum from the Director General of Political Affairs, Ministry of Colonies to the Governor General of French West Africa, c. May 1945.
104. Félix Eboué, Le Programme du Gouverneur Général, *Courrier Africain*, Edition de l'AEF, no. 25 (February 25, 1941).
105. *Centre des Archives d'Outre-Mer*, 1Affpol/2201/6.
106. Catherine Akpo-Vaché, *L'AOF et la Seconde Guerre Mondiale* (Paris: Karthala, 1996), 205–272.
107. Ibid.
108. The first draft constitution failed to muster enough votes to pass a referendum due to internal power struggle between de Gaulle (backed by the MRP) and the left: communists and socialists.
109. Gabriel Lisette, *Le Combat du Rassemblement Démocratique Africain pour la Décolonisation pacifique de l'Afrique Noire* (Paris: Présence Africaine, 1983), 158.
110. Ruth Schachter-Morgenthau, *Le Multipartisme en Afrique de l'Ouest Francophone Jusqu'aux Indépendances* (Paris: l'Harmattan, 1998), 53–54.
111. Lisette, *Le Combat*, 158.

112. Schachter-Morgenthau, *Le Multipartisme*, 53–60.
113. Gabriel d'Arboussier, "Question orale sur le franc," *Débats Parlementaires* (February 6 and 20, 1948), 131.
114. Schachter-Morgenthau, *Le Multipartisme*, 11–25.
115. Gabriel d'Arboussier, "Proposition concernant les événements de Bouaflé et de Bouaké en Côte d'Ivoire," *Annales de l'Assemblée de l'Union Française*, nos. 11, 12, and 13 (February 1950).
116. Ibid.
117. Ibid.
118. Ibid.
119. Félix Houphouet-Boigny, "Réponse à d'Arboussier," *Afrique Noire*, no. 27, July 24, 1952.
120. Ibid.
121. See, République Française, *Annales de l'Assemblée de l'Union Française* for the year 1947.
122. Gabriel d'Arboussier, "Propositions concernant les attributions de l'Assemblée de l'Union," *Annales de l'Assemblée de l'Union Française* (June 10, 1948), 488.
123. Gabriel d'Arboussier, "Propositions de résolution sur la répression des discrimination raciales dans l'Union française," *Annales de l'Assemblée de l'Union Française*, nos. 44, 45, and 46 (July 1949), 837.
124. D'Arboussier, "Attributions de l'Assemblée de l'Union," 486–487.
125. Schachter-Morgenthau, *Le Multipartisme*, 54.
126. Gabriel d'Arboussier, "Propositions de loi concernant l'élection des membres de l'Assemblée Nationale dans les territoires d'outre-mer," *Annales de l'Assemblée de l'Union Française*, nos. 72 and 73 (December 28 and 29, 1950), 1572–1597.
127. Ibid.
128. D'arboussier spelled out the models as "Federations of states, Federated States, ancients or moderns, like the United States of the Soviet Union, or the British Commonwealth." Ibid.
129. D'Arboussier, "Election des membres," 1572–1597.
130. Ibid.
131. Ibid., 1572–1573.
132. Ibid., 1573.
133. Ibid.
134. Ibid.
135. Ibid., 1574–1590
136. Ibid. 1574
137. Oumar Ba, "Assemblées locales dans les territoires d'outre-mer," *Journal Officiel*, no. 97 (December 31, 1951), 3605–3606.
138. Ouezzin Coulibaly, "Proposition de loi relative a l'élection des députés dans les territoires d'outre-mer," *Journal Officiel*, no. 64 (April 25, 1951), 3858.
139. Ibid.

140. Etienne Djaument, "Projet de loi relatif a l'élection des conseillers de la République," *Journal Officiel*, no. 85 (September 15, 1948), 3077.
141. Ibid.
142. Ibid.
143. Ibid.
144. Amadou Doucouré, "Assemblées locales dans les territoires d'outre-mer," *Journal Officiel*, no. 97 (December 31, 1951), 3581.
145. Ibid.
146. Ba, "Assemblées," 3605–3606.
147. D'Arboussier, "Attributions de l'Assemblée de l'Union," 487.
148. Ibid., 487.
149. Gabriel d'Arboussier, "Avis sur le projet de décret modifiant la réglementation de l'expropriation en A. O. F.," *Annales de l'Assemblée de l'Union Française*, nos. 66 and 69 (November–December, 1950), 1465–1473.
150. Gabriel d'Arboussier, "Proposition tendant a la Réglementation des Mesures relatives a l'Ordre Public," *Annales de l'Assemblée de l'Union Française* (March 18, 1948), 289.
151. D'Arboussier, "Attributions de l'Assemblée de l'Union," 487.
152. Ibid., 488.
153. Gabriel d'Arboussier, "Ratification de L'Accord Economique avec les Etats-Unis," *Annales de L'Assemblée de L'Union Française* (July 7, 1948), 668.
154. Ibid.
155. Boubou Hama, "Audition de M. Bollaert, Haut Commissaire Indochine," *Annales de l'Assemblée de l'Union Française*, no. 10 (January 1, 1947), 68.
156. Boubou Hama, "Débats sur un incident," *Annales de l'Assemblée de l'Union Française*, no. 21 (March 11, 1949), 360.
157. Ibid.
158. Boubou Hama, "Propositions concernant les rangs de préséances à l'Assemblée de l'Union Française," *Annales de l'Assemblée de l'Union Française* (February 4, 1949), 72.
159. Hama, "Audition de M. Bollaert," 68.
160. Hama, "Préséances à l'Assemblée," 71–72.
161. Ibid.
162. Hama, "Un incident," 360.
163. Boubou Hama, "Projet de loi portant création d'une Assemblée territoriale élue en Cochinchine," *Annales de l'Assemblée de l'Union Française*, nos. 19, 20, and 21 (March 1949), 334.
164. Hama, "Assemblée territoriale," 334.
165. Ibid.
166. D'Arboussier, "Assemblée de l'Union," 487. See also, d'Arboussier, "Election des membres," 1597.
167. See, Frank Costigliola, *France and the United States: The Cold Alliance Since World War II* (New York: Twayne Publishers), 44–78 and John S. Hill,

"American Efforts to Aid French Reconstruction Between Lend-Lease and the Marshall Plan," *Journal of Modern History*, vol. 64 (September 1992), 500–524.

168. D'Arboussier, "Accord Economique," 656

169. D'Arboussier, "Election des membres," 1573.

170. D'Arboussier, "Réglementation de l'expropriation," 1465.

171. D'Arboussier, "Attributions de l'Assemblée de l'Union," 492.

172. Ibid.

173. Assemblée de l'Union Française, "Union Française: Représentation au Conseil de l'Europe et a l'Assemblée Consultative Européenne," *Annales de l'Assemblée de l'Union Française*, Thursday (June 9, 1949), 700.

174. Ibid., 700.

175. Gabriel Lisette, "Politique Étrangère du Gouvernement," *Assemblée Nationale*, 2eme séance (March 11, 1948), 1653.

176. Ibid., 700.

177. Assemblée de l'Union Française, "Union Française: Représentation au Conseil de l'Europe et a l'Assemblée Consultative Européenne," *Annales de l'Assemblée de l'Union Française*, Thursday (June 9, 1949).

178. Gabriel d'Arboussier, "Avis sur des propositions et projets de loi relatifs aux assemblées locales des territoires d'outre-mer en qualité de rapporteur, et en son nom personnel," *Annales de l'Assemblée de l'Union Française*, nos. 43 and 45 (July 1948), 775.

179. Ibid.

180. Ibid.

181. Ibid.

182. Ibid.

183. Ibid.

184. Ibid.

185. D'Arboussier, "Réglementation de l'expropriation," 1465.

186. Ibid., 1473.

187. Ibid.

188. Ibid., 1465–1473.

189. Ibid.

190. Ibid.

191. Ibid.

192. Ibid., 1530

193. Gabriel d'Arboussier, "Proposition concernant le pourcentage d'attributions dans la répartition des apports du plan Marshall," Annales de l'Assemblée de l'Union Française, no. 40 (July 9, 1948), 710.

194. Ibid.

195. Gabriel Lisette, "Politique Étrangère du Gouvernement," *Assemblée Nationale*, 2eme séance (March 11, 1948), 1563.

196. Ibid., 1562.

197. Ibid., 1563.

198. Ibid., 1562–1564.

199. Walter Rodney, *How Europe Underdeveloped Africa* (Washington, DC: Howard University Press, 1981).

200. Gabriel d'Arboussier, "Avis sur un projet de loi concernant les accords conclus entre la France et les Etats-Unis d'Amérique," *Annales de l'Assemblée de l'Union Française*, no. 37 (July 1, 1948), 654.

201. Gabriel Lisette, "Politique Étrangère du Gouvernement," *Assemblée Nationale*, 2eme séance (March 11, 1948), 1563.

202. Ibid.

203. Dia, "Le Point IV Truman."

204. Ibid.

205. Ibid.

206. Ibid.

207. D'Arboussier, "Avis sur un projet de loi."

208. Gabriel Lisette, Avis sur un projet de loi concernant les accords conclus entre la France et les Etats-Unis d'Amérique *Annales de l'Assemblée de l'Union Française*, no. 37 (July 1, 1948), 653.

209. Ibid., 654.

210. République Française, "Avis sur un projet de loi concernant les accords conclus entre la France et les Etats-Unis d'Amérique," no. 37 (July 1, 1948), 646–657.

211. Ibid., 657.

212. Ibid., 650.

213. D'Arboussier, "Avis sur un projet de loi.".

214. République Française, *Annales de l'Assemblée de l'Union Française*, no. 37 (July 1, 1948), 650

215. D'Arboussier, "Pourcentage d'attributions," 710.

216. D'Arboussier, "Avis sur un projet de loi," 654

217. Ibid.

218. Ibid., p 488.

219. Fred Marte, *Political Cycles in International Relations* (Amsterdam: VU University Press, 1994), 49–141.

220. See, Victor Biaka Boda, "Projet de loi tendant a ratifier le Pacte de l'Atlantique," *Journal Officiel*, no. 65 (July 27, 1949).

221. Alioune M'Bengue, "Union Française: Espoir d'un peuple," *Condition Humaine*, no. 37 (April 26, 1949), 1 and 4.

222. Alioune M'Bengue, "Union Française," 1 and 4.

223. Léopold Sédar Senghor, "Appel aux lecteurs," *Condition Humaine*, no. 14, October 4, 1948, 1.

224. D'Arboussier, "Proposition," 289.

225. Houphouet-Boigny, "Réponse à d'Arboussier."; see also Felix Houphouet-Boigny, "Sur les thèmes de paix, fraternité et dialogue," *Centre de Recherche et de Documentation Africaine*, br.1.45./doss.7.

226. Gabriel D'Arboussier, "Lettre Ouverte à Houphouet-Boigny," Rapport du Rassemblement Democratique African (May 1, 1949).

227. Mamadou Dia, "Nos Erreurs Politiques," *Condition Humaine: Au service de la révolution sociale*, no. 1 (Wednesday February 11, 1948), 1.
228. Ibid., 1–2.
229. Ibid., 2.
230. Houphouet-Boigny, "Réponse à d'Arboussier."
231. Houphouet-Boigny, "Réponse à d'Arboussier"; see also Houphouet-Boigny, "Thèmes de paix, fraternité et dialogue."
232. Ibid.
233. Ibid.
234. Ibid.
235. Ibid.
236. Ibid.
237. Ibid.
238. Ibid.

Chapter 5   Daniel Ouezzin Coulibaly: Descartes Wasn't Always Right, Diderot Maybe

1. A reporter for the *New York Herald*, Henry Morton Stanley ventured in the Congo as philanthropist and anti-slavery abolitionist. He joined the Belgian International Congo Association and, later, advocated for the International Congo Commission, the forerunner to the Congo Free State—and later the Belgian Colony of the Congo. See Henry M. Stanley, *Despatches to the New York Herald, 1871–1872, 1874–1877*, Norman R. Bennett, ed. (Boston: Boston University Press, 1970) and *Through the Dark Continent; or, The sources of the Nile Around the Great Lakes of Equatorial Africa and Down the Livingstone River to the Atlantic Ocean* (New York: Greenwood Press, 1969).
2. Gary Younge, "No More Mr Nice Guy," *The Guardian* (London, September 19, 2002).
3. Ibid.
4. Ibid.
5. Ibid.
6. Ibid.
7. Cathal J. Nolan, *The Longman Guide to World Affairs* (White Plains, NY: Longman Publishers, 1995), 436.
8. On August 30, 1993, Nelson Mandela told the South African Institute of Civil Engineers that the "The ANC will abide by the Nuclear Non-Proliferation Treaty" and that his government "fully supports the declaration by the Organization of African Unity calling for the establishment of the African continent as a nuclear-weapons-free zone." David Albright, "South Africa and the affordable bomb," *Bulletin of the Atomic Scientists*, vol. 50, no. 4 (July/August 1994), 37–47.
9. Ibid., 230.

10. I illustrate this point in both French and Anglo-Saxon contexts through discussions of Tzvetan Todorov, *On Human Diversity: Nationalism, Racism, and Exoticism in French Thought*, trans. Catherine Porter (Cambridge, MA: Harvard University Press, 1993) and Anthony G. Hopkins, *The Future of the Imperial Past* (Cambridge: Cambridge University Press, 1997).

11. "Reverse ethnography" is an ethnography of the West conducted by the formerly colonized that parallels existing Western ethnographies of the other. Todorov, *On Human Diversity*, 88.

12. Ibid.

13. Hopkins, *Future*.

14. Todorov, *On Human Diversity*, 88–89

15. Hopkins, *Future*, 2–3.

16. Ibid., 85.

17. Ibid., 88.

18. Ibid., 1–88.

19. Todorov, *On Human Diversity*, xiv.

20. Ibid.

21. Ibid., xv.

22. Ibid.

23. Ibid., 1–88.

24. Hopkins, *Future* and Todorov, *On Human Diversity*.

25. Hopkins, *Future*.

26. Ibid., 30–42.

27. Ibid., 17.

28. Ibid., 30.

29. Ibid.

30. Ibid., 10–16.

31. Ibid., 14.

32. Ibid., 13–14.

33. Ibid., 14.

34. Ibid., 13–14.

35. Ibid.

36. Todorov, *On Human Diversity*, xv.

37. *Oxford English Dictionary* (Oxford: Oxford University Press, 1971), 1484.

38. Ibid., 2642.

39. Ibid., 2082.

40. Ibid., 2639–2642.

41. Ibid., 2639.

42. Ibid., 2642.

43. Walter D. Mignolo, *The Darker Side of the Renaissance* (Ann Arbor: University of Michigan Press, 1995), ix.

44. The Muslim press, for instance, came under particular scrutiny during World War II for its ironic and satiric treatises. See *Centre des Archives d'Outre-Mer*, 1Affpol 915–920, 1939–1945.

45. Hopkins, *Future*, 14.

46. Todorov, *On Human Diversity*, xv.
47. Ibid.
48. Ibid., 88.
49. Ibid., 83.
50. Ibid., 83.
51. Ibid., 83–88.
52. Michael J. Shapiro, *Violent Cartographies: Mapping Cultures of War* (Minneapolis: University of Minnesota Press, c. 1997).
53. For a historical account of social theory as theory of the self, see, for instance, Knud Haakonssen, *Natural Law and Moral Philosophy: From Grotius to the Scottish Enlightenment* (Cambridge: Cambridge University Press, 1996).
54. Ibid., 122–123.
55. Ibid., 74.
56. Ibid., 77.
57. Todorov, *On human diversity*, xiii.
58. Hopkins, *Future*, 7–13.
59. François-Marie Arouet Voltaire, *L'Ingénu et autres contes* (Paris: Bookking International, 1993).
60. Dénis Diderot, *Political Writings*, trans. John Hope Mason and Robert Wokler (Cambridge: Cambridge University Press, 1992).
61. Voltaire, *L'Ingénu.*
62. Ibid., 9–64.
63. Ibid., 45.
64. Diderot, *Political Writings*, 35–75.
65. Ibid., 44.
66. Ibid., 40.
67. Ibid., 46.
68. Ibid., 47–48.
69. Ibid., 61.
70. Ibid., 54–64.
71. Ibid., 52.
72. Ibid., 61.
73. Ibid., 74.
74. Ibid., 211–212.
75. Jean-Pierre Biondi and Jules Morin, *Les Anti-Colonialistes (1881–1962)* (Paris: Editions Robert Laffont, 1992), 223–307.
76. See, for instance, Maurice Merleau-Ponty, *L'institution dans l'histoire personnelle et publique; Le problème de la passivité, le sommeil, l'inconscient, la mémoire: Notes de cours au collège de France, 1954–1955*, Maurice Merleau-Ponty, Dominique Darmaillacq, Claude Lefort, and Stéphane Ménasé, eds. (Paris: Belin, c. 2003).
77. Perhaps the most important sign of Jean-Paul Sartre's connections to anticolonialists is his introduction to Franz Fanon's *Les damnés de la terre* (Paris: Gallimard, 1991).

78. See Jacqueline Lévi-Valensi's *Camus à Combat: Editoriaux et articles d'Albert Camus, 1944–1947* (Paris: Gallimard, c. 2002).

79. These denunciations were taken up later by French structuralists and functionalists, whether Marxists or not, most notably Louis Althusser. See, for instance, Louis Althusser, *The Humanist Controversy and Other Writings (1966–67)*, François Matheron, ed. (London: Verso, 2003).

80. Laurie Spurling, *Phenomenology and the Social World* (London: Routledge & Kegan Paul, 1977), 143–163.

81. For a similar analysis in the context of India, see Dispesh Chakrabarty, *Provincializing Europe: Postcolonial Thought and Historical Difference* (Princeton: Princeton University Press, 2000), 30; also 27–34.

82. Ibid.

83. Mohamadou Djibrilla Maiga, "Vote des crédits militaires pour l'Indochine," *Journal Officiel*, no. 33 (March 29, 1947), 473.

84. Etienne Djaument, "L'évolution de la Situation a Madagascar," *Journal Officiel*, no. 80 (July 24, 1947), 1066–1068.

85. Mohamadou Djibrilla Maiga, "Vote des crédits militaires," *Journal Officiel*, no. 92, vol. 9 (August 1947), 1726.

86. Maiga, "Vote des crédits militaires," 473.

87. Boubou Hama, "Débats sur un incident," *Annales de l'Assemblée de l'Union Française*, no. 21 (March 11, 1949), 360.

88. Mohamadou Djibrilla Maiga, "Vote des crédits militaires," *Journal Officiel*, no. 92, vol. 9 (August 1947), 1668.

89. Ibid.

90. Ibid.

91. Devalois Biaka, *La 'Disparition' du Patriote Victor Biaka Boda* (Paris: L'Harmattan, 1993).

92. Coulibaly was formally affiliated with the metropolitan Union Républicaine et Résistance (1947); Groupe Parlementaire Communiste (1948), and later USDR, the precursor to the French Socialist Party.

93. Ouezzin Coulibaly, "J'Accuse," *Réveil*, no. 327 (August 30, 1948).

94. Ibid.

95. Ibid.

96. Ouezzin Coulibaly, "Projet de loi portant ratification du pacte de l'Atlantique," *Journal Officiel*, no. 85 (July 27, 1949), 5296–5300.

97. Ibid.

98. Ibid.

99. Claude Gerard, "Interview with Professor Semi Bi-Zam," January 21, 1988 (Unpublished).

100. Ibid.

101. Ibid.

102. *Centre des Archives d'Outre-Mer*, 1Affpol/2201/6, 1–2.

103. Ouezzin Coulibaly, "Politique économique et financière dans les territoires d'outre-mer," *Journal Officiel*, no. 60 (June 22, 1949), 3588–3590.
104. Ibid., 3588.
105. Ibid.
106. Ibid.
107. Ibid.
108. Ibid., 3590
109. Ibid.
110. Ouezzin Coulibaly, "Projet de loi portant ratification du pacte de l'Atlantique," *Journal Officiel*, no. 85 (July 27, 1949), 5296.
111. Ibid.
112. Ibid.
113. Ibid.
114. Ibid.
115. Ibid.
116. Quotations from *La Gazette de Lauzanne*, the *New York Herald*, and so on.
117. Ibid., 5297.
118. Ibid., 5298.
119. Ibid., 5298.
120. Ibid., 5298.
121. Ibid., 5298.
122. Ibid.
123. Ibid.
124. Ibid.
125. Ibid., 5300.
126. Ibid., 5300.
127. Ibid.
128. Gerard, "Interview with Professor Semi Bi-Zam."
129. Ibid.
130. Ibid., 14
131. *Centre des Archives d'Outre-Mer*, 1Affpol, 2201/6, 1–15.
132. Among those notably tolerated in their criticisms of French policies were the *négritudistes* whose philosophical principles were in accordance with post-Enlightenment views that the "marriage" between France and Africa rested on two complementary capacities and faculties: French reason and science and African art and emotive expressions. For further reference see Lilyan Kesteloot, *Black Writers in French: A Literary History of Négritude*, trans. Ellen Conroy Kennedy (Washington, DC: Howard University Press, 1991) and V. Y. Mudimbe, ed., *The Surreptitious Speech: Présence Africaine and the Politics of Otherness, 1947–1987* (Chicago: University of Chicago Press, 1992).
133. Mudimbe, *The Surreptitious Speech*, 95–117.
134. Kesteloot, *Black Writers in French*, 15–89.

135. 1Affpol/2201/6, op. cit.
136. Coulibaly, "Pacte de l'Atlantique," 5296–5300.
137. See Michel Foucault's "Introduction" to Georges Canguilhem, *On the Normal and the Pathological*, trans. Carolyn R. Fawcett (London: D. Reidel Publishing Company, 1978). See also Gil Anidjar who quotes Jacques Derrida making similar inferences about the exigencies of anticolonial subjects in *The Jew, the Arab* (Stanford: Stanford University Press, 2003), 42–50.
138. *Centre des Archives d'Outre-Mer*, 1Affpol/260.
139. *Centre des Archives d'Outre-Mer*, 1Affpol/2230.

Conclusion

1. For supportive accounts, see for instance, Eric Cheyfitz, *The Poetics of Imperialism: Translation and Colonization from the Tempest to Tarzan* (Philadelphia: University of Pennsylvania Press, 1991), 142–213; Peter Hulme, *Colonial Encounters: Europe and the Native Caribbean, 1492–1797* (London: Routledge, 1986); Peter Mason, *Deconstructing America: Representations of the Other* (London: Routledge, 1990).
2. For illustrations, see R. B. J. Walker, ed., *Culture, Ideology, and World Order* (Boulder, CO: Westview Press, 1984).

INDEX

Printed and bound by CPI Group (UK) Ltd, Croydon, CR0 4YY